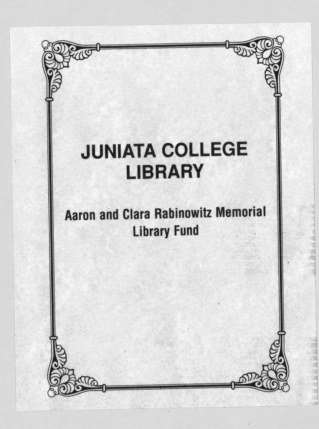

In memory of

C. Vann Woodward

Contents

Illustrations

Preface

The slur is notorious. It reads: "Strictly, the Southerner had no mind; he had temperament. He was not a scholar; he had no intellectual training; he could not analyze an idea, and he could not even conceive of admitting two."[1] These words come from *The Education of Henry Adams*, a book that first came into public view in 1918 and became rapidly an American classic of peculiar intellectual authority. The words used to be a fluorescent tattoo, stippled on to the foreheads of Southerners out in the world, by which they might be known and avoided by those confident of possessing minds, not just temperaments. Henry Adams himself did not stipple the words there. The labor of tattooing was chiefly undertaken by Wilbur Cash, whose *The Mind of the South* of 1941, itself in turn a work of peculiar intellectual authority, especially in the late 1950s and 1960s, took these words as definitive and founded an interpretation of Southern culture upon them.[2] Still, Adams composed the slur.

There is no need to interrogate whether these words were true, but it is of interest to learn where they came from, why they were written, and where they can be located in the landscape of American intellectual life in the nineteenth and early twentieth centuries. Though there is much in these words idiosyncratic to Henry Adams, there is much, too, that was not. Adams registered a wider shift in the standing of the South in American thought between about 1850 and 1918, when it passed from strength to weakness. How that transition worked, at least for those looking from the outside, invites understanding. One must ask, what cultural work was the South asked to perform by non-Southerners in these years?

For such a purpose, Henry Adams is useful. He mixed critical distance and proximity to what was then often called "the Southern Question," by way of designating a problem.[3] So there was, at the same time, "the Eastern Question" and "the Irish Question," and so, in the days of Antonio Gramsci, there would come to be in Italy a different "Southern Question."[4] Adams's distance is evident in the slur from the *Education*, the kind of words one could find in many writings by New Englanders of his generation, indeed of several generations. It is natural to see him as a representative New Englander, since he was born in 1838 in Boston, brought up there and in Quincy, educated at Harvard, indeed was later a professor of history there. He came, of course, from perhaps the most famous of Massachusetts families. For such a man, for such people, hostility towards the South was bred in the bone. But in this distance was a proximity, too. Being from an American political family in Massachusetts could mandate a grappling with the South. It had been so for his great-grandfather John Adams, who had struggled for the presidency with Thomas Jefferson of Virginia and won in 1796, then lost in 1800. It had been so for his grandfather John Quincy Adams, who had struggled with Andrew Jackson of Tennessee and won in 1824, then lost in 1828. It was so with his father Charles Francis Adams, who ran as the vice-presidential candidate of the Free Soil Party in 1848 and lost, but who later struggled with the Confederacy and, for the first time in the family's history, helped to win a lasting victory. Thinking about the South was part of being an Adams.

To this family tradition, Henry Adams formed no exception. In the four chapters that follow, how he considered the South in the phases of his life are traced.[5] First is Adams as a young man, who served as his father's secretary in the House of Representatives during the great secession winter of 1860–61 and in the American embassy in London during the Civil War and until 1868, and who wrote political journalism in Washington about Reconstruction. Second is an assessment of his 1877 move to Washington, D.C., a place that he and others understood to be Southern, or at least significantly influenced by Southern culture. Third is a close reading of the Southern history written in his middle years: his biography of John Randolph of Virginia, his nine-volume history of the administrations of Thomas Jefferson and James Madison, and his two novels, one of which was much occupied with the status of the South in postbellum America. In the late 1870s and 1880s, Adams wrote as much Southern history as anyone then and had a deep influence upon what Americans thought about the South. Fourth, the relevance of the South to the works of his old age, to *Mont-Saint-Michel and Chartres* and *The Education of Henry Adams*, is considered. Finally, returning to the words from the *Education* with which this book started, the concluding pages explore why Southerners like Cash were strangely disposed to embrace Adams's slur.

This book discharges a task deferred. When, as a very young scholar in the early 1970s, I became interested in writing about the intellectual culture of the American South, the dismissive words of Henry Adams stood like a boulder, barring the way. Then, however, it seemed easier to step unobtrusively around the boulder, while kicking aside the smaller rock that was *The Mind of the South*. This prudence arose from a respect for Adams. The *Education* had made a deep impression upon me, when as an undergraduate—my memory says it was March 1967—I was looking for vacation reading and chanced to take down from the shelves of Trinity Hall's college library the red, cheap edition published by Constable's of London.

I am not the first person to consider the relevance of Southern culture to an understanding of Adams, but no one (to my knowledge) has ventured a sustained analysis.[6] It would be idle to pretend that this work resolves the enigma of Henry Adams, for his life and intellect roamed richly, into places and interests to which Virginia and South Carolina, Thomas Jefferson and John Randolph, have little pertinence. Still, I hope this book will be of use to scholars of Adams. So I am greatly in debt to Mercer University for the invitation to give the Lamar Lectures. I discovered in Macon a kindly hospitality, orchestrated especially by Sarah Gardner, and the opportunity of valuable conversation. I confess to being unused to speaking in Baptist chapels, but both my audience and I survived the incongruity. And I am grateful for the tolerance, which permitted me to offer what is, mostly, a study in New England culture, albeit a study of how New England viewed the South.

I should add my thanks to the Arts and Humanities Research Board for a grant and research leave, the University of Cambridge for a supplementary leave, and William Dusinberre for a thorough, sympathetic, and searching scrutiny of the manuscript of this book.

CHAPTER ONE

The Sable Genius of the South

One must begin with the Adams family, which, in the way of families, was complicated. Henry Adams's paternal line had been in New England since the seventeenth century; its founder, the first Henry Adams, had come from Somersetshire in about 1632 and bred a line that included clergymen, farmers, lawyers, and politicians.[1] These were people of modest means, comfortable and staid. By contrast, our Henry Adams's maternal line was far richer; indeed his grandfather Peter Chardon Brooks was, if not the richest man in New England, close to being so in consequence of many years spent insuring merchant voyages and making shrewd investments. Henry Adams was the product of this convergence, for he inherited the cultural politics of the Adamses, but also the money of the Brookses, which enabled him to live a life of gentlemanly ease and scholarship.

But all families have branches and nuances, and even an Adams was more than a New Englander. John Adams and John Quincy Adams were compelled by their political lives to be wanderers, which meant their children often lived itinerant lives, too. John Adams, until old and retired, lived almost everywhere but Quincy—in Philadelphia, Amsterdam, Paris, London, and Washington. John Quincy Adams reiterated the pattern: the Hague, Berlin, Saint Petersburg, Ghent, London, and also Washington for many purposes, as senator, secretary of state, president, and congressman. Charles Francis Adams grew up in many of these places, especially Saint Petersburg and London, before he assumed the ancestral role by being a congressman in Washington and an ambassador to the Court of Saint James. This peripatetic pattern meant that an Adams, when he married, sometimes did so not to solidify local attachments but to mirror worldliness. Even Charles Francis Adams met his future Bostonian wife not in Boston but in Washington, where he was living with his father the president and she was visiting her sister, then married to a Massachusetts congressman.[2] More significant, for the Southern question, is the matter of Louisa Catherine Johnson, who in 1797 married John Quincy Adams at All Hallows Barking, close by the Tower of London. The Johnsons were a Maryland family. Louisa's uncle Thomas was a lawyer who served in the Continental Congress, where he became an ally of John Adams and the man who nominated George Washington as commander in chief of the Continental army. He later served as governor of Maryland from 1777 to 1779 and as a justice of the U.S. Supreme Court from 1791 to 1793.[3] It is a pretty fact, considering where his great-great-nephew Henry came to live, that it was Johnson who, when serving on the commission that was planning the new "Federal City," first proposed that it be called after Washington.[4] His brother Joshua was a merchant who went to reside in London and there probably married an Englishwoman called Catherine Young. So their daughter Louisa, save for a French interlude, grew up there. Joshua's fortunes faltered badly in the mid-1790s, and he moved his family back to Washington, where his children mostly settled and married into Southern ways. His son Thomas went to New Orleans, worked in the postal service and a bank, became very rich and somewhat mad. After 1825 he wandered inconsequentially around Europe, conveniently died in 1843, and left his seven sisters much money. Of Louisa's other siblings, only Harriet moved away from the South, by a marriage to someone who ended up as an Indian agent in northern Michigan. For the rest, Eliza married Senator John Pope of Kentucky in 1810 and died eight years later at his home in Lexington, in the Palladian villa that she had helped Benjamin Latrobe design.[5] Carolina married twice, on the second occasion to a Washington businessman called Nathaniel Frye. Nancy married Walter Hellen, a successful tobacco merchant in Maryland and Washington; she died in 1810, whereupon (to the consternation of many) Hellen married his sister-in-law Adelaide; he was to survive only until 1815 and left an estate of $60,000, which (though not without a fight over the will) carried his widow through to her own death in 1877. Catherine (or Kitty) became pregnant when with Louisa in Saint Petersburg and was obliged to marry the father, an alcoholic spendthrift called William Steuben Smith, then John Quincy Adams's secretary because the American minister's nephew. Later William and Kitty Smith migrated to Washington. So both Louisa and Kitty intermarried with the Adamses, and, in the next generation, it happened again. Mary, the daughter of Nancy and Walter Hellen, married her cousin John, the son of Louisa and John Quincy Adams. Indeed it was in Mary's house at 1601 I Street N.W. that Louisa and John Quincy settled when the latter came back as a congressman in 1831, just as it was at his aunt Mary's house that Henry Adams stayed when he came to Washington in 1868 to work as a journalist.[6]

Later it will be necessary to return, in greater detail, to the influence of Louisa on Henry Adams. For the moment it is relevant only to observe that, if one looks at the Adams family as a patriarchy, it seems to have an unstable center in Quincy, and Washington sits at the outermost point of the family's American orbit. But, if one looks at it as a matriarchy—and the Adamses were famous for their strong women, who asked not to be forgotten—part of the family looks very different.[7] Louisa Adams sat at the center of a family web that reached northward towards Quincy and southward towards New Orleans, but was mostly centered on Washington. In her early years, she much disliked Quincy and had to be dragged unwillingly there, though she felt more kindly towards Boston. Later, she grew more reconciled, but she founded her later life in the District of Columbia, where her family mostly lived, where in Rock Creek Cemetery most of them were to be buried (as Henry Adams himself was to be buried next to his wife), and where Louisa demanded her husband buy the house at 1333–1335 F Street N.W., around the corner from Lafayette Square, where Henry Adams came to live.[8] So, seen in a Johnson rather than an Adams family light, Washington was for Henry Adams in 1868 and 1877 a homecoming, not an expatriation. The first three chapters of the *Education* are entitled, in succession, "Quincy," "Boston," and "Washington," and each of these designated a childhood place, for he had visited his grandmother in the District.

In the *Education*, Adams was to single out Louisa's influence on him as a child, but the evidence from his early writings does little to support this claim. To be sure, there is evidence that, when young, he was drawn towards moving southward. There is the strange fact that, fleetingly, he thought of starting life as a lawyer in Saint Louis, in a slaveholding state. In 1858 in Berlin, he wrote of his plans: "Two years in Europe; two years studying law in Boston; and then I propose to emigrate and practice at Saint Louis. What I can do there, God knows; but I have a theory that an educated and reasonably able man can make his mark if he chooses, and if I fail to make mine, why, then—I fail and that's all." But this idea seems to have rushed by with the evanescence with which, in 1797, John Quincy Adams, out of sorts with his parents and his life, had contemplated retiring from the diplomatic service and giving "his life to literature, perhaps settling in the American South—where Joshua Johnson claimed to have a huge plantation in Georgia." More steady was Henry's impulse to live in Washington, at least in the late 1850s, when to move there would have meant staying close to his parents. (He was then an unusually devoted, if often sardonic son.) He told his mother in 1860 that he was planning to study law in Washington and explained his conflicting feelings: "I never knew before this how I liked Quincy and Boston and how sorry I should be to cut loose of them altogether; but this course which certainly is the one I should choose and follow, if it will go, finishes setting me afloat. I shall make up my bed in Washington, and no doubt it will be just as pleasant as anywhere else. At all events, whether it is or not, it's the place that my education has fitted me best for, and where I could be of most use."[9]

However, this ambition to move south seems then to have had no obvious connection with the heritage of Louisa Adams, despite what is said in the *Education*. Her name appears nowhere in his correspondence before 1869, and, before 1861, the existence of the Johnson link was more discouraging than inviting, for they were slaveholding.[10] An Adams, unlike a Johnson, was supposed to be antislavery. The theme had grown over the years and drifted from the margins of the Adams family's politics to its center. John Adams, like his wife Abigail, had thought slavery a "foul contagion," but had not been zealous in acting upon this opinion. John Quincy Adams, as a young man, had held office under slaveholders, but as an old man became publicly an enemy of the institution. From the first, Charles Francis Adams founded his political career upon antislavery politics. Both John Quincy and Charles Francis Adams, however, were moderates, not Garrisonians but politicians who wished to inhibit slavery's growth, so that it might begin to die. The latter had started his political life as a Whig, then became a Free Soiler, and eventually a Republican; he was the sort of politician who feared the aggression of the slaveholders (evident in the Mexican War) and wished to end slavery, partly for the sake of the slaves, but even more to restore the American political system to health. As he had put it in 1845, in the midst of the controversy over the annexation of Texas, "The question . . . is whether the government of the United States shall be an oligarchy, sacrificing one great portion of the community for the benefit of a small portion— or whether it shall be what it has always claimed to be, a republic, based upon the natural rights of all men."[11]

During the 1850s Henry Adams absorbed this moderate antislavery creed with a fidelity that is remarkable, when one recalls how much in later life he liked to be perverse.[12] There had been other options, notably that offered by the abolitionist Charles Sumner, who had been a family friend and an idol to Henry as a boy. Sumner had been more drastic and vivid, with his talk of the "lords of the loom" and the "lords of the lash" and his erotic evocations of slavery's whoremasters. But when Charles Francis Adams and Sumner split, Henry went with his father, notably into an allegiance to William Henry Seward, the quintessential Republican moderate and trimmer, a man whom Horace Greeley thought overly fond of "dexterity in politics." In December 1859, when living in Dresden, Henry expressed his support for Seward as a presidential candidate in 1860: "I would thank God heartily to know that comparatively conservative men were to conduct this movement and could control it."[13] Similarly, when the secession crisis came, it was Seward's manipulative gradualism, as well as Seward's contempt for the untested Lincoln, that Henry echoed.

One should not, however, be misled by this adjective, *moderate.* Even the moderate antislavery man was scathing about men corrupted by the possession of slaves and relentless in their drive for power. The words used by Henry Adams to describe Southerners, especially as the crisis of secession deepened in the winter of 1860–61 and he was in Washington as secretary to his father, are words like *insolence, meanness, rascality, braggadocio,* but especially *madness.* "I do not want to fight them," he wrote to his brother in early January 1861. "They are mad, mere maniacs, and I want to lock them up till they become sane; not kill them. I want to educate, humanize and refine them, not send fire and sword among them." The phrase about educating Southerners was symptomatic. Adams, like most New Englanders, felt the South was inferior in morals and education and believed that education was what gave New England its "moral power."[14]

There was a puzzle, though. New Englanders knew, too, that Southerners had been beating them in national politics for generations. Much later, Adams would be shown a letter that spoke of one instance of this running defeat. In 1837, John Quincy Adams had written to Charles W. Upham: "When I came to the presidency the principle of internal improvement was swelling the tide of public prosperity, till the Sable Genius of the South saw the signs of his own inevitable downfall in the unparalleled progress of the North, and fell to cursing the tariff, and internal improvement, and raised the standard of free trade, nullification, and state rights. I fell and with me fell, I fear never to rise again . . . the system of internal improvement by means of national energies."[15] Reading this in 1909, Adams was to be moved. He said to his brother Brooks: "Especially the letter to Upham . . . which is quite new to me, has given me cause for much thought. As I read, between its lines, the bitterness of his failure, and the intensity of his regret at having served the Sable Genius of the South, are immensely tragic—so much so that he shrank from realising its whole meaning even to himself."[16]

Puzzlement at, and fear of, this "Sable Genius" bred resentment. How was it that the Slave Power had taken a Constitution, "made for freemen," and perverted it into "an instrument discountenancing freedom and protecting slavery"? Had Southerners learned an immoral trick, unknown to the honest New Englander? Did the trick lie in charisma? In February 1861, Henry went to a "crush ball" given by Adele Douglas and Stephen, "her little beast of a husband," the senator from Illinois, and there Henry saw, with outrage, how people reacted to the appearance of John Tyler, the ex-president from Virginia: "A crowd of admiring devotees surrounded the ancient buffer Tyler; another crowd surrounded that other ancient buffer Crittenden [the senator from Kentucky]. Ye Gods, what are we, when mortals no bigger—no, damn it, not so big as—ourselves, are looked up to as though their thunder spoke from the real original Olympus. Here is an old Virginia politician, of whom by good rights, no one ought ever to have heard, reappearing in the ancient ceremonies of his forgotten grave—political and social—and men look up at him as they would at Solomon."[17]

In the spring of 1861, Adams wrote an essay on "The Great Secession Winter," intended for publication in the *Atlantic Monthly*, though eventually not sent there.[18] It was a starkly partisan piece, making the case for Seward and his stalling tactics, and also echoing Seward's standpoint on the illegitimacy of Southern political power.[19] Adams was vitriolic about Southerners, whose course was seen as "wild and suicidal," "coarse and drunken," in contrast to "the quiet New Englanders with their staid and Puritanical ideas of duty and right, of law and religion." The Confederacy was described as an imperial fantasy, "oriental" in its "magnificence." Around him Adams saw treachery and deceit, a conspiracy of dishonest men, a "methodical madness which seems to be part of the southern character." He spoke of "the semi-barbarous school of southern barbecues and stump harangues, gouging and pistol shooting." Seeing such words, it will seem odd to observe that Adams saw himself, like his father and Seward, as occupying the middle ground between the secessionists and those abolitionists who wanted "a violent destruction of the slave power; perhaps by war, perhaps by a slave insurrection." On that middle ground were those who wanted "to prevent a separation in order to keep the slave power more effectually under control, until its power for harm should be gradually exhausted, and its whole fabric gently and peacefully sapped away."[20]

The idea of the Slave Power lay at the root of this fiercely hostile view. Adams explained the phenomenon thus: "By the Constitution a great political, social and geographical or sectional power within the Government was created; in its nature a monopoly; in its theory contrary to and subversive of the whole spirit of Republican institutions." A republic could not survive such a challenge from "the grand corporation known under the name of the slave-power, peculiarly offensive as it was, not only to the spirit of our Government but that of our religion and whole civilization, did very shortly pervert the whole body politic, and as an inevitable result of its very existence, the nation divided into parties, one of which favored its continuing to control the Government; the other striving to rescue the power from its hands."[21]

However, Henry Adams in 1860, though concerned about the Slave Power, was little interested in the slaves themselves. Or, if he was, his surviving records bear little trace, except for a glancing remark in an 1860 letter. It was written in Dresden about a new book, which in its English edition was to be published as the *Letters of Alexander von Humboldt, Written between the Years 1827 and 1858, to Varnhagen von Ense.* (Its translator was Ludmilla Assing, the sister of Frederick Douglass's mistress Ottilie; Varnhagen, their uncle, was a Prussian diplomat and friend to Humboldt.) Adams's remarks read: "Apropos, American slavery comes in for it's notice: a letter of Baron Geroldt's is in it; antislavery but not up to our points; Humboldt's own ideas were ours."[22] The context is an 1856 letter to Humboldt by Friedrich von Geroldt, who served as Prussian ambassador to the United States from 1843 to 1871. In it, Geroldt had reported on the recent controversy about a new American translation of Humboldt's *Essai politique sur l'île de Cuba* (1826) by a Southerner called J. S. Thrasher, who had omitted from his edition a chapter in which slavery had been condemned. Humboldt's protest at this censorship had found its way to the American press and Geroldt had forwarded clippings from New York newspapers, wherein could be found Thrasher's "very lame" apology. These events prompted Geroldt to remark on John C. Fremont, the Republican candidate for president, and to observe that "the Slave Question becomes every day more serious," with "news . . . daily from Kansas of sanguinary conflicts between the freesoilers and the slaveholders." If Adams found this letter deficient in antislavery zeal, it was doubtless because Geroldt expressed a preference for Millard Fillmore, the candidate of the American Party, while acknowledging that Fillmore had little chance of success, for "the Knownothings have lost all their influence." Humboldt's letters, by contrast, were more forthright, if as complimentary to American democracy as might be expected of a Prussian aristocrat. There, he observed, "liberty . . . is but a dead machinery in the hands of utilitarianism, very little calculated to ennoble and rouse the powers of mind and heart, which, after all, ought to be the main object of political freedom. This explains their indifference to slavery. But the U.S. are a Cartesian vortex, carrying away and levelling everything to dull monotony." Later, in allusion to Preston Brooks's caning of Charles Sumner, Humboldt spoke of the Democrats as "the infamous party, which sells negro children of fifty pounds weight, and gives away canes of honour . . . proving that all white labourers had also better be slaves than freemen,—has triumphed. What a monstrosity!" This criticism arose from a general, if hedged, commitment to the equality of mankind. In its 1849 English translation, Humboldt's *Cosmos* of 1845 has a passage that reads: "Whilst we maintain the unity of the human species, we at the same time repel the depressing assumption of superior and inferior races of men. There are nations more susceptible of cultivation, more highly civilized, more ennobled by mental cultivation than others—but none in themselves nobler than others. All are in like degree designed for freedom; a freedom which in the ruder conditions of society belongs only to the individual, but which in social states enjoying political institutions appertains as a right to the whole body of the community."[23]

The wrongs and practices of slavery were not subjects that preoccupied Henry Adams. Radical abolitionists, especially those of a religious bent, cared about whipping, rape, forced labor, and chains. But Adams cared for slavery because, as an immense property, it conferred disproportionate power on a small number of men, whose interest was blindly aggressive and effective. In theory, any such interest—whether rooted in slaves or factories—would be a problem to what was, for an Adams, the heart of the matter, the Union as a republican nation. In "The Great Secession Winter," he was very clear on this point. A monarchy like England, he argued, might survive social hierarchies and maldistributions of power, but not a republic. "Its existence depends upon the absence of such distinctions, and all monopolies or corporations that exercise a direct political influence as such, are contrary to the spirit of the Government and hurtful for its integrity. They must be kept down or they will pervert the whole body politic."[24]

This sense that nationalism mattered more than slavery can be traced in his letters from London during the Civil War, mostly letters to his elder brother Charles Francis. The correspondence was not without a sibling tension, because Charles Francis was a serving officer and Henry was not; the former was fighting for his country in the elemental masculine way and the latter was a junior, unofficial diplomat who ventured not into mud and trenches but into salons and embassy balls. Henry worried about this, but Charles Francis was reassuring and Henry unsteadily repeated the reassurance to himself. Still, Henry was missing what Wendell Holmes, like many others, came to celebrate and mourn as the quintessential experience of his generation, the magic generation "touched by fire," and it is noticeable that, until he came to write the *Education*, Henry avoided the Civil War as a historical topic.[25]

This unmilitary experience had a consequence. In the battles of the Civil War, men like Henry's brother were often reminded of their immediate loyalties by their service in local regiments. In Charles Francis's case, this meant the Fourth Battalion of Massachusetts Volunteer Militia and the First Regiment of Massachusetts Volunteer Cavalry. But Henry worked as a representative of the nation and played as a diplomat the game of nations, and by this service his devotion to the principle of nationality was deepened. He tended to judge the policies of the Lincoln administration, not by their impact upon American society, but by their external effect. The British and European world, for example, supported the antislavery cause and hence he urged Assistant Secretary of State Frederick William Seward in 1862 to reverse the traditional policy that American embassies would render no services to African Americans abroad, because such a reversal would reassure Europeans about American antislavery credentials. And he cheered whenever Lincoln moved against slavery, especially by issuing the Emancipation Proclamation, an action that Henry judged had "done more for us here [in London] than all our former victories and all our diplomacy."[26]

This nationalism was competitive. The Adams family had an ancient quarrel with Britain, whose subjects often complacently hoped for the failure of the United States by way of vindicating the old Tory presumption that democratic republics were doomed ventures. This presumption was a grievance. Much as he took to English life (even to the extent of acquiring something close to an English accent), much as he liked London clubs and Wenlock Edge and ruined abbeys and listening to Swinburne, Henry Adams never lost sight of being an American and never acquired the common Boston vice of seeing England, as Charles Sumner had seen it, as the "land of my studies, my thoughts, and my dreams!"[27] Adams, rather, felt that military victory as a vindication of American exceptionalism would be a victory over Britain, as well as the Confederacy. "I assert my nationality with a quiet pugnacity that tells," he said in 1862. "No one treads on our coat tails any longer, and I do not expect ever to see again the old days of anxiety and humiliation." This commitment to exceptionalism ran very deep and would help later to structure his history of Jefferson and Madison, and still later to feed his skeptical commitment to the imperialist policies of William McKinley and John Hay. But, at both moments, he saw American exceptionalism as less the Union's exemption from the human condition but more the fruit of an advanced political ideology. Indeed, he was later to condemn Jefferson's foreign policy for presuming too much of human nature, for daring "to legislate as though eternal peace were at hand."[28]

A belief in exceptionalism required a mix of euphoria, folly, and prescience. In a striking passage, again in 1862, he conjectured that by victory "our good country the United States is left to a career that is positively unlimited except by the powers of the imagination." From this, he moved seamlessly to prophecy. He told his brother:

You may think all this nonsense, but I tell you these are great times. Man has mounted science, and is now run away with. I firmly believe that before many centuries more, science will be the master of man. The engines he will have invented will be beyond his power to control. Some day science may have the existence of mankind in its power, and the human race commit suicide, by blowing up the world. Not only shall we be able to cruize in space, but I'll be hanged if I see any reason why some future generation shouldn't walk off like a beetle with the world on its back, or give it another rotary motion so that every zone should receive in turn its due portion of heat and light.[29]

A Union victory over the South would seal the ability of the United States to devote its energies to a future controlled by an exciting science whose self-restraint even then he mistrusted. Gettysburg presaged Hiroshima, we might now put it.

More sanguinely, after the election of 1864, he wrote: "I never yet have felt so proud as now of the great qualities of our race, or so confident of the capacity of men to develop their faculties in the mass. I believe that a new era of the movement of the world will date from that day, which will drag nations up still another step, and carry us out of a quantity of old fogs. Europe has a long way to go yet to catch us up."[30] This equation, that to defeat the South was also to defeat Europe was, to be sure, a common-enough Northern view. To cast slavery as medieval, as the enemy of modernity, meant that the Northern way was the path to a rational and modern future.

Adams never ceased to believe in the moral project of democracy, though he often came to doubt the morals of the ruling democrats and the wisdom of the people. As has often been observed, he was a liberal aristocrat, a close reader and admirer of Alexis de Tocqueville and John Stuart Mill.[31] Like Tocqueville, he believed that democracy was unavoidable because intrinsic to modernity, though he went further than Tocqueville in conceding the moral cogency of the project. Indeed his later history of Jefferson and Madison was warmed by his care for the democratic project. But Adams was a sort of Fabian democrat. Things needed to proceed slowly, education and persuasion mattered, and leaders needed moral clarity. As he was to put it in 1867, "The public is a pretty contemptible thing; that I confess. I've no very high opinion of it myself; but men who propose to influence the public have got to be really great men; otherwise they find themselves talking a great deal of stuff in a vulgar jargon, which after all is only an echo of public talk. If I am to drive, I want to sit above my horses. If you are to address an audience you will do well to stand upon a platform, morally, intellectually and every other way." This much affected his view of slavery and emancipation. He wanted to go very slowly, indeed so slowly that it is unclear what progress might have happened in his lifetime, if his views had been adopted by the federal government. He had no patience with "extreme Abolitionists," whom he saw as "a rancorous set." He wanted "gradual measures," for he believed that "emancipation cannot be instantaneous."[32]

In May 1862, he offered the following as a plan:

We must . . . found free colonies in the south . . . the nucleus of which must be military and naval stations garrisoned by *corps d'armée*, and grouped around them must be the *emeriti*, the old soldiers with their grant of lands, their families, their schools, churches and Northern energy, forming common cause with the negroes in gradually sapping the strength of the slave-holders, and thus year after year carrying new industry and free institutions until their borders meet from Atlantic, the Gulf, the Mississippi and the Tennessee in a common centre, and the old crime shall be expiated and the whole social system of the South reconstructed. Such was the system of the old Romans with their conquered countries and it was always successful.

This "military system of colonies" needed to be "governed by the Executive" and be independent of the states in which they were placed. His exposition of this plan was not utterly clear, though he seems to have regarded it as, in part, the Port Royal experiment writ large. As such, one infers, he saw blacks continuing as dependent laborers, for, as he admitted, "the negroes would be extremely valuable and even necessary to the development of these colonies." For their pains, they would be elevated educationally by these schools and by proximity to these benign Northern families. Such an experiment, he thought, would require fifty years, and, in this time, the South would "become ten times as great and powerful and loyal as she ever was, besides being free."[33]

This conjecture was early in the war, which is some excuse for its strange impracticality. But little, in spirit, seems to have changed later. In November 1863, he was still speaking of a "slow social revolution which will outlast our lives" and speculating that "we shall never see the south thoroughly pacified." There is no evidence of what Adams thought about the actual events of emancipation, including the passage of the Thirteenth Amendment. What we do know is that he wanted the Republicans to lose the election of 1866, because he thought they had grown arrogant and imperious towards minorities, and he seems to have had little patience with radical Reconstruction. He worried much about the breakdown of social order in the postwar South, but he blamed radicals, rather than white Southerners, for this outbreak of "brigandage." He leaned towards what he called the "Conservative Liberalism of New England," which he regretted was being "whipped and kicked like a mangy spaniel by Sumner and his party." He favored proposals urged by his elder brother in 1869 to institute educational qualifications for the franchise that would have excluded the Irish, African Americans, and the Chinese.[34] And in 1869 he was opposed to the Fifteenth Amendment, not because he objected to the rights it asserted, but because the power it gave to Congress to enforce those rights was too much of a blank check.[35] Still, in 1869, he was not agitating for the repeal of radical Reconstruction, for then he considered "the questions resulting from the war" to be "practically settled."[36] He was, indeed, more than a little dismissive of the topic. "On the subject of Reconstruction little need be said," he wrote in the winter of 1869–70 for the *North American Review*. "The merits or demerits of the system adopted are no longer a subject worth discussion. The resistance to these measures rested primarily on their violation of the letter and spirit of the Constitution as regarded the rights of States, and the justification rested not on a denial of the violation, but in overruling necessity." These measures were undertaken reluctantly by politicians and the public alike, "and whatever harm may ultimately come from them is beyond recall and must be left for the coming generation . . . to regulate according to its circumstances and judgment."[37] So, mostly, he wanted to move beyond these matters, which he regarded as a distraction from the main business of government.

It will come as little surprise to note, then, that this indifference rested partly on the racism characteristic of his contemporaries. In July 1865, he remarked, "We have done with slavery. Free opinion, education and law have now entrance into the South. . . . Let us give time; it doesn't matter much how long. I doubt about black states. I fancy white is better breeding stock." By the standards of many in his time, this racism was not especially aggressive. He seldom spoke of African Americans with the hostility and venom with which he came habitually to speak of Jews after the fiscal crisis of the mid-1890s. Indeed he scarcely ever spoke of blacks at all, even though he became very interested in the historical significance of race, a word that occurs frequently in his writings after his going back to Harvard in the early 1870s turned him into a medieval historian. (There is more on this, later.) A rare exception earlier is an Orientalist letter of 1862, where Adams describes using a Turkish bath in London: "I am eastern in my tastes; a perfect satrap; and I affect the religious light, where you lie on marble, which, for marble, is perhaps not so very hard, and smoke your cigar and chibouc too, if you order it, and drink sherbet brought to you by grinning and perspiry Ethiop youths, especially imported from the east to minister to our effeminacy."[38] For the rest, there is mostly silence, which one might think the product of distance. There is no evidence that he then knew any free blacks in the North or any Southern slaves, beyond those he had seen on the streets of Washington.

This distance applied, less rigorously, to white Southerners, too, beyond the Johnson family. Before 1865, he knew a few Southerners, though only a few. In his Harvard set, there had been Rooney Lee, the son of Robert E. Lee, and James May, both of Virginia, as well as William Elliott of South Carolina.[39] In the secession winter, Adams came to meet more of them, but warily, because they were the enemy. (On February 22, 1861, he dined at the Lee mansion in Arlington, though with whom is unclear.)[40] Further, he had little or no acquaintance with the corpus of Southern writing. When, in 1869, he was asked by his English friend Charles Milnes Gaskell to recommend reading in American literature for a lecture Gaskell was to give on American culture, Adams mentioned a number of American authors, if often with skepticism: Irving, Cooper, Lincoln, Bryant, Longfellow, Lowell, Whittier, Hawthorne, Stowe, and Whitman. But he mentioned only one Southerner, and then perhaps only because Gaskell had asked about Jefferson, and Adams recommended reading "his famous Declaration of Independence as the best specimen of his style." We know that, as an undergraduate at Harvard, he checked out from the college library the works of Edgar Allan Poe, who was a sort of Southerner. But the catalog of Adams's small personal library, which he drew up with self-important formality in 1858, shows no Southern authors at all, but rather contains assorted classical texts, modern British and French literature, and the occasional New England work.[41] So he seems to have been untroubled by knowledge of Southern thought, which was a common enough condition for a New Englander of his generation.

This indifference did not always ill-serve the interests of white Southerners. When he came to Washington in 1868 and began writing on American political affairs, Adams was impatient with Reconstruction in the South. As he saw it, the task of reconstructing the Union lay, not in attending to the needs of freed persons or in punishing white Southerners, but in restoring the probity of the political system. "Our time and labor will be most usefully spent in a regular hand-to-hand fight with corruption here under our eyes," he told Edward Atkinson in February 1869.[42] Adams was interested in free trade, the currency, civil service reform, the diminution of political patronage, and fiscal matters. He wanted to achieve a sort of purified version of the antebellum republic, which he thought had been at its best before it was corrupted by Jacksonian spoils, the Slave Power, and the unconstitutional maldistribution of political power occasioned by the war and its aftermath.

Adams had a curious view of American constitutional and political history. As he explained in late 1869 to the readers of the *North American Review*, up to 1837 when Jackson left office, the United States had had "one continuous government; that is, the President, whoever he might be, stood as regarded the legislature and the political parties as merely the temporary head of a permanent executive system, which was meant to furnish and did in fact furnish, the necessary solidity and continuity without which no government can last. The President represented, not a party, nor even the people either in a mass or in any of its innumerable divisions, but an essential part of the frame of government," that is, the executive. After 1837, a succession of weak men in the White House undermined this integrity, and the Senate, as the most powerful branch of a legislature now dominated by party and patronage, became the center of "the nervous system of the great extra-constitutional party organizations," and, in time and during war and peace, the president became little more than the instrument of patronage decided by senators.[43] By this power, the system had been corrupted and so only reform could save it. It was central to Adams's scathing anger at Ulysses S. Grant that he thought Grant had botched this task of restoration, that Grant had not only not seen the problem but worsened it.

For Adams, the premise of the early republic, indeed of the American system of government, was the denial of power to the center. This was its great difference from the European system, which insistently located power and sovereignty at the center. In the Civil War, the American system had broken down and, so, the prime task of the postwar era was reasserting the ways of 1800. Without this, Europe was vindicated and American exceptionalism thwarted.[44] Not without reason, then, have some scholars seen Adams as a civic republican, pining for the Machiavellian moment.[45] Such wistfulness is important; the perspective features in his historical works of the late 1870s and 1880s.

In summary, then, looking at Henry Adams up to 1869, one sees a young New Englander with an ancestral tie to the South, but not a tie yet much valued; someone who had been a keen advocate of moderate antislavery politics, a mild racist, a constitutional conservative, and administrative reformer; someone who was attracted to living in Washington, but not someone who knew many Southerners or who had ever visited the South beyond the District of Columbia; and perhaps, above all, someone who was a dedicated nationalist, a predilection made partly by the Adams family's involvement in the making of the Union, and still more so by his own Civil War engagement in the making of American foreign policy. But there is another side to Adams's pre-1869 engagement with the idea of the South.

After graduation he had gone off to Germany, as Harvard men then tended to do. From October 1858 until the late spring of 1859, he studied at the University of Berlin, with a side trip at Christmas to Montpellier. In April, he migrated to Dresden and mostly stayed in southern Germany for the next year, until in April 1860 he started to move southward, via Vienna, to Venice, Bologna, Florence, Rome, and, eventually, Naples and Palermo, before returning to the North, to Paris and London. This, too, was a traditional enough venture for a Bostonian, indeed any wealthy young American of his generation. For a guide, the canonical American work was George Hillard's *Six Months in Italy* (1853), and Hillard was a family friend, whose writing Adams well knew.[46] Hillard's book was in the tradition of Madame de Staël and all the Romantics who had made Italy into a place that opposed and released the repressions of northern Europe. Hillard's preface speaks of his visit as "a brief and brilliant episode," of "images alike beautiful and enduring," and of Italy as "a land of promise." He writes of passing from Switzerland to Lake Como as passing from "the cold of icy summits and sleep in lonely chalets" to "the lap of the warm south" where one becomes "a mere passive recipient of agreeable sensations."[47] It had been essential to this moral tradition of traveling to see this liberation as double-edged. Italy released pleasure, but both morally and immorally. And it was in this spirit that Adams, when leaving Florence for Rome, wrote: "I'm rather afraid that it will grow darker as I get south. That's the way of the world."[48] Darkness and light, the two things went together; the lightness of feeling coupled the darkness of vice.

The experience of Italy was profound. In Berlin, Adams had been restive, interested in German culture (especially opera and art galleries) but struggling to establish any sympathy. He complained about the climate insistently. In December, there were fogs and chill. In February, "the weather [was] detestable." In March, "for nearly five months, I have seen very little but clouds, or rather a dead dull sandy sky, and dark, rainy or damp days."[49] Italy, by comparison, was the rapture it was supposed to be. Venice was "delicious," "splendid," and "stunning." It was "the only city I've yet seen which made me perfectly happy." He did not even mind rain there. "It was delicious to glide along over the water and bask in the sun, and the islands and the lagoons looked so charmingly." "There was music on the Piazza" and he "came back to sit in the sun, and drink chocolate, and smoke cigarettes, and look at the people, and listen to the seventy two musicians." Things were "pleasant," "warm," and "lively," if a "useless, ragged sort of liveliness." He was less convinced by Padua and only briefly in Ferrara, but the day on which he traveled on to Bologna was "pleasant, the trees just budding out into leaves and blossoms," and Bologna itself "charmed" him. In Florence "everything went beautifully" and he "felt as though I'd lived in Florence all my life." But Rome was what most intoxicated him. "In Rome I'm happy as the day is long," he told his mother. "It is utterly delicious here. I wander about and poke into churches and ruins and do what I please and don't care a rap for any man."[50]

There began to form in his mind, to the point where it became an instinct, that to move south was to move towards freedom and away from responsibility. The north was winter and chill and duty; the south was spring and flowers and renewal. "The weather here for two days has been something worth seeing," is how he spoke in 1860, when in Rome, after the hard work of Berlin and Dresden. "Upon my word it is intoxicating. I feel as if I were in the uppermost of the Heavens. The air is filled with the perfume of the roses, and that sort of Spring sensation that makes everything so delightful. The sky hasn't a cloud." "The air is soft and the orange and lemon groves full of fruit," is how he spoke of Sorrento in 1865, when he traveled south after four years of tense and bitter struggle in London.[51] This language recurred in later life.[52] To move southward was to move away from the crippling obligations of collectivity, of family and tribe, towards individuality, of self and whim. When life grew too much, instinct and habit would come to tell him to pack his bags and head for the south, which gave a sort of freedom, at least for a while.

This Romantic typology of North and South was, by 1860, old by about a half century. In the 1820s, it had been chiefly a typology applied by Europeans to themselves, but in the next several decades it was gradually applied by Americans to the American case, to the difference between Massachusetts and Virginia. But Henry Adams came from the generation that was to learn this language simultaneously about the European and American cases. What one learned of Boston and Washington, one applied to Berlin and Rome; by what one learned of Sorrento and London, you understood Charleston and Quincy. The dialectic was insistent. The moral geography of Europe advanced an American education, just as an American geography informed a European one. His sentiment quoted earlier—"it will grow darker as I get south. That's the way of the world"—though written of Italy, was also redolent of Georgia.

In his case, however, in the early years the American side of this equation was mostly latent. Italy refined his cultural vocabulary, but he was very slow to apply it habitually to the American South, far slower, for example, than his Harvard contemporary Charles Eliot Norton, who was drawing the analogy between Italy and the South as early as the mid-1850s, and who wrote warmly of "the yellow jessamine flowering in golden sweetness and profusion along the roadsides" during a South Carolina spring, and of the climate as creating a "Lotus island . . . [which] wooes one to voluptuous ease and indolence, and makes day dreaming the natural condition of life."[53] It took Adams until the 1870s to move towards using this language on and about the American scene. What inhibited him earlier was politics. The darkness of the Slave Power South was what compelled his attention in the 1850s and 1860s, not the spring flowers of Virginia. When later he noticed the flowers, he was to face an intellectual problem of much complexity. As a historian, what did one say of an American South, where one could see flowers and slaves at the same time? What was to be said of serpents in Eden?

Before turning to these matters, it will be helpful to recur to Louisa Catherine Johnson Adams. Henry Adams was to make much of her offering a link with the South. But did she? His four-page account in the *Education* is, as ever, sinuous. It starts with her in Quincy, when her husband was still alive, and Henry was very young. The *Education* speaks of her as remote, retired, and fragile, but gentle and refined, someone who did not belong in Quincy, but was exotic. Adams notes her faded literary tastes, her "writing-desk with little glass doors above and little eighteenth-century volumes in old binding." He briefly rehearses her early history and gives much of a paragraph to the mistrust felt by Abigail Adams towards her daughter-in-law, as someone too little fitted for New England. He remarks that Louisa's years in Berlin were "exciting," but also that "whether she was happy or not, whether she was content or not, whether she was socially successful or not, her descendants did not surely know." He adds that her life in Saint Petersburg was "hardly gay" because impoverished, that when her husband was secretary of state she did the "work of entertainer for President Monroe's administration," and that she was miserable in the White House. He returns to a description of how she seemed to him, when she was so old and he so young. She "seemed singularly peaceful, a vision of silver gray, presiding over her old President and her Queen Anne mahogany," but also someone "thoroughly weary of being beaten about a stormy world." He sets off his childish ignorance of "her interior life" against his mature historical knowledge that she

ouisa Catherine Adams. Painted by C. R. Leslie, engraved by G. F. Storm. From James
arton Longacre and James Herring, *The National Portrait Gallery of Distinguished
mericans*, 4 vols. (Philadelphia and New York: James B. Longacre and James Herring,
39), 4:252.

had lived a life "of severe stress and little pure satisfaction." He half suggests an influence: "He never dreamed that from her might come some of those doubts and self-questionings, those hesitations, those rebellions against law and discipline, which marked more than one of her descendants; but he might even then have felt some vague instinctive suspicion that he was to inherit from her the seeds of the primal sin, the fall from grace, the curse of Abel, that he was not of pure New England stock, but half exotic." This arose from his having, from her, "a quarter taint of Maryland blood." He ends by noting that his father, "half Marylander by birth," like his grandmother had come to New England later in life, though he does not assert that, therefore, Charles Francis Adams was likewise exotic.[54]

Many things in this portrait seem to rest on childhood memories— the furniture, her appearance, the colors—but its skill and deception rests in eliding the mind of the child Henry Adams with knowledge acquired much later, indeed several times made and transformed, first in the 1840s and 1850s, second in 1869, and again after 1900 when he was writing the *Education*. To be sure, all autobiographers do this, for autobiography would be useless without the fiction that old age can realize and communicate with youth. In fact, the demonstrable influence of Louisa Adams on Henry Adams begins in Quincy and Washington in 1869, when he came to examine her extant papers and gave thought to publishing an edition of them. As he put it to Gaskell, "An ancient lady of our house has left material for a pleasant story," a strange observation given the unpleasantness recorded in many of her papers.[55] In due course, he abandoned the project, though not before transcribing about a hundred pages of original manuscripts. This was Henry's first sustained venture into the history of the early American republic, and, though it yielded very modest immediate results, the long-term consequences of reading the jumble of her papers were, in their own way, profound.

The surviving bound volume gives no direct indication of what, if anything, he might have written as an introduction.[56] One can infer something, however, from his selective arrangement. Available to him were the diaries she kept, chiefly when she was in Saint Petersburg (1809–15), then in Washington when her husband was secretary of state (1819–25), and intermittently thereafter. She also left three memoirs: the "Record of a Life or My Story" of 1825, the "Narrative of a Journey from Russia to France, 1815" written in 1836, and "The Adventures of a Nobody," which she started in Washington in 1840. The rest of the papers consist of her poetry, a commonplace book, several plays, and assorted prose compositions. Much of this—the poetry, the drama, her religious reflections—he ignored.[57] Rather he deployed the texts to tell a selective story of her life, at least up to 1823.

He drastically abridged the period before her meeting John Quincy Adams, for he gave only five pages to her childhood memoirs of the London and Nantes years. By contrast, he gave thirty-two pages to the Berlin years, sixteen to the Boston/Washington period of 1801–9, and forty for Saint Petersburg and her journey from it in 1815. He then intruded twelve letters from Abigail Adams and two from John Adams, all to Louisa between 1811 and 1821. Next he transcribed some of her diaries from the secretary of state period, again interspersed with letters from Abigail and John Adams. Then there is a stern admonitory letter from John Quincy Adams in 1834 to his son John, which sits next to a whimsical 1826 poem by "J. B. Johnson" about the tedium of the Adams White House. But otherwise there is nothing after 1823, except a few letters from Louisa to her children between 1845 and 1847, all of which serve to narrate the decline in health of John Quincy Adams. The last document is a letter from Pauline Neale, an old Berlin friend: it offers condolences at the death of Louisa's husband, and speaks elegiacally of her own experiences of loss.

This selection suggests the young Henry was interested in Louisa for her own sake, to be sure, though not much as a Johnson from Maryland. There is no Johnson family correspondence to balance out the letters from Quincy. Mostly he seems to have been drawn to her as the wife of a diplomat (but not a president or an antislavery crusader) and as someone whose experience commented on the strengths and weaknesses of the Adams family. One infers he saw the strengths as mostly coming from Abigail and John, the weaknesses as coming from John Quincy, for their letters are sympathetic, while his sole letter is a priggish sermon. This was certainly Henry's opinion in 1909, when reviewing Brooks Adams's draft biography of John Quincy Adams: "I knew that the old man was in a high degree obnoxious to me . . . but I had no idea how acute the antipathy would be. . . . At the same time I am bound to add that it [reading the manuscript] has enormously increased my respect and admiration for his father and mother, whose criticisms are the foundation of my own. You have brought into violent light the contrast between their natures, wholly to the advantage of the father."[58] So his early sympathy for Louisa arose, mostly, from her sad plight of having married his grandfather. She focused the problem of family damage.

The portrait in the *Education* is likewise selective, though differently. In 1907 Adams nowhere mentioned that Louisa was an incessant, if unpublished, author and that for her day she was well educated. He shows her only as a social or familial creature, and, when mentioning her writing desk, he was interested in the piece of furniture and the books above it, not the manuscripts she wrote on it, which he had troubled to transcribe in 1869. In fact, in the 1780s she had attended various good schools in London and a convent in France, and she was fluent in French, an accomplishment of great use in Russia, where French was the language of imperial and aristocratic society. Throughout her life, she was a reader, if in a scattered way. The evidence of her reading only partially validates Henry's sense that she was eighteenth century, a sense much driven by his desire to see Quincy and his inheritance as immobilized in that century. As applied to her taste in drama, his judgment was almost wholly accurate. In her youth, she had made frequent visits to the London theater and there saw, among many others, the luminous Sarah Siddons, with the result that she often tried to write plays in the vein of the eighteenth-century drama. Her notebooks contain sustained criticisms of Shakespeare, but her compositions are closer to Gay, Sheridan, and Goldsmith than to the Elizabethan or Jacobean tradition; they have such titles as "The Wag" and "The Innocent Convicted." She also much liked memoirs, especially those of French ladies of the eighteenth century.[59]

But Louisa also tried to keep up. She read, for example, the newfangled periodicals. On the whole, she preferred the *Edinburgh Review* as an original, disliked the *North American Review* as a thin imitation ("very pedantic very affected full of conceit and without the proportion of talent visible in the [*Edinburgh*]"), and had mixed feelings about *Blackwood's* ("there are some admirably written things tho many of the pieces are arrogant, supercilious and inflated"). She had the usual taste for Walter Scott and in 1820 nearly missed a diplomatic dinner because she was so "deeply immersed" in *Ivanhoe*. She read Madame de Staël, at least her *Corinne*.[60] She was much drawn to poetry and liked Byron in the disapproving way that respectable ladies were obliged to affect (his "strong native genius . . . becomes a curse to the possessor and to mankind at large when it is used to bad purpose"). She once danced and sang with Thomas Moore ("He said that I sang delightfully but I wanted *Soul*") and insistently wrote verse of a sentimentality now hard to bear or read, but poised in spirit between the sensibility of the 1770s and the romanticism of the 1820s.[61] Certainly she lacked the instinct for control and repression, and the capacity for exuding competence, that the eighteenth century tended to prefer. She once said of herself, "I am precisely the Louisa Johnson I was when I married Mr Adams. The same romantic enthusiastic foolish animal as unfit for real life as I was then and as conscious of all my defects which as I rise become more striking."[62]

Still, she could admire control, even if she could not manage it. In 1821, she rode out with John Adams from the Quincy house, so that he could show her the "fine prospects." With some reluctance, she acknowledged that "they are in fact beautiful" and that "the natural scenery is lovely possessing all the charms that hills, Valleys rocks woods Water and forrest can bestow." But she had to add that, "there is a mellowness in the scenery of older Countries," which she preferred. "I do not know how to explain it unless it is owing to the artificial arrangement of the Parks and Gardens of Europe which ever and anon break into the rougher views of nature unadorned and operate like the fine passages in Byrons poetry to dazzle and astonish the imagination if not to satisfy the understanding." So she tended to mistrust the new modes and was sharply conscious that she lived in a changing world. She went in 1821, for example, to hear Henry Clay speak to the House of Representatives and remarked: "I was disappointed in him I confess—the style of oratory of the present day does not please me—it is too much studied; too theatrical, and, of course, too cold." She was too much of a Christian moral critic to be a thorough Romantic, since she preferred plain supernaturalism to the "natural supernaturalism" of Thomas Carlyle. Romantics did not, as she did, praise "solid and sterling merit" over "high sounding bombast and a considerable share of Rhodomontade." Nor did they observe, as she did in 1822, after hearing some lectures on rhetoric and belles lettres, "Is not this age run mad? What is modern poetry? a chaos of crude undigested thoughts preposterously metaphysical and soaring so far beyond the real conceptions of mortals belonging to this terraquous Globe that the mind is carried out of itself, and we unconsciously admire because we are sensible we understand cannot."[63] True to this, she once read Emerson with apoplexy: "I have just perused the Address of poor W. Emmerson!!! It is full of balderdash and that *conceit* which makes men mad!!!"[64]

Why Henry Adams in the *Education* disregarded his grandmother's literary gifts is unclear, for he knew from Marian Hooper that a woman could be intellectually gifted and once devoted a novel to exploring the phenomenon. But in 1907 he had weightier figures to help in carrying the story of how the eighteenth-century mind grappled with the nineteenth. (Himself, mostly.) Doubtless he saw Louisa's gifts as ramshackle, as indeed they were. She herself knew this. "I am incapable of research," she once said, though she did not seem to mind the incapacity. No bluestocking, she had little respect for formal learning and once praised James Madison for having "a mind so copious, so free from the pedantry and mere classical jargon of University Scholarship."[65] As fastidious a critic as Adams might have drawn back from her prose, which shows little command of form, but is impetuous, pell-mell, oddly punctuated, inconsistently spelled, but possessed nonetheless of a great vivacity and a relentless honesty, turned on herself and others alike. Still, it was in her prose that Adams will have discerned, whether in 1869 or later, "those doubts and self-questionings, those hesitations, those rebellions against law and discipline, which marked more than one of her descendants," which meant, at least, himself.[66]

Adams's portrait is of a retiring woman. Certainly, this was how she lived in her old age, a fact she herself lamented. In 1839, she observed, "When I retired to a private station, I resumed the privileges of an individual in the right to choose my associates—Was I right I fear not! for I have narrowed my circle of acquaintance to nothing; and what is infinitely worse it has led to an indulgence of feelings of dislike, and often antipathy; unsuited to christian charity."[67] But Adams also drastically underestimated her earlier sociability, other than in his laconic reference to her role as a hostess in Monroe's administration. This is hard to understand, since all her diaries testify to a woman drawn irresistibly towards fashionable society, about which she was anxiously and waspishly critical. To be sure, inaptly, she thought of herself as a social incompetent, as someone unpretty, shy, proud, and hysterical, and there is no doubt that she found society an ordeal. When very young, she had been terrified of venturing beyond the family parlor. As she remembered, "[I] thoroughly detested every thing like society beyond my own home unless it was an occasional visit to the Theatre. So decided was this trait in my character that I would shed tears for hours previous the going out to a party never open my lips while there and return to my home in . . . glee."[68] Later, she acquired a nervous ability to cope, but she was not a little paranoid about what people were saying of her, and eventually developed a contempt for the whole business of levees, balls, receptions, and dinners, at least insofar as they played too large a role in oiling the machinery of American politics. But, in fact, she was good at the game and at least one historian has suggested that Louisa self-consciously used her drawing room as a campaign headquarters that helped to turn the socially inept John Quincy Adams into a president.[69] Contrary to her self-image, society became her natural element, even from the time that her parents' home in London had served as a headquarters for expatriate Americans. Her problem, in fact, was rather that she was never very good at domesticity. One reason that there had been tensions between Louisa and her mother-in-law, the worryingly competent Abigail Adams, was that Abigail was good at domestic management and Louisa never did get the hang of what should go on behind the drawing room.[70] As Louisa remembered of the time when she shared Boston and Quincy with Abigail, "I hourly betrayed my incapacity; and to a woman like M[rs] Adams, equal to every occasion in life; I appeared like a maudling hysterical fine Lady, not fit to be the Partner of a Man, who was evidently to play a great part in the Theatre of life."[71]

Louisa was, indubitably, a "fine Lady," someone who dressed well and talked well, who could please a tsar and a president, and who would be offended if servants were impertinent. She had the habit of command, but also a sense of melodrama. She would lose her temper, retreat to her bedroom with the vapors, and brood on the world's ill-treatment. In many ways, she was socially a cut above the priggish and awkward American she married, for he came from a family notoriously befuddled about what society might demand of ladies and gentlemen, and she from a Maryland family of elegant social standing; her father's household in London had, at one point, eleven servants, which undoubtedly exceeded anything to be found at Quincy, where it was thought that debts ought not to underpin munificence. Abigail Adams, indeed, knew the Johnsons between 1785 and 1788, when John Adams was the American minister in London, and she deeply disapproved of their extravagance.[72]

Louisa's misfortune—tragedy was her own view—was that, just as she married, her father lost his fortune, and the handsome dowry of £500 promised to John Quincy Adams never appeared; indeed, John Adams as president was obliged dubiously to scavenge up a job for his son's father-in-law. She was mortified by this and claimed she carried the psychic scar for the rest of her life. There is no reason to doubt her. When she stepped out into the world, she remained troubled that someone would find her out, that they were saying behind their hands that she had no right to be there, that she ought to have married a Hackney schoolteacher and did not deserve membership in an American dynasty.

Henry Adams rightly spoke of the lateness of her introduction to American society. She was twenty-six when she first set foot in the United States and described herself as "a forlorn stranger in the land of my Fathers." But Adams did this, mostly as a way of explaining that she was not "educated . . . for a life in Quincy and Boston." She would not have disagreed with him on this score. Her memoirs exclaim about first seeing her husband's home: "Quincy! What shall I say of my impressions of Quincy? Had I steped into Noahs Ark I do not think I could have been more utterly astonished."[73] But Adams's explanation for this alienation had two aspects: the physical fact that she grew up abroad and the genealogical fact that she came from a Maryland family, and of the two it is the "Maryland blood" that is given more weight. So Adams gives the unclear impression that, as an American and a Marylander, she was therefore antithetical to New

England. This was because, in his narrative, she had been allocated a chief role as a siren enticing him away from Quincy and Boston, and only a minor role as someone who might draw him away from the United States.

There are many and grave difficulties with this emphasis, though they are historical, not autobiographical. Adams saw Louisa in her American years and saw her in Quincy and Washington, so it is natural that this was how his emphasis fell. But, as a historian and a reader of her manuscripts, he might have seen something more complex, though (in his defense) the complexity is easier to discern now than it would have been in 1869 or 1907. In Adams's day and life, the counterpoints between European and American, Southerner and New Englander, were very sharp, because proved by wars and rebellions. In retrospect, it is creditable that Adams saw that someone like himself might be a hybrid of Northern and Southern. Certainly his father never saw it, nor did his brothers. The autobiography of Charles Francis Adams Jr. makes nothing of Louisa, and Henry Cabot Lodge, in an explicit rebuke to the *Education*, observed that "the Southern blood brought in" to the Adams family by John Quincy Adams's marriage "seems to have had a sentimental rather than a real effect."[74] A hybrid Anglo-American or European American (to use a modern and anachronistic term) was harder to see, even with the example of Henry James, perhaps even because of the example, which the Adamses usually found discouraging. In 1882 Marian Adams reported laughingly to her father: "I had a farewell letter from Henry James, Jr., written Tuesday at midnight on the eve of sailing. He wished, he said, his last farewell to be said to me as I seemed to him 'the incarnation of my native land'—a most equivocal compliment coming from him. Am I then vulgar, dreary, and impossible to live with? That's the only obvious interpretation, however self-love might look for a gentler one. Poor America! she must drag on somehow without the sympathy and love of her denationalised children. I fancy she'll weather it!"[75]

The cultural identity of Louisa Adams is, in fact, surpassingly elusive, and Adams came nowhere near capturing its richness. That it was rich is readily explained by a reiteration of the migrancy of her life. She was born of an American father and an English mother in London in 1775; she moved to France in 1778 and back to London in

1783; in 1797 she married and spent the next four years in Berlin; in 1801 she went to live in Massachusetts and remained there until 1809, though after the election of John Quincy Adams to the U.S. Senate in 1803, she partly lived in Washington with her sister Nancy Hellen and, indeed, at first declined to accompany her husband back to Quincy when the senate was out of session, though in 1806 his earnings as a part-time Harvard professor bought a house in Boston, where she consented to live.[76] In 1809 she went with him to Saint Petersburg and stayed until 1815; then she lived in London until the summer of 1817, while her husband was the American minister. The years from 1817 to 1829 were mostly an oscillation between Massachusetts and Washington, but more Washington when John Quincy was president from 1825 to 1829. Two years were then spent solely in Quincy, but in 1831 he was elected to the House of Representatives and the Washington/Quincy shuttling resumed until his death in 1848. Thereafter she mostly lived in Washington until her own death in 1852. But this bare recitation underestimates the quicksilver quality of her life, for in most of these places she lived in many different houses, and, in her early and middle life, she seldom inhabited anything other than rented accommodation or the houses of relatives, often when her husband was somewhere else. Her possessions inhabited and her life was measured out in packing cases.

That her father was self-consciously an American was of great importance, for she doted on him, far more than his emotional instability, financial incompetence, and perhaps dishonesty seems to have warranted. "My father was the handsomest man I ever beheld," she remembered. "His eye or the power of his eye was indescribable; its usual expression was sweetness and benevolence; but when roused to anger, or to suspicion; it had a dazzling fixed severity that was absolutely awful; and which seemed by its vivid scrutiny to dive into the depths of the human heart—his temper was admirable; his tastes simple; his word sacred; and his heart pure and affectionate as that of the most unsophisticated Child of Nature—and the greatest fault he had was believing every one as good, as correct, as worthy as himself." He had come to London as a merchant in 1771, when he was twenty-nine, and was to stay (apart from his period in

Nantes) until his fortunes were ruined in September 1797 and he was obliged to return (or flee) to the United States. Upon Louisa's account, he stayed very close to the American expatriate community, traded with and for them, offered them hospitality, and, after being advised by his brother of its wisdom as a paternal policy, made sure that his daughters did not mix unduly with the English. Joshua Johnson was self-consciously a patriot, who named one of his children "Carolina Virginia Marylanda," and Louisa remembered being schooled in the heroic narrative of the Revolution ("I gloried in the heroic and General Washington was my idol"). So Louisa grew up in a sort of American immigrant ghetto, though not one that could be hermetically sealed. For one thing, her mother was English; for another, she went to English schools, attended English theaters, had mostly English servants, and read English books. For a third, she had spent six years in France, at an impressionable age. Like many children of immigrants, she had mixed feelings about the commandment to abjure the locals. Her memory of Thomas Johnson's advice was unenthusiastic: "In consequence of my Uncle's silly letter although we lived in the midst of the city of London we were kept almost entirely out of English society and visitted only one family in the street in which we lived." So it is not surprising that, in a passage where she spoke with disillusion of her marriage—"imprudent it is for a woman to form a connection in a foreign Country"—it is hard to know whether England or the United States is the "foreign Country."[77]

This sense of liminality may have been compounded by shame.[78] Louisa's mother, Catherine Young, was illegitimate, the daughter of a Mary Young and a "Mr. Nuth," and it is tolerably clear that Louisa knew this, for she would refer to her maternal grandmother as "Miss Mary Young" and not "Mary Nuth." Further, it is opaque whether Catherine Young and Joshua Johnson were ever legally married—at least, no record has ever been located, though several historians (including someone commissioned by Henry Adams) have tried. It seems that Johnson got the fifteen-year-old girl pregnant and they began living together. On balance, it seems more likely that a marriage did, in time, occur, though perhaps not in time for the birth of their first child on December 22, 1773. Still, there is evidence of what society then would have designated sexual impropriety for two generations in Louisa's maternal line, which may explain the occasional insistence in her diaries that she herself had always been chaste. There is little evidence, however, that she self-consciously identified with England, though she was a subject of George III. The law over citizenship was in a great muddle in these years, since the British enforced the doctrine of perpetual allegiance and the Americans of voluntary, but it is probable that, on either grounds, she was never an American citizen. She once described herself as "brought up a republican and living in a Monarchy." In 1796 Abigail Adams was less ambivalent, indeed rather cruel when observing of her son's fiancée, "I would hope for the love I bear my Country, that the Syren is at least *half Blood.*" By 1815, when Louisa was returning to live in London, Abigail was more kindly, but still indisposed to see the former as an American, in expressing the hope that Louisa would be "invigorated by the Air of your Native Soil."[79] True to this, in the federal census of 1820, the household of John Quincy Adams is shown as containing three "foreigners not naturalized," and it is probable that Louisa was among them.[80]

Nonetheless, her Englishness was oblique; it lay in habits, tastes, and occasional viewpoints. She had, as John Quincy Adams observed to his mother in 1796, "the habits of life necessarily formed" by growing up in England. Louisa worried, for example, a lot about class and hierarchy, about social behavior and etiquette.[81] Once, when traveling in Berlin, a servant was obliged to ride with her, and she remembered that, "I felt as if the greatest insult had been offered to me and set it down as another consequence of the downfal of my family—the American can never understand the sensation of mortified pride which I endured but an Englishman would blaze at the idea and you must remember that even my father had never seen America since she had become a Republick." She was very impatient with a "time serving democracy," and much preferred a world where hierarchies were clear and formal. Indeed almost her greatest trial was that an American drawing room was supposed to contain social equals, yet obviously did not, and she could never figure out how the American game of inequality should be played. When newly in "the little society of Washington" in 1804, she felt this sharply:

My manners were frigid, cold, and repulsive; and being naturally timid, and educated under much restraint; much was attributed to pride which was caused by fear of giving offence, or clashing with some usage which I did not understand, or some omissions of ceremonial with which I was totally unacquainted—At the Courts of Princes you get written instruction's to teach you the forms and ettiquettes—you are therefore seldom liable to give offence by erring—In a democratic government where all are monarchs; although *one* yourself, there is a perpetual struggle for a *position*, which gives rise to constant feuds, and demands utterly impossible to satisfy, which lay the foundations for absurd enmities that can never be reconciled.

But the sense never abated. Even in 1821, she was writing that social criticism of her as too courtly was exasperating, for she tried to "be as simple in my habits as nature originally intended me to be." In America, there seemed to be no ascertainable rules. "Could I ascertain what Republicanism is it would be possible to find some rules by which to regulate my future conduct but while the Nation itself appears to be wavering as to what the essence of this said Republicanism may really be it would be very difficult."[82] There is, in such a passage, more than a whiff of Mrs. Trollope.

But was she, as Henry Adams claimed, a Marylander? Her father was. He "was from Maryland, then considered quite a southern state and his politicks and his prejudices were all of the same cast of character," she was to note. These prejudices were significant in structuring those whom she was likely to meet, for "my father was not very fond of the Yanky and they were not much encouraged to visit at our house." This explained, for her, his dislike of John Quincy Adams: "He was a great favourite of my Mothers but I do not think father admired him so much. He always had a prejudice towards the *Yankees* and insisted that they never made good husbands." Later in life, she very occasionally expressed an explicit sense of identity with the South, which she regarded as somehow antithetical to democracy. "For my part," she said in 1822, when her husband was being accused of aristocratic tendencies, "I am very willing to show that I am the publick *servant* but I will never be the *Publicks Slave*—I have too much of the Southern Dominion in me." But Maryland itself had small meaning for Louisa. She had little to do with her father's family there, except that occasionally cousins would visit her in Washington. And she was not above working the family, if it helped her husband become president. In 1823, she noted: "I rode over to Mrs Frye's who was here last night with one of my cousins from Frederick as my connections in this State are of the most respectable and distinguished I am solicitous to secure them in his interest. Maryland it is said will be his." But she had essentially no link with her kinsfolk in Frederick, mostly because she inherited the tensions between them and her parents, for the former had not taken well to the latter's sharp and embarrassing decline in fortune. As Louisa noted, with some bitterness, in her memoirs, "I have been forty three years married and I have been but once since our first visit to Frederick and Mr Adams has never been there from the day that we left my father [who was dying]—My poor Mother was no favourite with her husbands relatives. She had been the spoilt child of excessive indulgence and her change of fortune came hard to her in her old age."[83]

The District of Columbia, on the other hand, did become very important to her, because it contained so many of her siblings. Her diaries are full of visits to especially her sister Kitty, the wife of William Steuben Smith (the grandson of John and Abigail Adams), but also to her sister Carolina, married in turn to Andrew Buchanan and Nathaniel Frye. In time, Louisa would be very close to and dependent upon her niece and widowed daughter-in-law, Mary Hellen Adams, of whom she wrote in 1836: "Mary has become my companion, my friend, and I find more pleasure in her society now that she has learnt to understand me, than in all the glare the world could proffer." But even this loyalty to place was segmented, for it scarcely extended even to Georgetown, where both "Sister Frye" and "Mrs Smith" lived. In 1821, Louisa went to a wedding party there and found herself "an utter stranger," because "the people of George Town and Washington associate so little that there were not more than half a dozen faces that I had ever seen before."[84]

But does "Southern" describe her? In some senses, no. In fact, her diaries show an instinct for standing equidistant between the two regions that mattered in her life, New England and the South. In 1822, a Mrs. Blackledge from North Carolina insisted to Louisa "that the Northerns were not so sociable as the Southerns which I endeavoured to make her believe was because she was not sufficiently acquainted with them." But such equidistance meant she was free to criticize both, which she did more often than she defended both. For example, she once criticized Caroline Langdon Eustis, the wife of a Massachusetts congressman and herself from New Hampshire, for having "too much affectation about her, and a sort of bending condescension which is more suited to the meridian of Boston, than to that of Washington." By contrast, she preferred "the good natured ostentation of Mrs Brown [which] produces more eclat"; Ann Hart Brown, the wife of a Louisiana senator, was a Virginian. And there are several passages where Louisa clearly associated Southern culture with social ease, with a greater willingness to laugh, and dance, and roll up the carpet, as her father used to do when she was young, and as they never did in Quincy. In the case of her sister Nancy Hellen's home in D.C., "The society . . . was delightful[.] Talent, Wit, Good humour, and an easy and general desire to please promoted freedom, without the familiarity of rudeness; and the young and the old, were received with equal respect and pleasure, with the security of the surest welcome—Music, dancing, Cards, or more frequently social and brilliant conversation, varied the Scene."[85] But it is notable that she felt less easy than the others, so this was a quality she admired, more than a trait she was confident of possessing.

By a reverse token, she could be very critical of Southerners, especially Virginians. In 1819 she dined with James M. Garnett and James Barbour, two of the leading Virginian politicians, and afterwards observed that "the one [was] an odd compound of liberality and V. prejudice and the other [was] formed only to breathe his own atmosphere as he appears to have a soul incapable of expansion fitted only to exist within a few given miles and willing to believe every thing beyond it a perfect chaos." "Prejudice" and "Virginia" seem to have been words that ran together in her mind, for a congressman called Archer was likewise "a disagreeable pedantic prejudiced Virginian."[86]

On the politics of slavery, too, she tried to be equidistant, though in her day evenhandedness tended to hint at the pro-Southern, especially if the views issued from the Adams household. During the Missouri crisis, she was mostly anxious that her husband should stay out of the controversy, and this remained her theme for many years, even when he became deeply engaged in antislavery politics. Mostly, she saw slavery as an economic issue, as a clash of interests, more than she saw it as a moral problem. Even later, she was to observe, "My reason tells me that much is to be said on both sides of the question. It is a great struggle for power and dominion equally subjecting the rights and privileges of both parties—And when the master passions of men are concentrated upon the vital interests of wealth and power reason loses her hold of the minds of men and the overweening stimulus of jealousy adds fuel to the fire." But she sensed in 1820, as most people did, that it was "a very portentous crisis" that might end in "some tremendous explosion." She could read and admire a proslavery argument, then read and admire its refutation. In 1835, she wrote:

The awful question of Slavery is before the publick and the question is of so fearfully exciting a nature it keeps me in a state of perpetual alarm. God has said blessed are the peace makers: then why should we to promote the end of a few factious politicians endanger the lives of thousands or occasion panics and alarms almost worse than death. . . . If in the wondrous wisdom of the Almighty Power the decree has gone forth may he mercifully grant that my husband may be spared from becoming the scourge through which the great event is to be achieved; and may heaven inspire my lips with persuasion to prevent mischief so threatening and awful.

Like her son and grandson, she saw the South as more powerful than vulnerable: "By the encrease and magnitude of the Slave States the Northern confederacies must in the end be over powered in so far as the influence of the Government is concerned." So "mortal emnities" were natural. She saw the dialectic of mistrust. The Northerners, being

wealthy, powerful, educated and religious . . . feel and disdain the manacled population of the South, and the good and respectable part of the community suffer the religious feeling of misguided sympathy to hurry them on to measures without observing the terrible results to which they really expose their haughty, but really afflicted brethren. And these in their turn arrogantly assume the imperial and dictatorial tone appertaining to the very nature of their jurisdiction, operating perpetually to exasperate the deadly feuds which irrisistably grow from the radical influences of their joint positions.[87]

Here, she seemed more sympathetic to the South, for the sympathy of the North for the slaves was "misguided" and occasioned unnecessary and unwise turbulence.

Elsewhere, however, she was more critical. She was unimpressed with those who argued that slavery was sanctioned by the Bible, and even denied that the Old Testament sanctioned the institution. The New Testament was still clearer to her: "It has been urged that Christ in the course of his ministry on Earth, did not preach against it as a part of Christianity. The basis on which the principles of Christianity are founded, militate so strongly against the system of Slavery, that it was utterly unnecessary and would have been an entirely superfluous thing, to have particularized that which in no possible way, could be analogous to the practical principles of the Christian Creed."[88] In general, she seems to have felt that slavery was wrong, but that the political instability occasioned by its agitation, let alone the personal dangers that any abolition would cause slaveholders, necessitated quietism.

Her own personal experience helps to explain this abstract stance. She had grown up far from the institution and had first seen a slave only when two children of Charles Carroll of Carrollton (the younger Charles and Kity) had passed through London on their way to a Dutch school and been accompanied by a "black woman [who] was to be sent back immediately." "The slave was a novelty to us," she remembered, "and the treatment of that Slave by her young M^rs was a thing we could not comprehend as we had always been severely punished for improper conduct to servants and this matter produced many unpleasant scenes while the woman staid between us young people." This Jeffersonian impression that proximity to slaves was corrupting persisted. In the summer of 1821, she was on a packet taking her to Providence, Rhode Island, and aboard were "Mr & Mrs & Miss Hunter of Charleston, SC." Of the youngest of these, Louisa tartly observed: "Miss Hunter is a pretty little Girl whose language and manner indicate her thorough acquaintance with Negro waiting maids."[89] Nonetheless, in Washington, Louisa consistently had black servants. One of them, whose name was Nelson, accompanied her to Russia.[90] There is an entry in her diary for December 21, 1819, where, complaining of having to make so many social calls, she wrote of leaving behind "often only a little black Girl to take care of house and family during our absence or perhaps a set of Slaves who would delight to see the whole fabrick destroyed during our ceremonious excursions." Consistent with this, the 1820 census shows that the household of John Quincy Adams in Washington contained a female slave under the age of fourteen.[91] It does not follow that she was the property of either Louisa or her husband. He, at least, as a Massachusetts politician would have been unlikely to have risked such a possession, nor she as his wife. But if someone else in the household did own the girl, or if she was hired in, it meant that the Adamses would have availed themselves of her services, as they availed themselves of the services of slaves when visiting Louisa's relatives.[92] Later, in 1850, the slave schedules give no evidence of her household containing any slaves, but the population schedules do show the presence of a forty-year-old black male called Overton Barnes. It seems likely that there were more than him. In the early 1840s, at least, she had a steward, a butler, "two boys," a porter, a housekeeper, a cook, and certainly more, for she inscribed this domestic rule: "The coloured females [are] to apply to Housekeeper for permission to go out and to be sent away if they are not at home at ten o oclock at night or for impudence or disrespect to any of the White people in the family." Certainly, she seems to have been a conventional racist. She once laughed when James DeWolf, the U.S. senator from Rhode Island, who was from a family that had made its fortune in the slave trade, showed himself to be socially inept: "He is probably better versed in *Affrican politeness* than in Senatorial dignity. . . . two or three millions of dollars will wash out many stains especially if those stains are *black*."[93]

On all of this, Henry Adams was silent, though he had once read the manuscripts. As telling is that, in the *Education*, he said nothing of Louisa Adams as an observer of American politics. Yet her diaries and memoirs had offered him in 1869 instruction in the politics of the early republic, which was to become his subject matter. Even more striking is that many of her judgments and preoccupations were to find echoes in his scholarly writing. She was, for example, fascinated by the bizarre spectacle of John Randolph, some of whose last days as a politician coincided with her own time in Washington. Randolph provided her with a supply of amusing gossip, but she also was moved to pity. In February 1820, she dined with her husband and Daniel Pope Cook, a congressman from Illinois, and the topic of Randolph came up, for the Virginian had been holding forth in the House of Representatives for some four hours that morning. "Poor man he has so entirely sunk in the publick estimation, that he is by many thought to be partially insane; and a mere wreck of what he once was great in intellectual power," she wrote in her diary. She surmised that Randolph sensed his situation. "There is a sort of painful consciousness about him of this fact, which excites compassion, and it is impossible for a feeling and reflective mind not to witness such a debasement, without being grieved at the awful changes which a few short years [have produced]." He was, she thought, living upon his vanity and pride: "He barely exists upon the recollection of his former greatness and is dying at the loss of it—a perfect hypocondriac at one moment revelling in the fairy dreams of gratified ambition the next sunk into gloomy despair and sending for friends to close his eyes."[94] She seldom saw him, except from the visitors' gallery in Congress, but she liked to set down the tales of his antics, his jokes, and his increasingly few moments of intellectual power when he "spoke with all the fervour and real eloquence which he most certainly possesses." In her memoirs, she tried to sum him up; the verdict is worth quotation.

Full of all the attributes of mind which *forms* great men, his temperament was irritable and sensitive almost to madness; and he was incessantly goaded on in his political career by a wild ambition, ill regulated passions, petty jealousies and indomitable perseverance—Every act was a phrenzy though the purpose was often good, and there was a sort of method in his Speeches; yet like Hamlet 'tis difficult even to this day to prove that he was insane—Even in extremes he was at times a delightful companion; or an insolent bully—in fact every thing by starts and nothing long enough to learn to love him or respect him. Surrounded by admirers who loved the excitement produced by his waywardness and his brilliant rhapsodies; he appeared to be the great man of his day, for he ruled the timid and amused the weak, till his *duties* produced the most serious consequences; in the shameless persecution of men infinitely superior to himself; and to whom, the Nation owed a debt of gratitude for long and faithful services To sum up the whole he was to congress what Shakespeares *Fools* were to a Court. He kept Congress awake with "his quips and cranks" and made the *Ladies* smile—peace to his manes.[95]

Elsewhere in her writings are judgments as acute, sometimes close to what Henry Adams was later to say, sometimes not. At first, she was susceptible to the charm of Henry Clay, as many were: "There is something about Mr Clay that pleases me in spite of reason—and it is this: that if you watch his character; you almost immediately discover that his heart is generous and good, and that his first impulse is almost always benevolent and liberal." Still, she was not deceived by this charm, for she also observed that "a neglected education, vicious habits, and bad company, united to overweening ambition; have made him blush to act the better part, and covered with foul blots that which might have been made perfect." Later, in 1821, she was more struck by his bullying vanity: "From the habits acquired by leading a party he is always domineering and arrogant and usurps by his dictatorial manner the greater proportion of the discourse which he generally contrives to make offensive to some one or other. Altogether he is the oddest compound of vulgarity and courtesy I have ever met with." Towards Calhoun, when secretary of war, she was more sympathetic: partly because she saw him *en famille*, she grieved at the death of his child, and she sympathized with his struggles with inconveniently strict and Calvinist parents; and partly because she saw him as young, put-upon, and as yet out of his depth. "Poor Calhoun is most direfully persecuted," she noted in 1821. "He has some great political enemy who is working his ruin and he requires a great fortitude to get through it—It is whispered that he is intriguing for the Presidency and that this has aroused many who would otherwise support him but they think him too young a man to have pretensions such." Later, about a dinner party attended by Clay, Webster, and Calhoun, she reported: "This is what we call a snarling dinner composed of such opposite materials it was not possible to prevent sharp speeches Mr Clay assumed a very high tone and forced our Secretary of War completely into the back ground." She was not above a little snarling on her own account. The campaigns of 1824 and 1828 did little to endear Andrew Jackson to her: "The vice of ingratitude and the basest injustice is the foundation of my disgust of this man's character," she said in 1836.[96]

But she had been in Washington in 1803, so she had opinions about the older generation, too. Towards Jefferson, she was consistently scathing, even though her father had once been a Jeffersonian. It did not help her good opinion that, notwithstanding, Jefferson had removed Joshua Johnson from his office as superintendent of stamps and she judged the disappointment had hastened her father's death. (She seems to have forgotten that it had been Jefferson's casting vote as presiding officer of the senate that in 1800 had accomplished the appointment in the first place.) For the rest, she saw Jefferson as a hypocritical and scheming demagogue, without principle and courage, "a jest among brave men," and someone who had only "the sneaking greatness of mere good fortune attained in a lucky hour; and by a concurrence of propitious events." "Every thing about him was *aristocratic except* his person which was ungainly ugly and common," she insisted, when remembering dinners at the White House. "His manner was awkward, and excessively inelegant; and until he fairly entered into conversation, there was a sort of peering restlessness about him, which betrayed a fear of being scanned more closely by his visitors, than was altogether *agreeable* to his self complacency—while conversing he was very agreeable, and possessed the art of drawing out others and at the same time attracting attention to himself." Madison, however, she admired, though she tended to see him as a sort of worthy bureaucrat, with a career "neither brilliant, nor calculated to dazzle the senses," but a peacemaker by conviction and instinct. (His death in 1836 prompted a sense of contrast with Jackson, not a peacemaker by instinct.) Still, she had some sense of Madison as a Founding Father, for she observed that he had "the simplicity of mental greatness." And she had much preferred his company and manners to Jefferson's. For her, Madison "was a *very* small man in his *person*, with a *very* large *head*—his manners were peculiarly unassuming; and his conversation lively, often playful, with a mixture of wit and seriousness so happily blended as to excite admiration and respect. . . . his language was chaste, well suited to occasion, and the simple expressions of the passing thought, and in harmony with the taste of his hearers."[97]

For John Adams, of course, she was obliged to have special feelings, which transcended politics. (Indeed, nowhere in her writings does she discuss the old man's politics.) While her relations with Abigail had been complicated and tense, with "my father," as she came to call him, they were warm and affectionate. She felt especial gratitude that he had gone out his way, even at some political cost, to accommodate Joshua Johnson. She wrote some of her diaries in the form of a journal, written for his eyes, in which he was asked to respond to her comments and questions.[98] That for December 1819 begins, "I shall attempt to renew our correspondence in the old form, in the hope of enabling you in some measure to participate in our pleasures and troubles, which [we] must expect to have intimately blended." And if, indeed, he did read her journals, her frankness did much credit to their relationship, for it showed her confidence that "the old gentleman" of Quincy cared for her. Once she remarked, "I am a very good diplomat—You may laugh but it is so—Egotism is the quintessence of journalizing so that I need make no apologies; and I am so silly as to believe that nothing is more agreeable to an affectionate correspondent than a full history of ourselves and all the little events of our lives." In retrospect, she could say, "From the hour that I entered into his family, the Ex-President John Adams never said an unkind word to me; but ever to the hour of his death, treated me with the utmost tenderness, and distinction the most flattering—I loved him living, and venerate his memory."[99]

All these judgments and memories can be found in the manuscripts of Louisa Catherine Johnson Adams, which her grandson sat down to read in 1869. Few of them can be said to have found their way into his own memories and judgments of her, at least in the *Education*. But it is easy to see how much she might have influenced his trajectory as an American historian, for much of her world became his subject matter, and in her writings are portraits of men whom he would labor to realize and whom she had brought to life, perhaps for the first time in his experience. For, above all, Louisa understood that politics and history were an intimate matter of fallible human beings, and, even when Henry Adams most aspired to the role of the dispassionate scientist, this was a truth he did not neglect.

CHAPTER TWO

The Little Society of Washington

In the sixty years between his departure for Germany in 1858 and his death in 1918, Henry Adams lived in New England for only eight, of which seven were spent teaching history at Harvard. The years from 1870 to 1877 constitute the only period during which he submitted to the Adams family obligation to serve Massachusetts and New England. As was usual with him, self mattered more than family, though in 1870 he was still a bachelor and felt the pull of home more strongly than when, later, he had married. Further, he was at a loose end. His career as a journalist in Washington had not been a success, though there had been odd if insufficient moments of influence. Remaining very interested in political influence, he conjectured that he might exercise it more effectively as editor of the *North American Review*, which was the second part of the job he was offered at Harvard, the first being the task of teaching medieval history. He had spent much of his intellectual apprenticeship in the world of the great British periodicals and knew their power. Certainly, it was arguable then that the *North American Review* was the most influential organ of intellectual opinion in the United States and plausible now to think that this editorial chair mattered more to Adams than his professorial one, though he threw himself into the duties of both. His letters show a man eager about finding contributors, editing essays, setting priorities, dispensing advice to writers, but also a man puzzled about what a professor or a student was for, diffident about his historical knowledge, bored by the rhythms of an academic year, and little enchanted by those he met. In both Cambridge and Boston, he found "no society worth the name, no wit, no intellectual energy or competition, no clash of minds or of schools, no interests, no masculine self-assertion or ambition." His family offered little respite. "My family muddle on in a stupid way out at Quincy," he observed soon after his return in 1870, "and I go over there every Saturday and pass Sunday with them." In 1871, he wrote: "My family has migrated again to Quincy where they live merrily or at least soberly in their pig-stye, and I go over once or twice a week to see them." So he was often solitary and was prone to taking "long walks" to see the spring flowers.[1]

Adams disliked the New England climate, for he hated being cold and damp, especially cold. He was a man who watched thermometers, bundled up warm, lit fires, and pined for winter to end. Like many wealthy people, he would come to migrate to preserve himself from ever experiencing a chill: in his last years, he would spend the winter and spring in Washington, summer and autumn in France. One reason he disliked England, though he liked a good many English people, was the stubborn English indifference to bodily comforts. He was among that generation of Americans who began to cultivate the womblike amenities of modern plumbing and heating, and thereby to lose touch with their stoic transatlantic cousins, who saw nothing problematic in the cold toilet seat and the stuttering faucet. In 1892, Adams took a Channel steamer from Calais to Dover and shivered over "cold foot-warmers of the last century," as the steamer was wrapped in "an icy fog that froze my back-bone." "I shook with cold," he told John Hay. "Seizing a state room and shutting myself up, I wrapped every coat and rug I had, or could find, round me, and lay down under a heap, and rang for hot tea." Surely, he asked, "a steamer might be warmed"? The train to London was cold, the customs house at Charing Cross was cold. And the English did not seem to care. "I can understand," he said, "that their art should be bad and their literature rotten and their tastes mean, but why the deuce they should inflict on themselves cold and hunger and discomfort, hang me if I can understand."[2] Such a man was not a natural inhabitant of Boston, partly because in this small matter, as in larger matters, he was not a Puritan (except very obliquely) or indeed even a latitudinarian Christian of the Emersonian sort.

So Adams's characterizations of New England history and culture were unsympathetic. In 1871 he spoke of Harvard as "this curious corner of the world, which only the perversity of human nature ever could have conceived to be fit for the existence of animated objects," where in January the temperature could vary from zero to seventy. In 1875, he observed, "Our New England climate and soil do not even breed picturesque situations or incidents. We are but a rather improved low-country Scotland and our lives and deaths are too absolutely unimaginative to adorn a tale." He told a story of a neighbor's suicide and noticed that "there was no flourish, no pathos, no moral, and except for his poor children and his old father and mother, no tragedy about it." This was so because, "We are a practical people. We are sternly conscientious." Young women were taught to improve themselves and be strangers to innocent amusements. They were starved of emotional nourishment to the "poor little hard thin, wiry, one-stringed instruments which they call their minds." The men were little better, just "harmless intellectual prigs" who "in the same devoted temper talk 'culture' till the word makes me foam at the mouth."[3] In 1877 he told Hugh Blair Grigsby, the Virginian historian, that the New Englander was "narrow, nervous, self-distrustful often, always introspective, uneasy, and till lately, intolerant." In later years, this habit of disparagement was not to die away, although he rallied in the *Education* to offer a more affectionate portrait, at least of New England as experienced by a child. Still, in general, it was more typical of him to refer to Boston's intellectual provincialism, "green with mental mould" as he was to put it in 1906. The stifling uniformity habitually vexed him. As he remembered it in 1887, "in the New England of that day [his youth], there was little divergence of condition, and not much of character." In Samoa in 1890, he reflected on the puzzle that there a sensual climate had not created a passionate people, but rather one which lived "a matter-of-fact existence that would scare a New England spinster." This flinty empiricism in New Englanders could, on occasion, evince a little more than disregard, but it was grudging. "I admire" the Puritans, he told Henry Cabot Lodge in 1876, "but I shall not deny that they were intolerant even according to the age in which they lived."[4]

So there was much to push Adams away. Even his marriage to a Bostonian in 1872 did not alter this, which was in some ways odd, not least because she was fiercely tied to her Bostonian father. As

Adams acknowledged, marriage traditionally pushed one deeper into the cycle of Bostonian loyalty. "Boston is a curious place," he told Charles Milnes Gaskell in 1876. "Its business in life is to breed and to educate. The parent lives for his children; the child, when educated himself, becomes a parent or becomes an educator, or is both. But no further result is ever reached."[5] But Marian Hooper Adams, too, liked to travel. And it became relevant that they never became parents. Why, we do not know. Conjectures have roamed widely and wildly. It has been claimed that he was sexually impotent, a favorite charge to bring against New England men whose marriages ended badly, for it was said of Sumner, too. But there seems no evidence of this, for either of them.[6] That Adams had a copy of J. Marion Sims's *Clinical Notes on Uterine Surgery with Special Reference to the Management of Sterile Conditions* (1873) in his library has led to the more plausible speculation that she was infertile.[7] Of late, we have had the assertion that they did not want children and, curiously, practiced a mysterious form of birth control, taught exotically to those in the Sturgis and Hooper families who had plied the China trade. There is more evidence for the former claim than the latter, for Adams did once confess to a friend, "I have myself never cared enough about children to be unhappy either at having or not having them, and if it were not that half the world will never leave the other half at peace, I should never think about the subject."[8] Whatever the reason for childlessness, one result was that the pressure of tribal loyalty, occasioned by having added to the kinship network, was not brought to bear on them, except in the form of guilt. So it may be no accident that they left Boston five years after their marriage, long enough to indicate the possibility of childlessness if not its certainty, and they migrated to a place where bachelors and itinerants were the norm and where society did not revolve around family hearths.

But why Washington? Departure from Boston was one thing, arrival somewhere else was another. The Adamses could have settled in many places, even if they had confined their choice to the United States, which their friend Henry James would have thought unnecessary. Given their class and tastes, many places were impossible or deeply unlikely, but New York and Philadelphia were not. Many New England intellectuals were beginning to be drawn to New York, which was making itself a sort of national literary capital. But Adams, though he set his novel *Esther* there and had the heroine of his other novel *Democracy* come from there, does not seem to have regarded New York as much more than a hotel and a dock, from which one went to Europe; its commercialism and bloated vulgarity did not offer what he wanted from a city. This was not so of Philadelphia. Fairly consistently, Adams was an admirer of the city and its culture, and he even tended to see Pennsylvania as the best, most balanced of American places. But Philadelphia had declined since 1800 and Adams in 1877 was interested in attaching himself to a place that was growing, vibrant, fluid, malleable. In truth, what he would have preferred was an American London or Paris, a great city at once the capital of the arts, politics, finance, and high society. But there was no such place in the United States. Washington had national politics, but no art or finance. New York had finance, a middling-to-high society, and a little art, but no national politics. Philadelphia had no national politics and a diminishing quality of society, finance, and art. So, in choosing Washington, Adams said something about what mattered most to him, politics. As Henry James was to observe of Adams's fictional counterpart, Alfred Bonnycastle, he "was not in politics, though politics were much in him." An ambition to be, if not a statesman, then (as he put it) "a stable-companion to statesmen" was much alive.[9] But politics was also amusing and he was a man easily bored, much in need of amusement and gossip, and certainly no place lives and dies more by gossip than a political capital. Still, for most Bostonians, the choice was inexplicable, since they mostly agreed with Horace Greeley's famous judgment: "Washington is not a place to live in. The rents are high, the food is bad, the dust is disgusting, and the morals are deplorable."[10]

Further, Adams had his family connections, sufficient that on a visit in 1874 he referred to Washington as "my native asphalt." The phrase was accurate. The immediate area of Lafayette Square was textured with associations, both his and Marian's. It was not just that his father, his grandparents, and his great-grandparents had lived across the square in the White House. But Louisa and John Quincy Adams had also owned a house around the corner at 1333–1335 F Street N.W., when the latter had been secretary of state and again (after an interregnum in which it had been rented out) after 1838. When Henry had come to Washington in 1868, he had briefly stayed with William Evarts at the corner of H and 14th Streets, which was one block east of Lafayette Square, before moving in with his aunts Catherine Johnson Smith and Mary Hellen Adams, who lived on the corner at 1601 I Street, which was two blocks away. (Louisa and John Quincy Adams had lived there, too, while he had served as a congressman after 1831 and before their return to F Street in 1838.) In October 1868, Henry had moved to a rented apartment on G Street, west of 20th Street, which was about four blocks west of the square.[11] The previous tenant of 1501 H Street (one block east), which he and Marian first rented in 1877 from William Corcoran, had been Marian's uncle Samuel Hooper, the Massachusetts congressman. In 1875 as a married couple they had visited the house, but Marian had also inhabited its attic in the spring of 1865, when in the lower rooms had temporarily lived Andrew Johnson, who in the immediate wake of Lincoln's assassination and in the midst of Mary Todd Lincoln's distress had opted to delay his possession of the White House. And there was another Hooper who haunted the neighborhood. Alice Mason Hooper, the widow of William Sturgis Hooper (the son of Samuel Hooper and so Marian's cousin), in 1866 had married Charles Sumner, moved into a rented house at 322 I Street, then built a house at the corner of Vermont Avenue and H Street, where a view of Lafayette Square was intended. (Only intended, because the marriage, to the great satisfaction of the discontented many who knew Sumner, ended with splendid acrimony and a speedy divorce in 1872, and she never saw the inside of the new house.) Further, moving beyond family to patrons, William Henry Seward had from 1861 rented a house on the east side of Lafayette Square. In 1874, George Bancroft moved to 1623 H Street. Later, of course, the square drew and was populated by Henry's friends, by Elizabeth and Donald Cameron, and by Clara and John Hay.[12]

So Lafayette Square was a sort of New England village green, around which the Adams familiars and their ghosts walked and lived. And, in the way of village greens, enemies were nearby, too. The successor to Seward in the three-story red brick mansion, which Adams could see from his window at 1607 H Street, was James G. Blaine, whom he and Marian refused to call upon, for the sake of reprobating his notorious corruption. "I am glad indeed that we never broke the man's bread nor so much as pulled his doorbell," she told her father in 1882. "Mr. Lowndes and we alone in this society took that stand, and for eight prospective years to cut the Secretary of State was a measure which brought on us much criticism and some ridicule, I fancy, but let me say that we are not now the only three who cry 'Stop thief'—not by a long sight. He's down now and so they can safely jump on him."[13]

This clinging to the neighborhood of Lafayette Square was eloquent of Adams's connection to the geopolitics of the District. From its foundation, the city had had two centers, the Capitol and the White House, each connected and divided by the long spine of Pennsylvania Avenue, which for many years was but a "desolate country road" vulnerable to flash floods and traversed only twice daily by a stagecoach. In the early years of the republic, in the days of Washington's "village simplicity," around the Capitol had crowded the many boarding houses where from December to March every year senators and representatives had lived, in raucous remoteness from their families at home. Approximate to the presidential palace were the executive departments (state, war, navy, treasury) and their employees, who lived nearby.[14] So it was no accident that Seward, as secretary of state, had lived on Lafayette Square, as it was no accident that the Adams family had clung to the western side of the city, because John Quincy Adams had first bought property there when he, too, was secretary of state. To be sure, by the late 1870s, this pattern had much broken down. The muddy roads had turned to asphalt, trams connected neighborhoods, and wives and children had started to appear. Still, the shadow of the old pattern could still be seen and, so, Adams's haunting of Lafayette Square said something about his allegiances. However much he might despise the caliber of the presidents who came to live opposite him, and however many senators and representatives he might take for friends, nonetheless the Washington of his moral imagination revolved around the White House and its diaspora.[15] In Adams's mind, the executive branch was supposed to be worthy, so its failure occasioned regret and comment. But he seldom imagined that a congressman could be other than wretched, so any transcendence of this miserable standard was notable. One of his favorite quotations exemplified this bias. He first told it in 1881: "A friend, in high administrative office, said to me the other day when I recommended tact as a means of dealing with legislators: 'Tact is of no use! A Congressman is a hog. You must take a big club and hit him on the snout!'" He told it again, with aesthetic adjustments, in the *Education*: "One never expected from a Congressman more than good intentions and public spirit. Newspaper-men as a rule had no great respect for the lower House; Senators had less; and Cabinet officers had none at all. Indeed, one day when Adams was pleading with a Cabinet officer for patience and tact in dealing with Representatives, the Secretary impatiently broke out: 'You can't use tact with a Congressman! A Congressman is a hog! You must take a stick and hit him on the snout!'" As for senators, they "passed belief."[16]

This need not have been so. John Quincy Adams had, after all, been a senator and a representative, just as Charles Francis Adams had sat in the House, and the former had been a senator before ever he became a secretary of state. But John Quincy Adams between 1803 and 1808 had lived not near the Capitol and in a boarding house, but with his wife and Hellen relatives in Georgetown, still more westward from the Capitol than even the White House. And Charles Francis Adams in 1860 had lived at the Markoe House, near the triple intersection of I Street, Pennsylvania Avenue, and 20th Street, which was five blocks west and one block north of Lafayette Square.[17] An Adams went to Congress as a condescension, even when an elected member of Congress, for everyone knew (or thought they knew) that an Adams could only be passing through, on their way to or from the other part of town.

Beyond the specificity of neighborhood were other enticing considerations. The climate mattered greatly—the mildness of the winter, the beauty of the spring, the flowers. (Adams was devoted to flowers.) In the nearby fields and woods of Virginia and Maryland, he and Marian would ride, and on the Potomac they would gently sail. Henry James was to write, after visiting them, of "those soft, scented days of the Washington spring, when the air began to show a southern glow, and the little squares and circles . . . to flush with pink blossom and to make one wish to sit on benches."[18] The summers, to be sure, were stifling, but they and he never spent summers there. And there was the practical consideration that Adams needed the archives of the federal government for his histories of the early republic. But, in choosing Washington, he chose more than he bargained for, perhaps even more than he understood, for he entered a place with special dynamics, in which the matter of Southern culture was important. He was forced in unexpected directions, and his writing acquired a new structure.

Before the Civil War, Washington had been a Southern small city, which, as a recent historian has observed, felt much more like Mobile and Richmond than like Hartford and Albany.[19] The District was located on Southern soil, was slaveholding, and mostly dominated not only by the Southern politicians who came and went but by those Southerners who were its permanent residents.[20] Charles Francis Adams Jr. was to remember the "unkempt barracks" of the boarding houses where the congressmen lived, which "all had the third-rate, Southern-slouchy aspect and atmosphere," and to recall that "the social element was altogether Southern in sympathy and in expression."[21] Of this element, the Adams brothers' maternal ancestors, the Johnsons, were typical. They were among the many families— the Burneses, the Carrolls, the Tayloes, the Dorseys, the Lewises, and their ilk—who had owned much of the land, rented the houses, provided the boarding houses, run the local newspapers, built and administered the churches, founded the orphanages, run the industries and the schools, and threw many of the parties.[22] The war had disrupted this Southern hegemony because many in the social and economic elite were forced to leave, but many returned and reclaimed their property.

In the years after 1865, the city expanded. In 1860, it had had 75,000 people, but in 1870 this had become 132,000, in 1880 178,000, and two years after Adams's death it was 438,000.[23] The city was attracting migrants, and Adams was typical, as someone who moved to town, rented a house for a while, then built his own. Nonetheless, in Adams's early days in the city, it remained demographically a Southern place. In 1880, the city had 88,278 white residents: about 18.3 percent of these were foreign born, but of the Americans, 53.9 percent had been born in the District, another 25 percent came from Southern states (almost all from Maryland and Virginia), and only 20.9 percent came from the rest of the United States.[24]

Further, there were 43,404 African Americans, who formed about a third of the population: of these, a third were born in the District, and two-thirds came from the rest of the South, again overwhelmingly from Virginia and Maryland.[25] As they had in the days of Adams's grandmother, these furnished the servant class, and in using them, he was typical, too. Over the years, his domestic household in Washington came to consist of a fluctuating black population of cooks, maids, and the like—Marian Adams called them "our African adjutants"— though it has been suggested that they had first unsuccessfully attempted to use white servants.[26] These black faces discomfited Henry James when visiting. He complained in 1882 of the absence of the liveried servants to which he was accustomed in England and invidiously remarked that "Washington is too much of a village . . . [and] too niggerish." But he shrewdly observed, in a short story describing the Adams salon, that the servants had "a complexion which served as a livery."[27]

Early on, there was a cook called Margery Talbot, who at 1607 H Street perhaps lived in the building set apart in the back and so, presumably, inhabited what had once been the slave quarters.[28] It is unclear how long she was employed, but it was at least as late as 1892, when Adams complained to Charles Milnes Gaskell, that "my old negro cook demands £10 a month."[29] In the autumn of 1885, in preparation for the migration to 1603 H Street, she had been joined by Maggie Wade as a housekeeper.[30] Since 1882, there had also been William Gray, a mulatto who has been variously described as butler, valet, and majordomo, and who doubtless was all of these things.[31] In addition, there was Brent the groom, who was employed as early as 1881 and was still in the household in early 1901.[32] Most important, though, were Gray and Wade. They cared for Adams's comforts when he was resident, but also indispensably looked after the house when he was away.[33] As far as one can tell, on only one occasion did Gray travel with Adams, when in 1892 the latter went to England and, in anticipation, wrote lightly to Sir John Clark: "I shall bring with my importance my own colored valet or major-domo, a bright mulatto youth who is wild to see the world, and has been so faithful to me

Portrait of an African American woman (identified as "L.S."). Photograph by Marian Hooper Adams. Courtesy of the Massachusetts Historical Society.

for ten years that he now thinks he has a right to ruin his morals and manners by foreign travel. He will take charge of the establishment as far as his duties extend, and if he is not taught to drink and steal, may smash to his heart's content. I never interfere with the destruction of my porcelain."[34]

These flit in a ghostly fashion through Adams's letters, not much as human beings, mostly as conveniences, people who were to be given orders, mostly orders to offer conveniences to grander, whiter folk. Of William Gray, Adams never spoke with much sympathy, though his references to Maggie Wade show more humanity, at least when she grew older. "I must come home soon to nurse William and Maggy in their old age," said from Kent in 1898, was doubtless ironic. A remark from 1907 has a more sincere ring: "Maggy had vertigo, fell, ruptured a blood-vessel in the head, and has been occupied for the time since by trying to get straight. She improves always, and is about, but needs care and time. How much time she will need, I don't know. No more does anyone." Still more humane were words written after her death: "Maggie and I were long ago prepared for the end. She was very low about herself, especially since her stroke two years ago, and I tried to encourage her by the happy hope that I would go first. I can't say that the prospect helped her much, but I still think it was a fair race." This sympathy was personal, not generic. Adams was a man who could write casually, as he did in 1892, that when out riding near Rock Creek Church, "my horse shied at a nigger."[35]

As is the way with servants, these were present at many intimate moments. It was William Gray who announced to the world the death of Marian Adams, when a friend of hers came to the door, asked for the mistress, and was told "Mrs Adams is not at home," because "Mrs Adams is dead." It was Gray who in 1912 picked up Henry Adams, who had had a stroke, helped to carry him upstairs to a bed, and fetched the doctors. And it was Gray who sardonically and usefully suggested to a medical consultant that the bevy of three doctors, one medical student, and three nurses who buzzed around the sick Adams might be motivated by impulses extrinsic to the Hippocratic oath. "They are living on terrapin and his champagne here," he whispered in Dr. Worcester's ear. This care by Gray does not seem to have been reciprocated. In 1914, he went suddenly insane and Adams delegated

Powhatan [with groom, Brent]. Photograph by Marian Hooper Adams. Courtesy of the Massachusetts Historical Society.

the problem to a niece, who arranged for the servant of thirty years to be committed to an asylum. Adams's account of the affair was typically self-absorbed. "I have been met by a domestic collapse," he told Elizabeth Cameron, "for my man William Gray has broken down and gone to hospital. How I have outlived everything!"[36] Indeed working for Henry Adams does not seem to have been good for one's health. Of the four most-important members of the Adams household in Washington, two lost their grip on reason, a third was frequently anxious and ill, and a fourth often aspired to oblivion.

Of Maggie Wade, it is possible to know more, for twelve letters of hers survive, all but one written to Louisa Hooper between 1898 and about 1908, and so they cover some of the later years when Adams was a widower. Being letters from a black servant to a white surrogate-mistress, they need to be interpreted with caution. Nonetheless, they were written with some freedom, intimacy, and confidence, qualities that suggest Wade felt she had a respected, even a warmly regarded place in the household, at least in the eyes of Adams's nieces. She seems to have seen 1603 H Street as her "home." In 1898, she wrote of a holiday at Malcolm, in the Maryland countryside, "It is about 25 miles from Washington & quite a pleasant place to be, but I feel like a stray cat in a garret I have not left off thinking of home & it is time for me to go back."[37] She felt free to use the house's stationery, the same used by her employer.[38] The letters show someone attentive to her domestic duties, for there is much talk about looking after decorators and builders, of sewing and hanging curtains, of putting out a vase of flowers in spring, and of hiring extra staff to care for visitors. Wade was a frugal housekeeper, beyond the necessities of so affluent a household; in one year, she took care to buy cheap coal in the summer, to spare Adams the expense of expensive coal in the winter.[39]

But she was often ill, of chills and the "grippe," and spoke of being "run down." To help, she tried to lose weight, had massages, and drank Lithia or Poland mineral water. Work was a therapy, too, especially when she was grieving for a younger sister, who had died suddenly in the midst of the wedding preparations for another sister. "I have relied on hard work which give me little time for thought," she said, because "to tell the truth my hands and brain has been so full at times I hardly know what to do."[40] Religion helped, too, by offering a formula of words, since otherwise "when I want most to express myself I loose the power of speech & am forced to silence."[41] There is evidence that she worried about the imminence of death, for when she died intestate, Adams wrote that he was "surprised she did not leave a will, for she has been expecting some such end for years."[42] So Wade's letters are marked by insistent anxiety.

They are also marked by neediness, especially for affection and company. The latter need was noticed even by Adams. "As for my Washington house, the more you use it, the better," he told Brooks Adams in 1898. "William and Maggy are longing for company." She often complained of solitude when Adams was away—"everywhere has a look of loneliness here"—and so hunted for clues that he might be returning, and glowed when the house had the excitement of guests and she could be busy with tasks and the possibility of conversation. Though, to be sure, sometimes the white people came so thick and fast that she could not distinguish them: "We had stay with us for two weeks Mr & Mrs Brooks Adams. and after they left we had Mr Arthur Adams for three days, with a friend of his. I cant remember his name." She especially liked visits by the Hooper nieces, who gave her presents (pin cushions, a broach, family photographs), with whom she could gossip, who shared womanly concerns (dressmaking, flowers), and to whom she could freely express her "very best love." She liked them, even when they occasioned untidiness, the housekeeper's bane. To "Miss Loulie," she wrote during one January, "I do not want to find you changed even if does mean tidiness. I for one love to see your things lying around. so be a little careless whilse here. I shall count the days until you come."[43] She did not like it when they married and so visited less. Mabel Hooper married a son of John La Farge on September 8, 1898, and two days before, Wade wrote to Mabel's sister: "Another thing is I feel that another one of you will be marrying soon, & so I shall hear of my little girls slipping through my fingers as tight as I may try to hold them, one by one."[44]

Her attitude towards Henry Adams was cooler, more solicitous than affectionate. He wrote to her occasionally, presumably with instructions, and sometimes gave her presents. And sometimes she liked his letters. In 1898, "he wrote a sweet letter to us the last time telling us of his trip up the Nile & Turkey & then to Anthens to see Mr Rockhill I think he felt we was looking for him home." But she had more often to complain of his silence when away from H Street, and of having to prepare the house for a deadline he did not trouble to disclose. "As I have said we have no news," is a common sentiment. Still, living with him, she seems to have understood his exasperating nature. She knew his reticence about private ills, even trifling ones. So, "Mr Adams has a cold but of course he wont own it."[45] She looked after him, even when he was oblivious of her discreet support. One of her letters has this: "Miss Loulie I think Mr Adams is looking for a letter from you, of course I don't know it, but he shows more eager for mail each morning. And said 'no mail for me' when I entered with a card this morning."[46] As he sat and wrote about the world's disorder, she quietly surrounded him with regularity.

Beyond the household was the city. In Adams's early days, Washington society was divided between the descendants of the older residents, known as the "Antiques," and the newcomers. As a newspaperwoman observed in 1873, "The old provincial Southern city is no more. From its foundations has risen another city, neither Southern nor Northern, but national, cosmopolitan."[47] This transition created tensions. The Antiques were self-consciously defensive and in 1865 had even created their own organization, known quaintly as the Association of the Oldest Inhabitants of the District of Columbia, which was officially dedicated to keeping "alive the reminiscences of the past" (which Adams certainly did), but also to civic improvement and, tactfully for 1865, the disregard of "section or political distinction."[48] So it is pertinent to ask where Adams stood in this divided world, since he might have been regarded as the heir of Antiques or a newcomer. The answer seems to have been: a little of both. He and his wife were welcomed by the Antiques when they arrived in 1877 and rented a house owned by an eminent Antique, the banker William Corcoran. Some sniffed at them, to be sure, especially for their sharp and irreverent tongues. Violet Blair Janin, who lived in Lafayette Square too, was more than sniffy. "The Adams [*sic*] . . . run altogether on the fact of having two dead presidents in the family," she said in 1883. "Still as those who went before the great grandfather were very plain people, we of older blood do not think him [Henry

Adams] such a great aristocrat."[49] Nonetheless, in general, they were admissible.

On the other hand, they were among the newcomers. So the easiest way to understand their position in Washington society is to see them as intermediaries. This is evident in his novel *Democracy*, where there is a portrait of Washington society. In it, all the elements mix: the politicians from various sections like Senator Ratcliffe, the foreigners who staffed the embassies like Aristarchi Bey, the social newcomers like Madeleine Lee, and the old hands like the Virginian John Carrington. These sorts mingled in the Adams salon, too, and Henry showed sympathy for almost all of them, except the politicians, and this disdain was typical of an Antique, for Antiques looked on the passing herd of senators, congressmen, and presidents as ephemeral and vulgar people who did not know their way, as country cousins who wore white gloves awkwardly at inaugural balls.[50] It is a disdain that survives, though today the Antiques are known as "cave dwellers." Their literary expositor now is Gore Vidal, who rightly sees Henry Adams as his spiritual ancestor.[51]

Living in Washington brought Adams, for the first time, into sustained intimacy with Southerners. He became especially close to three of them, and had more than an acquaintance with a fourth: General Richard Taylor of Louisiana, Lucius Quintus Cincinnatus Lamar of Mississippi, James Lowndes of South Carolina, and Sarah Nicholas Randolph of Virginia. These were, for the most part, his contemporaries or older.[52] This was of consequence, for it meant he dealt with the survivors of the old order. With younger Southerners, especially those of a New South persuasion, he had little or nothing to do.

Adams may have first met Richard Taylor in November 1868, when the former called upon the widow of Zachary Taylor in Washington.[53] Their friendship rested partly on their sharing of a familial connection with the White House, since Taylor was "a son of a former President of the United States." More important was the younger Taylor's being "a first-rate raconteur and whist-player," as well as a "brother-in-law of Jefferson Davis, himself one of the best of the rebel Major Generals, [and] a great friend of the Prince of Wales."[54] In truth, Taylor was precisely the sort of Southern planter, politician, and soldier whom Adams always claimed to abominate.

Richard Taylor. Courtesy of T. Michael Parrish Papers, MSS. #4513,
Louisiana and Lower Mississippi Valley Collections, LSU Libraries,
Baton Rouge, La.

Taylor had been a lazy, undisciplined, and handsome student at Yale, before assisting his father in the Mexican campaigns.[55] In 1850 he inherited 147 slaves and a Louisiana sugar plantation called (aptly) Fashion, about twenty miles north of New Orleans. This he administered with some kindness—even Frederick Law Olmsted admitted— but he eventually ran it into the ground, by a mix of overinvestment (he had expanded to 197 slaves by 1860), too many loans, a few bad crops, and too many expensive amusements, especially race horses.[56] In the politics of the 1850s, Taylor had started as a Whig like his father, then migrated to the American Party, and then become a Democrat who supported James Buchanan, opposed Stephen Douglas and popular sovereignty, and eventually voted to leave the Union. In all this, he was never preeminent, but was usually important. He was among the dozen Louisianians who attended the Democratic convention in Charleston in 1860 and with reluctance joined those who seceded from the meeting and, eventually in Baltimore, nominated John C. Breckinridge. As chair of the Committee on Federal Relations of his state's senate, it was Taylor who sponsored the bill to authorize the Louisiana secession convention of January 1861, which he attended. When hostilities began, he was at first reluctant to do more than advise on military affairs at a distance, but he was quickly drawn in, fought with "Stonewall" Jackson in the Shenandoah Valley campaign, and ended up as commander of the Department of Alabama, Mississippi, and East Louisiana, where he is usually thought to have struggled with skill and imagination against odds too great to be defeated by those qualities alone. Immediately after the war, he worked for leniency towards the South, not least towards his brother-in-law, partly in ineffectual conversations with Andrew Johnson—the Taylor name could still gain an access to the White House—as well as with Thaddeus Stevens and Charles Sumner. He also tried to repair his fortunes, especially in undertaking the lease of the New Basin Canal, which was to link New Orleans with Lake Pontchartrain. This venture proved ruinous. In 1873 the state legislature annulled his contract and required him to pay back several hundred thousand dollars, which he declined to do. Wisely, he removed himself to London for a year, which is how he came to know the Prince of Wales. Albert Edward of Saxe-Cobourg-Gotha much took to Taylor, had him as a houseguest at Sandringham, and had him elected to the honors beloved of those country gentlemen, planters, and royalty who liked whist, horses, and gambling, that is, to membership of the Marlborough Club and the British Turf Club. Back in the United States, Louisiana remained a risk, so Taylor went to live in Winchester, Virginia. He drifted into being a political lobbyist, mostly working for Samuel Latham Mitchell Barlow of New York, an attorney of great wealth who had since the 1850s worked the Democratic side of the political scene. So lobbying was Taylor's occupation when Adams came to know him. In 1878, he was working to gain subsidies for Thomas A. Scott's Texas and Pacific railroad. He had also begun to write his memoirs.

A lobbyist, a rebel, and a shady entrepreneur was not a man whom the Adamses ought to have cultivated, but the lobbying seems to have been gentlemanly, the rebellion gallant, and the entrepreneurship more incompetent than venal, so his wit, skepticism, gossip, and charm compensated.[57] A careful man like Henry Adams seems to have liked someone who was reckless and went on "with indifference to consequences." (It was part of the attraction of Clarence King, too.) Taylor's early death left a considerable void. Marian Adams observed in January 1881 that "we all miss General Taylor sadly and no one takes his place."[58]

Charm seems to have been the indispensable quality for a Southerner to gain entry to the Adams salon. Taylor laid it on with a trowel, especially with Marian Adams. In 1879, for example, he gave her a small, clay pot, "once in the possession of John Randolph, whose mental aberration ended in his drivelling idiocy," and his letter conveyed it with a literary arabesque: "Hitherto, you have strewn with flowers every path in the garden of hospitality, and I have been permitted to gather the golden fruit without hearing the growl of Cerberus. May this wretched 'échantillon' of the arrested intellect of China serve to allay the wrath of the monster." Lamar, too, could end letters with flourishes: "During your absence my thoughts often wandered to you & always, let me say, with great affection; for you have been *so* kind to me, & I am proud to be your friend, L. Q. C. Lamar." As Henry was to put it, Lamar was a man well able to turn the "grandly courteous Southern phrase," indeed was "one of the calmest, most reasonable and most amiable Union men in the United States, and quite unusual in social charm."[59] Indeed Lamar was so charming that Adams judged that if the Confederacy had had the wit to send him as an envoy to London, instead of futilely to Saint Petersburg, Lamar's tact and humor might have prevailed against the Adams family in influencing the British government. In 1877, Lamar was the junior senator from Mississippi; the senior was the black politician Blanche K. Bruce, with whom Lamar managed a cordial relationship, if scarcely an alliance.[60] Before the war, Lamar had knocked around between Georgia and Mississippi. In Georgia, where he had been born in 1825, he had worked as a lawyer (mostly in Macon), and married a daughter of Augustus Baldwin Longstreet, the Methodist college president best known for writing *Georgia Scenes*. In Mississippi, Lamar had taught law at the state university (where his father-in-law had become the president) and briefly tried his hand at being a planter, at a place inaptly named Solitude, for solitude was scarcely Lamar's way. He operated at a lower social level than Taylor's, in that Lamar had only twenty-six slaves in 1857, but like Taylor he seems not to have prospered, though his failure was less spectacular. Their differences are instructive. Taylor was a sort of Southern aristocrat, but Lamar was more a representative of the new Southern middle class. The former, with brilliant casualness, wrecked his world and had the self-confidence not to repine for it, but the other (if with smiles) worked to hold things together. Lamar was a dogged officeholder: a Mississippi congressman from 1857 to 1861, the Confederacy's envoy to Russia, again a congressman from 1873 to 1877, then U.S. senator until 1885, when he became Grover Cleveland's secretary of the interior, before in 1888 undertaking an obscure stint on the Supreme Court.

Adams spoke of Lamar in 1878 as "the most genial and sympathetic of all Senators and universally respected and admired." The former might have been true, but the latter is very doubtful, not least because Lamar was frequently absent from his duties. But Northerners often liked him, sometimes more than his constituents did, for he was a proponent of the New South and had made his postwar congressional reputation by giving a eulogy on the death of Charles Sumner. It is a nicety whether, in this speech, generosity outdid hypocrisy, but each facilitated the will-o-the-wisp of sectional reconciliation. Still, it is doubtful that in 1874 Lamar was accurate in observing

L. Q. C. Lamar. Photograph by Marian Adams, 1884. Courtesy of the Massachusetts Historical Society.

that "Mississippi regrets the death of Charles Sumner, and sincerely unites in paying honors to his memory," or that Mississippi admired Sumner's splendid intellect, high culture, elegant scholarship, varied learning and, above all, "those peculiar and strongly marked moral traits . . . which gave the coloring to the whole tenor of his singularly dramatic public career," unless Mississippi chose to dwell on the word "peculiar." But the world applauded Lamar's temerity, and even James G. Blaine, that connoisseur of hypocrisy, was seen to weep in his speaker's chair.[61] Henry Adams was well aware how hard it might be to coin a judicious phrase about Charles Sumner.

The warm admissibility of Lamar, as well as Taylor, to the Adams household said things about a tendency towards political amorality. It was not merely that Lamar did his share to disfranchise and brutalize his African American constituents, especially when the scrutiny of the North lessened in the 1880s, though even as late as 1879 he had prudently thought disfranchisement a "political impossibility." (Henry Adams was himself indifferent to this matter.) It was that he, like Taylor, was an energetic proponent of subsidizing the Texas Pacific Railroad and was fond of promoting federal internal improvements in the South, and that these policies, while they probably did not line Lamar's own pockets, certainly helped to line those of many others, whom Adams was in the habit of deprecating. So charm, the ability to be "chatty and in good spirits" at dinner, counted for much among the Adamses, perhaps more than policy. A connoisseur of gossip is seldom able to sustain an unambivalent probity, as Henry James was to observe. During his 1882 visit, James reported to E. L. Godkin that the Adamses sometimes disapproved of the company James was keeping; he had dined with Blaine, for example. However, "I notice that they are eagerly anxious to hear what I have seen and heard at places which they decline to frequent."[62] Still, both Taylor and Lamar were independent spirits, capable of disobeying a party line and doing the surprising thing, not always in their personal interest, and that was a quality that went far in the Adams salon, further than the political virtue that Charles Sumner had humorlessly represented.

Of the third Southerner, James Lowndes, much less is known. He was a South Carolinian, descended from a family most notable for having produced William Lowndes, who in the 1810s had competed

James Lowndes and Boojum. Photograph by Marian Hooper Adams. Courtesy of the Massachusetts Historical Society.

with John C. Calhoun and Henry Clay for preeminence in Congress.[63] Of him, Adams was graciously to observe that "no better example could be offered of the serious temper which marked Carolinian thought, than was given by the career of this refined and highly educated gentleman, almost the last of his school." This was a judgment that in 1823 Louisa Catherine Adams had anticipated.[64] James Lowndes himself was born in 1835, served as a colonel in the Confederate army, and became a lawyer in Washington. After 1882 he was the commissioner of Spanish claims, a piece of patronage given to him by Chester Arthur. He died in January 1910.[65] The genealogists seem divided on when he married; one gives 1870 and Rhode Island, another Washington and 1891; the latter seems more probable, since none of the letters of Henry and Marian Adams in the 1870s and 1880s mention a Mrs. Lowndes, who first appears in Henry's correspondence in 1895.[66] But there is agreement that his wife was Laura Wolcott Tuckerman, whose father Lucius was an iron manufacturer in Stockbridge, Massachusetts, and that she was descended on her mother's side from Oliver Wolcott, a Connecticut signer of the Declaration of Independence. Lowndes's functional role for the Adamses was to serve as their lawyer, and, here and there, one can read letters in which Henry gave him instructions, even on minor matters to do with the employment of servants. But Lowndes's main role, at least in the 1870s and 1880s, was as a companion, a bachelor available to complete a dinner table, someone to amuse Marian Adams when her husband was busy or she was disinclined to go out. So in 1881, she wrote to her father, "Last night a reception at the Evartses'; I backed out and sent Henry, while Mr. Lowndes, who dropped in to dinner, kept me company by the library fire." He was someone to whom one could go for tea or with whom one could go to the theater. Lowndes performed these services not only in Washington, but also at the Adamses' summer retreat at Beverley Farms in Massachusetts, for a letter of 1883 reads: "The gentle Southron James Lowndes is now our guest. Today he has run off with my wife to visit the Pacific Mills at Laurence." By these Northern visits, Lowndes came to know Robert Hooper and not the least of the former's charms for Marian Adams was a sympathetic interest in her father.[67] Indeed, it is possible that Lowndes was more Marian's friend, for the Southerner's name occurs with far greater regularity in her letters than Henry's. This may not have gone unobserved. If Lowndes was the model for John Carrington in *Democracy*, it may be no accident that in the novel Carrington interacts almost exclusively with women.

In one sense, Lowndes's friendship with Marian Adams was curious, for she was even more inclined to be anti-Southern than her husband and to see the South as a place in need of missionary redemption. In 1883, she was urging various New England relatives and friends to send money to fund "a school of art for Charleston, S.C." and was observing, "We must help educate and cultivate a vanquished foe. Allston and Richardson show that there is seed worth forcing in that barren land."[68] (Washington Allston had been a friend of the Sturgises, her maternal family, who had bought some of his paintings, while H. H. Richardson the architect had been her husband's classmate at Harvard.)[69] This evangelicalism ran in the family. Her cousin Robert Gould Shaw had famously commanded the black regiment the Massachusetts Fifty-fourth and died in its assault upon Fort Wagner. Her brother Edward had worked as an unpaid volunteer in Beaufort for the Port Royal Experiment. There he served first as secretary to Edward L. Pierce, the person whom the secretary of the treasury had asked to organize the slaves left unsupervised by the flight of their masters in 1862. There Ned, as he was called, had sung hymns and "John Brown's Body" with the missionaries as their steamer had approached Beaufort. There he had promised the slaves that in exchange for "faithful work . . . they might expect . . . good care, justice, and to be taught to read" and told them the story of Saint Christopher and the Christ child to draw out "the moral about faithful work in small things." There he had tried to propagate the principles of "liberal Christianity" (he was a Unitarian) as a remedy for black vices. And there, against great odds, he had argued that freedmen could successfully make the transition to free labor. Later he was a stalwart of the New England Freedmen's Aid Society, for which he served as treasurer. Marian herself had worked as a nurse for the Sanitary Commission during the war, and in May 1861 she had used stationery emblazoned with the Stars and Stripes and the legend "Stand By the Flag."[70]

So she tended to see Southerners as, on balance, less than a moral and cultural asset. In 1883, she went to William Corcoran's eighty-third birthday party at the Louise Home, his "almshouse for some forty decayed gentlewomen." She found the occasion "really very pleasant," but felt moved to note the presence of "the Solid South of course, but others beside." The "but" was telling. An account of a dinner party in March 1882 is still more so:

> Dined Wednesday at Randall Gibson's of Louisiana; sat between Mr. Bayard and Eugene Schuyler. A curious dinner: Wade Hampton; Judge Cox; a Kentucky widow with powdered face and hard, loud voice; Carlisle, who is coming to see me, alas! the wife of Senator B., hard-featured, ill-dressed, common-looking woman, like our overworked New England farmer's wife. The tradition of Southern culture, voices, manners, etc., is ill-supported in these post-bellum days; Mr. Lowndes seems "a bright particular star"; Mr. and Mrs. Gibson are better than any I have seen socially, quiet and well-mannered.[71]

So, for her, it was not that Lowndes's charm represented the South, more that he was the exception to the rule, at least the rule since 1865.

However, the rule was broken with regularity. Taylor, Lamar, and Lowndes broke it. John Randolph Tucker of Virginia, a congressman and lawyer, and his wife, Laura, came often and were "quite pleasant." They had, for Henry, the added advantage that the husband was the great-nephew of John Randolph and so the bearer of family gossip, but also someone who had seen Calhoun upon his deathbed.[72] Randall Gibson of Louisiana, another Democratic congressman, was "a quiet, gentlemanly, attractive man." Marian certainly liked and respected their Louisianian architect H. H. Richardson, "gay as always." Southerners were thought capable of "amusing talk and good stories" and she was not loath to repeat even dubious yarns. "MacVeagh told a good story which he just got from Judge Harlan of Kentucky," she wrote in 1883. "A week or so ago a man from Kentucky came back from Washington and when he was asked what was going on in Washington, said, 'Nothin'.' 'Nothin'!' said one of his friends. 'Why, there's a nigger in the Senate, Mahone has jined the Republicans, there's four Yankee schoolmasters in the Cabinet, and the country's goin' to hell.'" In 1884, she could write, "Heaven helps those who help themselves as the darky said when he stole his neighbors hen."[73]

Old Sweet Springs, Virginia, June 1885, Rebecca Dodge, Clifford Richardson, H.A. [Henry Adams]. Photograph by Marian Hooper Adams. Courtesy of the Massachusetts Historical Society.

Included among the admissible Southerners was Sarah Nicholas Randolph, who ran the Patapsco Female Institute, a Maryland girls school in Ellicott City, a little to the west of Baltimore. In 1877, when working on his Gallatin biography, Adams was advised by Hugh Blair Grigsby that Miss Randolph would be helpful in fathoming the history of Virginia and, in particular, locating the papers of Wilson Cary Nicholas, her grandfather. More notably, she was also the great-granddaughter of Thomas Jefferson, about whom in 1871 she had published a book, *The Domestic Life of Thomas Jefferson*. (Her father, Thomas Jefferson Randolph, had been the son of Thomas Mann Randolph, who had married Jefferson's daughter Martha.) The book had been made possible because in 1848 her father had sold the papers of Thomas Jefferson to the federal government, upon the understanding that the "private" papers would be separated from the "public" ones and the former returned to the family. Eventually this happened and in time these papers passed into Sarah's possession after her father's death in 1875.[74] So Adams, in search of the elusive Thomas Jefferson, had many motives for commencing a correspondence with Miss Randolph. In time, something halfway between an acquaintanceship and a friendship developed. She came to dine, she sent (or sold) the Adamses some horses—no small matter for a household so devoted to horse riding—and in May 1878 they stayed at her birthplace (Edgehill, near Charlottesville) and from there, under her guidance, visited Monticello.[75] She would have shown the Adamses the weed-choked graveyard where she knew she would rest, where her great-grandfather was buried, and where over him stood "an ugly misshapen column" with its marble epitaph missing, a ruined obelisk that she had once remarked was "a standing monument to the ingratitude of a great republic."[76] Randolph was an engaged campaigner for the historical importance of Jefferson, an importance that the mid-nineteenth century had been much reluctant to grant, considering how many Christians there were then to dislike deists, how many nationalists there were to mistrust proponents of interposition, how many conservatives there were to frown at the conjecture of democracy. Henry Adams himself was among those who restored Jefferson to centrality in the American story, but also to humanity, and in both of these ventures he was encouraged by knowing Miss

Randolph. Her book was, doubtless, benign to the point of fantasy, but it did try to capture Jefferson the man, and Adams had a use for the stories she told, if not for all the perspectives she embodied.

So, taken all round, Washington provided a steady supply of Southerners for Adams and his wife to study and know. One should not overstress the intimacy of this. For one thing, the link seems to have been strongest in their early Washington years, when they were finding their way and Southerners could help. Taylor died in 1879, Randolph in 1892, and Lamar in 1893, but the last reference to Lamar in Henry's letters is in 1885, the last to Randolph in 1881, and Marian does not mention her after 1882.[77] Lowndes seems to have persisted, though marginally, and his death in 1910 prompted a remark that indicates some difficulty, if not necessarily between Adams and Lowndes: "This morning we buried James Lowndes. I could not help gaily wondering which of us would like most to change places with the other, but I admit that I would make a bad bargain by changing places while he was alive."[78] In truth, the Adams salon was large and many people moved through it. Its core—the so-called Five of Hearts, which consisted of Henry and Marian Adams, John and Clara Hay, and Clarence King—contained no one who was a Southerner, since John Hay was born in Indiana and grew up in Illinois, Clara came from Ohio, and King grew up in Rhode Island and Connecticut. Rather, it is that, through knowing the likes of Richard Taylor, Adams began to see Southerners as real people, with histories and problems, not just as demonic abstractions of the Slave Power. This was the social equivalent of the intellectual process that Adams was undergoing in these years. By deciding to write about the early republic, he was obliged to understand Southerners. To do this, he had not only to read their texts, to understand their politics and culture, and so forth, but also to talk and correspond with those Southerners who were the region's historians. So it is that, when after 1877 he was breaking bread with Taylor, Lamar, and Lowndes near Lafayette Square, he was also exchanging letters with Hugh Blair Grigsby, the greatest living historian of Virginia, to try and fathom the mysteries of John Randolph and Thomas Jefferson.[79]

CHAPTER THREE

American Types

Henry Adams's positioning in Washington society occasioned an implication. The District was preeminently the place in the United States where the making of nationality, at least politically, was being most advanced, and this fact was a fundamental reason for his going there. In Washington, there were the Southerners, but also the New Englanders, the Midwesterners, the New Yorkers, out of whose interrelationships an American nationalism might be constructed. But in this commitment was also a negation. Adams was uninterested in the making of New England culture, which seemed troublingly complete to him, a thing to be evaded.

After the Civil War, nationalism became intertwined with regionalism. Earlier there had been no such phenomenon, because the idea of regionalism rests upon the acknowledged supremacy of the nation state, to which regions are thought to stand in a subsidiary relationship.[1] Before 1865, the Union was not a nation state, but a federal republic in which the states were understood to be coequal with the federal government, hence the political and cultural hierarchy to mandate the imagining of regions did not yet exist.[2] The political triumph of the Union after 1865 and its increasing centralization, a thing Adams observed and partially mistrusted, required many things, but amongst them was the necessity to reinvent places like New England, the South, the Midwest, and West as regions. So precisely his nationalism freed Adams to imagine regions. But, because he did it from Washington and not Boston, he was not engaged in developing a fragment of the picture, but in imagining the United States as a whole, if a whole segmented by regions, a whole unintelligible without those segments.

Adams was not alone in this venture. The invention of regionalism is a great theme of late-nineteenth-century American culture. One can find it in the "local color" fiction of Sarah Orne Jewett, George Washington Cable, Mary Murfree, and Hamlin Garland; in the organization of American corporate capitalism, where the new national corporations often came to organize their branch offices and divide up the country by regions; in the fine arts and in popular culture, in advertising and in Wild West shows. Historians were inventing regionalism, too. But it became customary to write regional history under the guise of national history, and vice versa. This was, usually, a habit of Northern historians, who claimed to write books about the American mind or American politics, while actually writing books about the New England mind or New York politics. This conflationary custom worked within a fairly strict cultural and economic hierarchy, arising from the postbellum political settlement. Roughly speaking, the South was thought most regional, the Northeast most national, with the West and Midwest poised unstably in between. One could not write a book about, say, the social history of Macon and entitle it *The Making of an American City: Macon, Georgia, 1820–1890*, but one would be obliged to call it *The Making of a Southern City*. (In fact, one is still so obliged.) Regions other than the South were less marginalized, but unevenly. In Adams's day, a book about the Far West was more likely to be thought an exercise in regional history, but might be national, especially after 1893 when Frederick Jackson Turner persuaded many that Western history was the clue to national history. A book about the Midwest was usually national, unless seen as a precursor to the Far West, but one about the Northeast was obliged to be thought national.[3] So, for generations, thousands of books were produced that, in practice, used a single region to define American national culture. And that region was, more often than not, New England. As Stephen Nissenbaum has observed, "It was a New England version of American history . . . that penetrated the schools for the better part of the century after the Civil War." Indeed, in this interpretation, "New England is the nation: the 'regions' are everywhere else."[4]

An example of a historian plying this hegemonic trade is Charles Francis Adams Jr., who, after making his fortune in the railroads and real estate investment, set himself up as a gentleman historian like his brother.[5] In worldly terms, Charles was a success in this venture: he published widely, was president of both the American Historical Association and the Massachusetts Historical Society, and in 1913 was invited by the University of Oxford to lecture on American history. While Henry shunned honors, refused invitations to speak, and even evaded an honorary degree at Harvard, Charles liked nothing better than to give addresses to distinguished audiences. "The year ended very pleasantly," he wrote at the end of 1912, "the sound of applause still ringing in my ears."[6] He flattered himself that such historical writing and speaking exercised a salutary public and political influence.[7]

As children and young men, the brothers had been close. Most of Henry's surviving early letters are to Charles, and their free candor speaks to an intimacy. But, in later years, they drifted apart. Henry became reclusive, subtle, ironic, while Charles became public, direct, and a personage. Their differing temperaments bred tension. The elder brother had not much liked Marian Adams, and he was later to acknowledge that the antipathy had been mutual: "Me she never liked; nor can I blame her much for that:—I trod all over her, offending her in every way." He gave an account of her suicide in which he claimed to have prophesied its coming, contended that she had "inherited a latent tendency to suicidal mania," and insisted that in her marriage she had moved between periods of "excitement and unnatural action" and those of "depression and morbid reaction." He execrated the Saint-Gaudens statue as looking like a "mendicant, wrapped in a horse-blanket" and set up his own interpretation against that of the widower. None of this assisted fraternity. But there was also an element of competition between the brothers as historians, at least on the elder's side. Charles was often critical of Henry's writings. The former was shown drafts of the *History* and threw around adjectives like "obscure," "dull," and "verbose," a criticism by which Henry was unimpressed. After the nine volumes were published, Charles's diary was a little more sympathetic: "[Henry] has used his time better than I have mine." Still, the work was only "surprisingly good."[8] Certainly Charles had no sympathy with Henry's later writings, and in the 1915 memorial address given by Henry Cabot Lodge (who had also fallen out with Henry), Lodge was true to Charles's perspectives by speaking disparagingly of "paradox-makers" who displayed "some cleverness" and offered "some passing amusement," but who were "shallow" and "tiresome." Instead, Lodge praised Charles for his "uncompromising vigor," "blunt sincerity," and "absolute conviction," qualities little in favor at 1603 H Street. This lack of sympathy was reciprocal. When Henry sat down in 1909 to rake through Brooks Adams's inept prose, he often used Charles's writing as an awful warning. "By so doing" was a phrase that "always sounds to me like your brother Charles." "'Moved thereto' sounds like Charles." "'To so use' raises all my worst passions. Your brother Charles used to be given to all these 'so' and 'gotten' and things of naught, till I hid in the attic."[9]

The contrast between the brothers has not diminished over the years, though few now would turn from Henry to Charles and think themselves removed to a higher intellectual or aesthetic plane.[10] To go from the prose of Henry Adams to that of Charles Francis Adams Jr. is like passing from a painting by Georges Seurat to one by Sir Edwin Landseer.

Their personal quarrel is less important here than their differing views on American history and regionalism, for Charles saw New England as the core of American history. Charles was not simplistic in this preference, for he was sharply critical of the Puritans, saw little or nothing of value in their legacy, was formally dismissive of ancestor worship, and understood the colonial experience in Massachusetts as, for the most part, "a monotonous period of slow, provincial growth," an ice age in which Jonathan Edwards had lived as "a vast glacial boulder." For Charles, Calvinism was "an outrage on human nature," happily displaced by Unitarianism. He was pleased to record, in Comtean fashion, the moment when the "theological period passed away, and the age of scientific enquiry gradually replaced it."[11] This limited skepticism towards New England was accompanied by his willingness, as a Union veteran, to hold out a friendly hand to the postwar South. In 1902 he went to Charleston and argued for the ethical cogency (if not the historical wisdom) of secession, and in 1907 he stood in the chapel of Washington and Lee University to praise the general, who lay entombed near him, for declining the option of guerrilla warfare.[12] These were sentiments he was prepared to endorse not only to Southerners, but to audiences in Massachusetts, in England, and elsewhere.[13] In all this, he was much influenced by

Charles Francis Adams Jr. Photograph by Marian Hooper Adams. Courtesy of the Massachusetts Historical Society.

his fierce and unapologetic belief in the Anglo-Saxons as a master race, which led him (among much else) to see wartime slaves as submissive, to deprecate the experiment of Reconstruction, to vindicate racial segregation, and to defend Manifest Destiny. Nonetheless, Charles was clear that in New England lay the key to American development, indeed to the history of the world. To observe that "the passage of the Red Sea was not a more momentous event than the voyage of the Mayflower; and the founding of Boston was fraught with consequences hardly less important than those which resulted from the founding of Rome," was to state the matter unequivocally. Since he was not impressed with the religious errand into the wilderness as the foundation of American culture, Charles needed a different grounding for this claim.[14] He found it in New England's eventual commitment to the republican, legal tradition of popular government and toleration, a commitment stifled by the Puritans but flowering in the mid-eighteenth century when the lawyers took over from the ministers.[15] As Charles saw it, the historic mission of "we of the Anglo-Saxon race" was "the Emancipation of Man from Superstition and Caste." And "Massachusetts was the peculiar and acknowledged champion" of "that long struggle for the recognition of the Equality of Man before the Law." He was especially impressed by the Massachusetts constitution of 1780 (drafted by John Adams), because in it "the lines of Anglo-Saxon development" were "for the first time" reduced to a philosophy, "correctly divined, and then and there reduced to form and practical working." Indeed he thought the American Constitution of 1787 was founded upon its Massachusetts precedent. To be sure, Virginia had contributed the Declaration of Independence, but the Massachusetts constitution was "infinitely the more important production of the two." Hence, over the years, Massachusetts "enjoyed an easy American supremacy." Virginia, by contrast, was obliged to be inferior, because it stood for "privilege and aristocracy."[16]

Charles's portrait of the antebellum South was sorrowfully sympathetic, if dismissive. The sympathy arose partly from his being only mildly troubled by slavery. It was predictable that he should have said of New England slavery, "[it] existed for a time; but it was only in its least objectionable form." But it was more unexpected that he thought that "African slavery, as it existed in the United States ante-rior to 1862, was an evil institution at best, yet constituted a mild form of servitude, as servitude then existed and immemorially had almost everywhere existed." However, his dismissal of the South was more important than his sympathy. For Charles, Virginia and the South in 1860 constituted a conservative, patriarchal, agricultural, and provincial society, rooted in intolerance and privilege. Because of this, in "complete provincialism and childlike faith," Southerners remained "eighteenth-century reactionists" and thereby labored under a "curious and complete misapprehension, material and moral." The point they missed, the experience they never had, was that of nationality, or what Charles called "nationalization." The compact theory, states rights, individualism, all these had lingered in the South, while the North had changed. The Northern community, being "very fluid in its elements, commercial and manufacturing in its diversified industries" and being welded together by "the railroad, the common school and the newspaper," had coalesced into "a harmonious whole," which stood for the nation. Charles was very anxious to be generous about this. He did not impugn Southern integrity; he acknowledged that Lee had no option but to stand with his state. Still, Southerners were on the wrong side, and so did not belong to the essential story of American and world history. This was despite white Southerners being Anglo-Saxon. The difference, for Charles, lay in the fact and legacy of slavery, however mild. As he put it in 1911, in an addendum to his 1902 Charleston address, "the Southern people have a dead-weight of Africanism tied to them, which is tending perpetually to hold back or pull down."[17]

Important to his analysis, therefore, was a view of how race structured dominion. One might expect that Charles would have been, in the heyday of William McKinley and Theodore Roosevelt, an imperialist. Like his brother Henry, Charles came from a long line of expansionists. To be sure, John Quincy Adams had famously observed in 1821 that the United States "goes not abroad in search of monsters to destroy. She is the well-wisher to the freedom and independence of all. She is the champion and vindicator only of her own."[18] But "abroad" did not encompass North America, and, even as a Federalist senator, John Quincy Adams had voted for the Louisiana Purchase.

As secretary of state, he had negotiated the annexation of Florida, arranged a westward adjustment of the American boundary with Mexico, and had wished to acquire Texas. His later opposition to the annexation of Texas and the Mexican War was driven less by any opposition to American imperialism (for he was pleased by Polk's acquisition of Oregon) than by his growing hostility to slavery. Likewise given to imperial reverie was the later Adams family's political mentor, William Henry Seward, who was to buy Alaska from Russia. In 1853, he had conjectured that "the borders of the federal republic . . . shall be extended so that it shall greet the sun when he touches the tropics, and when he sends his gleaming rays towards the polar circle, and shall include even distant islands in either ocean." Further, "mankind shall come to recognize in us the successor of the few great states, which have alternately borne commanding sway in the world."[19]

Charles Francis Adams the younger, in some dissent from this tradition, was in the 1890s formally an anti-imperialist, though in a way which tended to erase his distinction from imperialists. He was opposed to formal empire, because he believed that "race elevation, the capacity in a word of political self-support, cannot be imparted through tutelage. . . . A 'wise and salutary neglect' is in the end the more beneficial policy; for, with races as with individuals, a state of dependency breeds the spirit of dependency." (He was very fond of Edmund Burke.)[20] So the British Empire in India could never breed a race of self-reliant Indians, any more than the United States could train up the Filipinos or, for that matter, advance blacks in the American South in 1868.[21] Rather, progress was driven by advanced races tending to their own affairs and ethics. Inferior races might, upon seeing the example, choose to emulate and advance, or (being stubbornly inferior) they might fail, even in the act of emulation. Most crucially, the advanced race must refuse amalgamation with lesser breeds; this had been the wise policy in North America of the Anglo-Saxons, unlike the French and Spanish.

These two views—declining formal imperialism and refusing assimilation—had a brutal corollary, which Charles did not refuse to expound, in his social Darwinian way.[22] The Anglo-Saxons tended to kill their enemies, and this was a good thing. As he put it in 1898, being "unchristian, brutal, exterminating" was "the salvation of the

race," for it saved the "Anglo-Saxon stock" from the hideous consequences of miscegenation. "The Canadian half-breed, the Mexican,
the mulatto . . . are not virile or enduring races; and that the Anglo-
Saxon is none of these, and is essentially virile and enduring, is due to
the fact that the less developed races perished before him. Nature is
undeniably often brutal in its methods." This was not pretty, this fact
that for the English in North America, "the knife and the shotgun
have been far more potent and active instruments in his dealings with
the inferior races than the code of liberty or the output of the Bible
Society." Still, "the record speaks for itself."[23]

Nonetheless, Charles thought the master race needed to look to its
own ethics, though they applied only to itself. "Our fundamental principles of equality of human rights, and the consent of the governed
as the only just basis of all government" were "true, when confined
and carefully applied to citizens of the same blood and nationality,"
but were "questionable, when applied to human beings of different
race in one nationality [and] manifestly false, in the case of races less
developed, and in other, especially tropical, countries." The old stock
of New England, preeminently, had looked to these principles, which
necessarily had triumphed in the American experience, because race
and principles were coterminous. So, "the history of Massachusetts
is . . . the record of the gradual and practical development of a social
and political truth of the first importance," which was, in turn, radi-
ated to the rest of the United States. In 1865, "at the cannon's mouth,"
New England's mission was fulfilled, and then "Massachusetts, intellectually as well as politically, merged in that larger community of
which it had always been a part, though ever a distinct part and, at
times, one exercising, and never more than towards the close, a dom-
inating influence."[24]

Such presumptions were not idiosyncratic to Charles Francis
Adams Jr. Barrett Wendell of Harvard, whose *Literary History of America* (1900) became a standard work, was equally willing to assert intellectual hegemony: "In America, I believe, only New England has
expressed itself in a literary form which inevitably commands attention from whoever pursues such inquiries as ours. What else has
been written in the periods of American life . . . may almost certainly be brought within generalizations based on the literature of

New England."[25] In this certainty, his predecessor was Moses Coit Tyler, whose four volumes on American literature from 1607 to 1783 were likewise canonical in their day. Tyler's story is instructive. Born in Connecticut, he was taken as a boy by his family to Detroit.[26] He graduated from Yale in 1857 and proceeded to the Andover Theological Seminary and, for some years, tried his hand as a Congregationalist minister in upper New York State and Boston, before in 1863 oddly venturing to England as a salesman for "musical gymnastics" and there branching out into lecturing on American culture. This, in turn, led to his appointment in 1867 to a professorship of rhetoric and English literature at the University of Michigan, where he stayed until a migration to Cornell University in 1881, where he coequally taught American history and literature.

Tyler's reputation was made by the *History of American Literature, 1607–1765* (1878). It is an earnest, enthusiastic work, arguing the centrality of New England to colonial literature. It starts, to be sure, with three chapters on early Virginian writing, which consider John Smith and a few lesser lights. But Tyler considered that the promise of the first twenty years after 1607 was rapidly dissipated and that "for the remainder of the century, nearly all literary activity in Virginia ceased," which was not the contemporary experience of New England. His explanation was social. The New Englanders settled in "groups of families forming neighborhoods, villages, and at last cities; from which it resulted that among them there was a constant play of mind upon mind; mutual stimulation, mutual forebearance also: likewise an easier and more frequent reciprocation of the social forces and benefits; facility in conducting the various industries and trades; facility in maintaining churches, schools, and higher literary organizations; facility in the interchange of books, letters, and the like." Virginians, by contrast, lived like English "territorial lords" on large, scattered, isolated estates, and "the social structure of Virginia was that of dispersion," a condition hostile to intellectuality. The colony developed towards "a sort of rough extemporaneous feudalism, toward the grandeur and the weakness of the patriarchal state, rather than toward those complex, elaborate, and refined results which are the achievements of an advanced modern civilization." Such improvised feudalism depressed freedom of thought, as much as (if not more than) did intolerance in New England, though Tyler was anxious that his pages be not "stained by any apology for religious intolerance in New England."[27] So in Virginia, with no community, no clash of minds, no schools, no religious or intellectual freedom, no libraries or presses, and with a society riven between "haughty landowners" and "impoverished white plebeians and black serfs," "how could literature have sprouted and thriven amid such conditions?" How could Virginia produce anything other than "country-gentlemen, loud-lunged and jolly fox-hunters, militia heroes, men of boundless domestic heartiness and social grace, astute and imperious politicians, fiery orators, and by and by, here and there, some men of elegant literary culture, mostly acquired abroad"? So it was logical for Tyler to devote eleven further chapters to the literary accomplishment of New England, to its "extraordinary" learned men with their "not provincial" minds, its "great trait of intellectuality," its "very sprightly and masterful" writings, which constituted "monuments of vast learning, and of a stupendous intellectual energy." Only towards the end of his second volume did Tyler give a single chapter to the "Middle Colonies" and another to the South in the eighteenth century.[28]

Not all flowed in one direction, however, towards simple cobblers in Aggawam. Even Tyler's enthusiasm could flag. Calvinist disquisitions were "of course, grave, dry, abstruse, dreadful; to our debilitated attentions they are hard to follow; in style they are often uncouth and ponderous . . . they are devoted to a theology that yet lingers in the memory of mankind only through certain shells of words long since emptied of their original meaning."[29] Still, he mostly stood in reverent, lyrical awe at what his forebears had done and but darted a contemptuous glance on the lonely monuments of the South.[30]

Such neglect was not merely condescension. It so happened that the professionalization of American literary studies, as well as of American history, occurred when an infrastructure for scholarly endeavor was developing rapidly in the Northeast and Midwest but not in the South. When Tyler sat down to read about early American literature, he had to hand a new body of critical texts written by Northerners about other Northerners, and he could use libraries from Boston to New York and Ann Arbor to furnish him with the original sources. Moreover, he was impelled by teaching new courses on that new subject, American literature, in universities either new or revitalized. Cornell University was richly founded in 1865 from land sales authorized under the terms of the Morrill Act and an endowment of $500,000 from Ezra Cornell, who had made his money from being a major shareholder in Western Union, the telegraph company. The University of Michigan had been founded in 1817 and was inconspicuous before the Civil War, but it grew dramatically afterwards (1,255 students in 1866, 1,534 in 1880, 2,692 in 1891), so that it became the largest university in the country, larger if not greater than Harvard. By comparison, almost all Southern universities in the late nineteenth century were marked by poverty, dissent, and the exigencies of a segregated educational system. In 1901, "the total available income for the sixty-six colleges and universities of Virginia, North Carolina, South Carolina, Georgia, Alabama, Mississippi, and Arkansas was $65,843 less than that of Harvard." So, it was not merely that most Northern scholars were then hostile to writing about Southern culture, though they were. It was that no one could have written then with any rigor about the topic, for the means were not available. And effort, even for Southerners, was incapacitated by this awareness of inferiority. As William P. Trent, once of the University of the South but then at Columbia University, put the matter in 1909, "Neither the Old South nor the New can fairly be said to have rivalled New England and the Middle States in contributing to the intellectual development of the nation, nor have Southern writers been discreetly zealous in making known what their section has actually accomplished."[31]

Charles Francis Adams Jr., Barrett Wendell, and Moses Coit Tyler were examples of a type, which had originated with Federalists like Jedidiah Morse and Timothy Dwight who, at the turn of the nineteenth century and in conscious competition with the South, had made a case for New England's superiority. Part of the case had been achieved by relocating the New England narrative from the Puritans-as-Calvinists to the Puritans-as-Pilgrim-Fathers, who by the *Mayflower* Compact had sponsored American republicanism. Further, Dwight in particular had transmuted the religious idea of the Puritans as a "peculiar people" to the cultural premise of New Englanders as an ethnicity, with distinctive customs and ideological preferences, even physiognomies. These ideas were taken up by such as Daniel Webster, who in 1820 stood at Plymouth Rock for a bicentennial celebration and declaimed on the modern New Englanders' "attachment to those principles of civil and religious liberty which [the Pilgrims] . . . establish[ed]." This claim flowed into Webster's Unionism, for on New England's "regional nationalism" (to use Joseph Conforti's modern phrase) the project of the United States was to be grounded. Two thousand miles westward from Plymouth, as Webster put it, "may now be found the sons of the Pilgrims, cultivating smiling fields, rearing towns and villages, and cherishing, we trust, the patrimonial blessings of wise institutions, of liberty and religion." So, in time, the nation should be a consistency of honest villages, white clapboard houses, steepled churches, moral commerce, and turkey dinners. But, to achieve this, another America, the one elaborated in Virginia, needed to be defeated. Before 1861 this was an ambition, but after 1865 an accomplishment.[32]

It was not that Henry Adams was innocent of the foregoing perspectives; fragments can be seen in his work. But, on the whole, he saw the American story differently and, as Earl Harbert has suggested, understood "that regionalism was not only a dangerous bias in historical judgment . . . but also a particular form of prejudice from which the Adams family could not easily escape."[33] Yet Charles was more in the mainstream, so Henry's writings of the 1880s represent a road not taken by most of American historiography. For Henry offered, instead, a thoroughgoing regionalist version of American history. He did not take the history of New England and imagine it to be definitive of American history. No doubt, for this impulse, his revulsion from New England culture was crucial, but also his physical location in Washington, the chief American place whose existence depended upon the reality of American nationalism and whose social life was peculiarly a mix of the national and the regional.

This regionalist vision is to be found in Adams's fiction, where the dramatis personae are identified by their locality and as, what in *Esther* he calls, "American types."[34] So, in *Democracy*, Senator Ratcliffe is the Midwesterner, the congressman C. C. French and the diplomat/historian Nathan Gore are the New Englanders, Hartbeest Schneidekoupon is from the Middle States, and John Carrington is the Southerner. (Adams was antique enough to think that Pennsylvania was in something called the Middle States, a regional category much alive in the nineteenth century, though it vanishes during the twentieth.) In *Esther*, the Westerner is Catherine Brooke, the vivacious ingenue from Colorado. Significantly, the central character in *Democracy*, Mrs. Lightfoot Lee, is given a mixed regional identity. She is described as having been born in Philadelphia, but her late husband was a Southerner, and she had lived for most of her marriage in New York, before coming in her widowhood to Washington. It is precisely this embodiment, but also this transcendence of regionalism, that in Adams's account earns her the right in the novel to be the moral arbiter of American politics and life. Nationality, for Adams, rested in the awareness of regions, but also in a remoteness from them.

This sense of balance located Adams in the spectrum of regionalism's inventors in the late nineteenth century. The French in 1875 had coined the term *régionalisme*, but they had from the first understood regionalism as a means to conserve local and traditional societies against the dangers of a centralized and modernizing state. The British, who started to talk about regionalism in the 1880s, saw regionalism not as a fortress by Viollet-le-Duc but as a bridge, along which wise planners might usher incoherent, premodern localities towards a better future, especially as a way to preserve the British state from the centrifugal tendencies of Scottish, Irish, and Welsh nationalisms. The British tended to see regionalism—and still tend to see it—as a problem in social scientific management. The American tradition has wavered between these two poles. Conservatives have often seen regionalism in the French way, as notably did the Southern Agrarians, B. A. Botkin, and Russell Kirk from the 1930s onwards. Liberals have as often seen regionalism in the British way, as, for example, did the sociologist Howard Odum and the cultural critic Lewis Mumford.[35] Adams was, on the whole, closer to the British view. He had very little sense of the value of traditional customs and resisted the allurements of community.[36] In his historical writings, it was habitually a criticism on his part to observe that a local society—Massachusetts or Virginia—was persistent in its old ways. This alone distanced him from the French tradition. The British experience of centrifugal nationalisms was, moreover, closer to the American experience, and Adams, especially in the

1870s and 1880s, was much interested in the possibilities of science for ordering society upon consistent principles.

So Adams narrated American history as a mix of regionalism and nationalism. His nine-volume history of the United States during the administrations of Jefferson and Madison begins with two chapters on "physical and economic conditions" and "popular characteristics," both of which are national in scope. He then turns to three regional chapters on the intellects of New England, the Middle States, and the Southern states. (The Western states he ignored.)[37] He then recurs to the national with a chapter on "American Ideals" before settling to his task of narrating American political and diplomatic history. The form betrays the presumption. For Adams, an American story required a historian to identify this dialectic between the regional and the national. However, as is not surprising, Adams did not achieve equidistance. Sequence indicated partiality. In the three opening chapters, he started with New England, then went to the Middle States, and lastly talked about the South. This was, in fact, the traditional ordering, as old as Jedidiah Morse's *The American Universal Geography* of 1793, which had divided the United States into "three grand divisions, denominated the *Northern*, or more properly *Eastern*, *Middle* and *Southern* States" and allocated the individual states to these divisions as Adams was later to do.[38] So, by Adams as by Morse, the reader's mind was asked to run from North to South, and hence to know North before knowing South, although it would have been as logical to start with the South and then proceed northward. Indeed, given Adams's understanding that Virginia was the preeminent actor in the American drama of 1800, this would have been more logical. But it was very rare for a nineteenth-century American to think in this way. In its early days, even when it had been run by Southerners, the U.S. House of Representatives had called the roll of the states, not by the alphabet, but by starting with the northernmost state of Maine and proceeding southwards.[39]

To see how Adams described the South in his historical writings of the 1880s, his descriptions of New England and the Middle States are pertinent too, because Adams saw regionalism as contrapuntal.

New England had fixed qualities: an excellent if antiquated educational system, a powerful and conservative religious establishment losing ground to as-yet inchoate liberal tendencies, a deep Federalist mistrust of democracy much deepened by the response to the French Revolution, a profound provincialism (what he called the absence of any "tendency in its educated classes to become American in thought or feeling"), an old-fashioned literature inadequately challenged by newer writers like Timothy Dwight and John Trumbull, a feebleness in scientific thought, but still a few weak signs of the liberalism to come.[40] This was a bleak portrait, unsurprising when one knows much about Adams's personal history. Occasionally, to be sure, he showed defensiveness. He permitted himself to be amused at the ignorance of Jefferson about the theocratic tendency of the region and scoffed at the president's notion that the defeat of New England "was necessary not only to his own complete triumph, but to the introduction of scientific thought." He especially scoffed when, in a loose moment, Jefferson compared New Englanders to Native Americans, for their propensity for superstition. And there was a sort of defensiveness in the inconsistency with which Adams appraised New England's acceptance of democracy. In his early chapter on the region, he observed of the late 1790s that "the steady progress of democratic principles in the Southern and Middle States" left Connecticut and Massachusetts isolated in their undemocratic ways. But, later, when his irritation with Jefferson and the South had gathered pace, he introduced a distinction. The democracy of Virginia and the South was, he asserted, not so much democratic but more a republican antimonarchism that valued freedom and independence. Seen in this light, New England did better, for the "Virginia school" (to use Adams's habitual referent) "had nothing in common with the democracy of Pennsylvania and New England, except their love of freedom; and Virginia freedom was not the same conception as the democratic freedom of the North."[41] But the inclusion of New England in this sentence was uncharacteristic, for it was in the Middle States, especially Pennsylvania, that Adams usually located the democracy coming to govern the American way.

In fact, the preoccupation of his account of New England was treason, the sullen dissidence from national policy and bitter jealousy of Virginian power that eventuated in the Hartford Convention. The pattern was steady, from the late 1790s onwards. So, "Hamilton thought that disunion, from a conservative standpoint, was a mistake;

nearly all the New Englanders, on the contrary, looked to ultimate disunion as a conservative necessity." So, in early 1814, "The attitude of New England pleased no one, and perhaps annoyed most the New England people themselves, who were conscious of showing neither dignity, power, courage, nor intelligence. Nearly one half of the five New England States supported the war, but were paralyzed by the other half, which opposed it." The best to be said of the treasonous Federalists was that they were muddled, more so than their opponents: "Whatever was the true object of the Hartford Convention, all Republicans believed it to be intended as a step to dissolve the Union, and they supported the Administration chiefly because Madison represented the Union. Federalists might deceive themselves. Probably the men who voted for the Hartford Convention saw its necessary consequences less clearly than they were seen by the men who voted against it."[42] But Adams was very anxious that the reader see the consequences with the utmost clarity, for he took treason seriously, whether it issued from South Carolina or Massachusetts. He had, after all, spent his early manhood in fighting it. The first book that bore his name, the *Documents Relating to New England-Federalism* of 1877, contained as its centerpiece John Quincy Adams's 220-page allegation "that influential Federalist leaders had countenanced secessionist activities before and during the war of 1812."[43] Even in old age, Henry was touchy. There is a story of a dinner party at 1603 H Street in late 1917 during which Henry Cabot Lodge was scathing about the war policy of Woodrow Wilson. According to Aileen Tone, who was present, Adams stopped his old student by saying, "Cabot, I've never allowed treasonable conversation at this table and I don't propose to allow it now." The dinner ended in "icy silence."[44] So, on balance, Adams's portrait of New England between 1801 and 1817 is vexed, for he could find little on which to fasten his sympathy. A nationalist, an agnostic, a democrat, a cosmopolitan, he had few qualities that matched the instincts of his old home.

The Middle States did much better, indeed better than any other region, although the extent to which this was a region is opaque in Adams's account. He first described New York and then turned to Philadelphia, and he was clear that these were very different places. New York had little in the way of a religious establishment, scant literature or science, a weak educational system, but (unlike New England) a willing disposition towards innovation and change, as well as towards democracy, and an enthusiasm for commerce. Philadelphia, by contrast, formed the best of American places, if one too little and unjustly regarded by the rest of the country—a place moderate, tolerant, democratic, committed to the national project, wisely ecumenical in religion, perhaps not intellectually swift but "never committed to serious follies," and fairly indifferent to political theory. Still, Philadelphia was "the intellectual centre of the nation." And Pennsylvania was "the only true democratic community then existing in the eastern States." In this, as elsewhere, Adams's analysis was social. It was because Pennsylvania "contained no hierarchy like that of New England; no great families like those of New York; no oligarchy like the planters of Virginia and South Carolina" that this democracy arose, not because talented individuals willed or imagined democracy. Indeed, he tended to see Pennsylvania as instinctive, not reasoning. (And so he implied that the presence of intellectuals in Philadelphia was more decorative than effective.) Once, when writing of John Randolph's berating the Pennsylvanian delegation for dissent, Adams observed, "Punishment of Pennsylvania Democrats was waste of time and strength; sarcasm did not affect them; social contempt did not annihilate them; defeats made no impression upon them. They had no leaders and no well-defined policy, but they gravitated like inert weights to an equilibrium. What they wanted they were sure in the end to get." In the short run, this "want of the habits of leadership" was a disadvantage, for they were driven to "accept the guidance of aristocrats" like the Livingstons, Jefferson, or John Randolph. This diffidence, too, Adams understood to have social origins. A Northern democrat (for this was a wider issue than Pennsylvania alone) "had never been used to command, and could not write or speak with perfect confidence in his spelling and grammar, or enter a room without awkwardness."[45] Later, when democracy taught that awkwardness might not matter, even that a plain gaucherie might be evidence of superiority, things changed.

The South in 1800 had bad communications, an indifference to manufacturing and finance, but an energetic commitment to westward expansion. Its great planters were not very great in wealth, but moderate in means, if not in pride. They were country gentlemen in the English mode, simple and straightforward, truthful and hospitable, mistrustful of urban guile, genial but ambitious. They had little literature not legal and political, but in politics and constitutional reasoning, as well as in oratory, they excelled. So, "without church, university, schools, or literature in any form that required or fostered intellectual life, the Virginians concentrated . . . upon politics." They were, on the whole, a static people, for "their character was stereotyped, and development impossible." Hence they were Arcadian in instinct, although Adams did concede that South Carolina, especially Charleston, was more energetic than Virginia because more urban, more cosmopolitan, innovative, and even "brilliant," but both states were handicapped by "the squalor of nine hundred thousand slaves."[46]

With the partial exception of the Middle States, these regions are not flattered, but criticized. Though it has been customary to isolate Adams's characterization of the South as especially hostile and invidious, Adams was as hard on New England as on the South, and kinder to the Middle States because there alone he saw unambiguous evidence of modernity. Elsewhere he saw much primitivism. Indeed Adams saw the United States in 1800 as quasi-medieval. Most of his contemporaries and predecessors as American historians, of course, saw the United States in 1776 and even earlier as modern, indeed revolutionary in 1776 because modern.[47] But Adams, who had recently spent years at Harvard teaching and reading and even writing medieval history, was struck by how little early American social and economic life was altered from that of England in the tenth century. As he put it, "America was backward. Fifty or a hundred miles inland more than half the houses were log-cabins, which might or might not enjoy the luxury of a glass window. Throughout the South and West houses showed little attempt at luxury; but even in New England the ordinary farmhouse was hardly so well built, so spacious, or so warm as that of a well-to-do contemporary of Charlemagne."[48] So Adams's sense of the United States from Thomas Jefferson to John Hay is of a society emerging from medievalism. It is common to think of this contention, so prominent in *The Education of Henry Adams*, as a playful metaphor, but (though it was not without mischievousness) his was a serious argument. A major part of his historical project was, first to identify the transition from medievalism to modernity in American life, but then to ask what sort of modernity was accomplished, when one remembered that there were several paths that might have been taken and that not all roads must lead to corporate capitalism.

However, the early Adams was a casual medievalist. Oscar Cargill in 1940 was too strong in insisting that Adams was "a mere controversialist" and that "if a realization of his limitations as a medieval historian never came to him, some real knowledge of the arduousness of the labors in that field had been borne in upon him" by his Harvard experience.[49] But Adams himself would not have dissented from the verdict. For in the 1870s Adams published no sustained work on medieval history, but contented himself with a lecture (on the "Primitive Rights of Women") at the Lowell Institute in 1876, which he only got around to publishing in his collected *Historical Essays* of 1891, plus a piece on the Anglo-Saxon courts in an 1876 volume of essays on Anglo-Saxon law, edited by himself and containing the studies of his Harvard students. But otherwise he expressed his views only in occasional reviews for the *North American Review*, where he commented on several works by recent luminaries, among them Edward Freeman, Henry Sumner Maine, William Stubbs, Fustel de Coulanges, and Rudolph Sohm. His remark in the *Education* that in 1870 "he knew no history; he knew only a few historians" is not inapt to describe his knowledge of the medieval, at least then.[50]

This casualness did not, in itself, make an awareness of medievalism any less important to his intellectual development. Ignorance of details left him the more vulnerable to the self-convinced generalizations of the new medievalists, whose numbers were growing, in conscious opposition to the established authority of the classicists. (Adams was never to show much interest in antiquity, despite his regard for Gibbon.)[51] The essay on the Anglo-Saxon courts is full of refractory details and the debates of anxious medievalists, but is framed by assertions of laser clarity. "The long and patient labors of German scholars," it begins, "seem to have now established beyond dispute the fundamental historical principle, that the entire Germanic family, in its earliest known stage of development, placed the administration of law, as it placed the political administration, in the hands

Virginia Farmhouse. Photograph by Marian Hooper Adams. Courtesy of the Massachusetts Historical Society.

of popular assemblies composed of free, able-bodied members of the commonwealth." This undisputed principle allowed the historian to pass backwards through the "vicissitudes and dangers" of two millennia, if only by a "slender thread," and so evade "the confusion of feudalism, or the wild lawlessness of the Heptarchy" and reach "safely and firmly . . . the wide plains of northern Germany," where this principle had been first established. Most significant was the idea that there, in Germany, a basic division was established: on the one side, "within its own sphere, the family was uncontrolled," and, on the other, for political purposes, "the state was already supreme."[52]

Under the medievalists' influence, Adams became more sensitive to the links between society, culture, and history. A habit grew of seeing history as a series of social stages, each with its distinctive social configuration. This was, in part, an anthropological insight, arguing that societies and historical moments could coexist in time. Adams, for instance, thought the North American Indians to be still primitive, though they shared a continent with modern Americans: "the entire race of American Indians from Behring's Straits to the Straits of Magellan were, and to a certain extent still are, in the stage of communism." In this analysis, Adams did not aggressively favor the modern. In his essay on the "Primitive Rights of Women," he was anxious to be generous to primitive cultures and expressed a tempered regret at the loss of their world: "Within the bounds of their own society they succeeded in constructing a social fabric that compared with any that succeeded to it for successful adaptation of means to ends." He was disenchanted, for example, with the retrograde role of the medieval Church in abridging the rights of woman and driving her into being "the meek and patient, the silent and tender sufferer . . . submissive to every torture that her husband could invent, but more submissive to the Church than to her husband."[53]

What contributed, however, to his flickering sense that history and society moved forward was the idea of race. The discourse that had invented the Indo-European and Aryan, a construction everywhere to be found in the new historical science, much influenced Adams, as did the allied notion that medieval culture arose from the dialectic between the barbarian invasions and Roman society, between a "northern" culture and a "southern" one. None of this was original; indeed its rudiments had been available in American intellectual culture since the 1820s and had, as we have seen, influenced Adams's approach to Italy in the 1850s. But the idea of the Aryan race had by the 1870s acquired an awful majesty. The Aryans were the people who, as Adams explained, had preeminently fused patriarchalism, property, law, and the family by an unmatched energy and "intellectual versatility"; they were "the strongest race and the best fitted to conquer." From this, he took the premise that history was a contest between cultures and races, in which the more advanced destroyed the less advanced. So a historian's first obligation was to appraise any given culture's location in the arc of human development by interrogating how that culture defined the relations between men and women, how it structured laws, whether it knew only the tribe or had risen to comprehend the state, what kind of religion it practiced, and especially whether it had made a nation. The interest of medieval English history was that it encapsulated the essence of these developments by way of a test case. As Adams put it in a review of Stubbs's *Constitutional History of England in Its Origin and Development* (1874), the "seven centuries between the first establishment of the Germans and the adoption of Magna Charta" had a "scientific interest [that] is very great," for "the constitutional changes . . . were more radical than any which have occurred since their close. They include the entire conversion of an archaic, pagan community into a nation which was only waiting for the masterly touch of Edward I. to become a model in history." By this logic, cultures had coherence, but were always under challenge. There was "the incessant and always intricate struggle between the old that was passing away and the new that was at hand."[54] Self-evidently, this was a habit of analysis easy to transfer to the American scene, where a nation had also been made by an incessant and intricate struggle.

Nonetheless, Adams did not straightforwardly transfer to American history the medievalist preoccupation with institutions, especially that of the law. One of the curiosities of his *History* was that, though he was greatly concerned with constitutional logic and probity, he showed relatively little interest in what eclectically American courts did, except by some attention to the Supreme Court of John Marshall. This is a little surprising, since his essay on the Anglo-Saxon courts shows that, even then, Adams was sensitive to the implications of medieval history for the modern problem of constitutional federalism. In deciding, for example, what to call "the political and territorial unit[s]" that made up the ancient German polity—tribe, pagus, canton, shire, and gau were the options—he decided, "The idea to be conveyed is entirely expressed . . . by the American use of the word *state*, as in the term *United States*, signifying, as it does, not merely definite territorial boundaries, but confederated political organizations." He was also clear that the modern problem of nationality and states rights was, equally, a medieval issue. In commenting on the refusal of the English to adopt "the hundred constitution of Charlemagne," he observed that such conservatism was "the distinctive peculiarity of England as compared with Germany," for "the development of Germany was in the path of political consolidation; that of England was in the path of political confederation."[55] Such had been the language of Thomas Jefferson, Daniel Webster, and Robert Hayne in their own day.

Rather, in his American history, Adams gave prominence not to law but to people. In one sense, this was unexpected, for he was formally convinced that individuals mattered less than demography, economics, and what the nineteenth century vaguely denominated forces. In his essays of the 1870s, where he imagined how history should be written, he discerned a lyricism in these abstractions. "If the historian will only consent to shut his eyes for a moment to the microscopic analysis of personal motives and idiosyncrasies," he wrote in 1876 of Holst's *History of the United States*, "he cannot but become conscious of a silent pulsation that commands his respect, a steady movement that resembles in its mode of operation the mechanical action of Nature herself."[56] Matters looked different when he moved from prolegomena to action. In the 1880s, it proved more congenial to offer respect to mechanical actions than to center a narration upon them. To be sure, such extra-human compulsions frame his *History*; they appear at the beginning of the first volume and return at the end of the ninth. But, in between, are thousands of pages about people acting, succeeding, failing, moving. Adams seems to have been conscious of the contradiction and tried in his final pages to explain himself.

By 1815, he argued, the United States was a democratic nation and, as such, something new in the world: "The national character had already diverged from any foreign type . . . [and] the American, in his political character, was a new variety of man." This "methodical evolution of a great democracy" affected the possibility of history becoming "a true science," for science required regularity and "North America was the most favorable field on the globe for the spread of a society so large, uniform, and isolated as to answer the purposes of science." Europe and Asia ("except perhaps in China") would not do for achieving scientific history, because there "undisturbed social evolution had been unknown." Matters there were and had been too much in flux, too disturbed, too complicated. Hence, in the Old World, historical narrative was drawn to the individual, the hero, as a distraction from "the helplessness characteristic of many long periods in the face of crushing problems." In the New World, "war counted for little, the hero for less; on the people alone the eye could permanently rest."[57]

Yet this lack of "European movement and color" was hard to bear, for "without heroes, the national character of the United States had few charms of imagination even to Americans." So even in the United States "historians and readers maintained Old-World standards." The moment of cold dispassion might come, but "no historian cared to hasten the coming of an epoch when man should study his own history in the same spirit and by the same methods with which he studied the formation of a crystal." This resistance, however, did not change the underlying, fixed character of the American democratic society, which Adams compared to a Swiss glacier. Hence his emphasis on individuals was a sort of protest against the earnest sameness of an American world stripped of "kings, nobles, or armies; . . . church, traditions, and prejudices," and his gesture against becoming only a glaciologist. But he had an extra excuse, more scientific. A look at individuals offered insight into the American race or nation, necessary because "the chief object of interest was to define national character." So "in the story of Jefferson and Madison individuals retained their old interest as types of character, if not as sources of power."[58]

In these ways, he rationalized his love for making portraits. Very near the center of his analysis of the South, for example, was John Randolph, of whom there are portraits in the biography of Albert Gallatin, again in the biography of Randolph himself that Adams wrote for Houghton Mifflin's American Statesmen series in 1882, again frequently in the pages of the *History of the United States.* The biography of Randolph has often been dismissed as a lesser work; indeed Adams himself was dismissive of it for tending to overrate someone whom he described as a "lunatic monkey." When the volume was published, he told John Hay: "Do you know, a book to me always seems a part of myself, a kind of intellectual brat or segment, and I never bring one into the world without a sense of shame. . . . This particular brat is . . . the only one I wish never to see again; but I know he will live to dance, in the obituaries, over my cold grave. Don't read him, should you by chance meet him. Kick him gently, and let him go." Still, he knew that Randolph was "the type of a political charlatan who had something in him," and he obviously felt that understanding such a something would tell significant things about the South.[59]

Focusing on Randolph was, in many ways, an odd and cruel decision. Over the years, most historians and biographers have seen Randolph as a splendid eccentricity, not a paradigm. But Adams often saw Virginia, at least, as a continuation of the English society of the eighteenth century, and he saw the English as eccentric, even to his own day. Later, when writing of his London years, he entitled one of his chapters "Eccentricity" and, in it, observed that "English society was eccentric by law and for sake of the eccentricity itself." Indeed, "The commonest phrase overheard at an English club or dinner-table was that So-and-So 'is quite mad.' It was no offence to So-and-So; it hardly distinguished him from his fellows. . . . Eccentricity . . . made the chief charm of English society as well as its chief terror." Likewise, Southern society was eccentric, alternately charming and terrible, but best studied by the scrutiny of an acknowledged eccentric. As Adams was to put it in the *History*, no one else in the Virginian political firmament "could express so well as Randolph the mixture of contradictory theories, the breadth and narrowness, the aspirations and ignorance, the genius and prejudices of Virginia."[60]

The Randolph biography is among Adams's best works in the earlier years. Written when he was newly in Washington, in vigorous early middle age, and as happy as he was ever to be, the book has joie de vivre. It is preeminently about the relationship between talents and accomplishment, and so was (more than any other) the book in which Adams gave thought to how his own promise might be fulfilled or betrayed. Adams sketches Randolph's Virginian childhood, surrounded by "dogs and negroes," as a scene of indulgence and ill-discipline, as a world creating individuality, but also vice and irresponsibility. The Virginian aristocracy is shown as "violent, tyrannical, vicious, cruel, and licentious," a class coarse and provincial, but also sociable, well read (if in old-fashioned texts), and courteous. Out of this world, Randolph emerged as a representative man, "exaggerated but genuine," respected in his world and long regarded as Jefferson's most likely successor.[61] That is, Randolph (unlike Jefferson) was a true Virginian, evidence for an American type. The book follows Randolph's meteoric rise as a Jeffersonian politician and parliamentarian, his estrangement from the ruling powers, his growing misanthropy and rhetorical violence, then his final years of meandering self-caricature.

Adams had the highest regard for Randolph's gifts, especially of rhetoric. He is loving and exuberant in detailing Randolph's speeches, which are variously called "astonishingly clever," "wonderfully striking," "keen, terse, vivacious," though also, especially later, "wicked and mischievous beyond all precedent." He is also very respectful of Randolph's powers of analysis, especially in his early years. Adams regarded Jefferson as a slippery sophist, but he saw Randolph as the Jeffersonian who was willing to admit an error or confess to an inconsistency, especially when, during the congressional debates over the Louisiana Purchase, Randolph acknowledged that the bargain disavowed all true Jeffersonian principles. This honesty came at a price. Indeed the biography is a study in how political disappointment can breed emotional shipwreck, in how Randolph declined into drink, rhetorical brutality, and willfulness. In that sense, it is a study in how a warped heart can wreck an able mind. In this analysis, Adams is prim. He observes that a man like Randolph would never have been tolerated in New England, because he was so much the individualist, whereas New England stood for the principles of collectivity. Adams ends the book with a complaint about Randolph's "habitual want of self-restraint." One might expect, therefore, that Adams would have argued, simply, that the impetuosity of Virginia had occasioned Randolph's failure. In some parts of the book, he does imply this. But, elsewhere and inconsistently, Adams locates Randolph's madness not in the heart, but in the mind. He says explicitly that, "Randolph had an ugly temper and a strong will; but he had no passions that disturbed his head." It was Randolph's ideas that were wrong.[62]

Crucial here was Adams's curious impression that Randolph, in his later years, was the master strategist of the antebellum South's linkage of states rights with the proslavery argument, the linkage that led to secession and war. As Adams saw it, Randolph explained what Calhoun then carried out.[63] Very few historians since have seen this connection, but it was deeply important to Adams to see the Jeffersonians chiefly as democrats and philosophers of states rights, not as proslavery politicians, because he wanted to use the Jeffersonian years as a way to interrogate whether such democratic principles were workable in the modern world. The answer turned out to be no, but it was given with much regret, even anguish, because it suggested that ever since the bankruptcy of Jeffersonianism the United States had been doomed to moral and political failure. So, in Adams's narrative, Randolph, like Jefferson himself, is only lightly connected to slavery. It is later, after Jeffersonianism is dead, that Adams focuses upon the pertinence of slavery.

This issue of democratic decentralization lies very close to the crux, at least of political philosophy. Adams was a nationalist, but he was not unsympathetic to locality. He took no pleasure in the defeat of states rights in 1865, because he knew full well that what had destroyed local power in South Carolina had also destroyed it in Massachusetts, that the old New England died in victory as much as did the Old South in defeat. In the Randolph biography, he was insistent that there was no logical relationship between states rights and slavery, that making such a connection was, not merely an intellectual blunder, but the prostitution of a moral idea to an immoral interest.

But more was at stake in the Randolph biography than political philosophy. It was also a preliminary judgment by Adams on what should be regarded as the proper relationship between the heart and the head. As his earlier study of Gallatin had suggested, Adams was then most in favor of the head, or at least of a heart much under the control of a sensible head, for his great admiration for Gallatin, as for Pennsylvania, lay in Gallatin's responsibility, restraint, moderation, wisdom, and discretion. This preference embodied Adams's view in the early 1880s, when his life was in good order and he was as yet only lightly unacquainted with life's blind cruelty. In the Randolph biography, he says at one point that Randolph had "a nature that would have made for itself a hell even though fate had put a heaven about it" and that had Randolph "been an Italian he would have passed for one possessed of the evil eye." This is said dispassionately, with no especial sympathy. Later Adams would come to see himself as such a person, though he was never to abandon his preference for self-restraint and, in the matter of personal tragedy, silence. There is a striking sentence in the Randolph book, where Adams writes that Randolph had "some private trouble," but that "since he chose to make a mystery of its cause a biographer is bound to respect his wish."[64] It is a dictum Adams was to follow with fierce fidelity when accounting for his own life in *The Education of Henry Adams*.

The figure of Randolph recurs insistently in the *History*. There, too, Adams did not lack for indications of Randolph's instability, of his being "a freak of Nature," a man "ill-balanced, impatient of obstacles, incapable of sustained labor or of methodical arrangement, illogical to excess, and egotistic to the verge of madness," but also a man "sparkling and formidable in debate or on the hustings." In general, this portrait was more benign, for a Randolph of substance and sense had exquisite usages as a Greek chorus in Jefferson's enactment of *Oedipus at Colonus*, the more so as Randolph came from Thebes, too. And Randolph even tempted Adams to lyricism, an impulse he was usually anxious to suppress in the 1880s: "With all of John Randolph's waywardness and extravagance, he alone shone among this mass of mediocrities, and like the water-snakes in Coleridge's silent ocean his every track was a flash of golden fire."[65]

But, in the *History*, Randolph shares the stage with a crowd of Southerners. This congestion was necessary, because, as Adams admitted, "During the administrations of Jefferson and Madison, the national government was in the main controlled by ideas and interests peculiar to the region south of the Potomac, and only to be understood from a Southern stand-point." But there was a contradiction between Adams's portraits of Southerners and his understanding of the South. He was often insistent that the South was intellectually static and incapable of change, that it was "satisfied" and "helpless to produce . . . literature, science, or art." Yet he, as often, was obliged to spend time on Southern thinkers who were intellectual, imaginative, forces to be reckoned with. Thomas Jefferson, James Madison, John Randolph, John Marshall, John C. Calhoun, these were not fools and Adams knew that. To evade the contradiction, he did what historians often do. He spoke of "contradictions." He observed at one point that "the elements of intellectual life existed without a sufficient intellectual atmosphere." He tended to characterize exceptionally bright Southerners as atypical, not Southern. So Jefferson, Adams could hardly not admit, took "true delight . . . in an intellectual life of science and art," but Jefferson was not "at ease in the atmosphere which surrounded him" and "was singularly out of place." He was isolated by preference: "with manners apparently popular and informal, he led a life of his own, and allowed few persons to share it." He was a sort of "liberal European nobleman" displaced among raw, crude, backward Virginians, who little understood what he stood for and were little changed by his liberal schemes. Likewise, Calhoun might not be best described as South Carolinian or Southern, but as a man whose "modes of thought were those of a Connecticut Calvinist; his mind was cold, stern, and metaphysical."[66] Nonetheless, Adams had too much the biographer's instinct to slight idiosyncrasy. His Southerners differ more than his South is variable.

At the center of the narrative in the *History* is the ill-dressed violinist from Monticello, whose "rambling and often brilliant conversation, belonged to the controlling influences of American history, more necessary to the story than three-fourths of the official papers, which only hid the truth." As has often been acknowledged, Adams's portrait of Jefferson is among the finest efforts of American historical literature. As Adams knew, to capture Jefferson required extraordinary subtlety. "A few broad strokes of the brush would paint the portrait of all the early Presidents," he observed, even of his own great-grandfather. "But Jefferson could be painted only touch by touch, with a fine pencil, and the perfection of the likeness depended upon the shifting and uncertain flicker of its semi-transparent shadows."[67] There seems little doubt that, on the whole, Adams liked Jefferson. Later, he was to grow irritated when his brother Brooks too freely used Jefferson as a punch bag. "You can blackguard Jefferson till the cows come home," he insisted, "but Jefferson was better than his people."[68] The man had charm of style and "moderation of tone," a kindly nature that was "sensitive, affectionate," a deep honesty and a "pliant and conciliatory" aversion to conflict, which meant he was "not apt to be violent, nor . . . despotic in temper." Further, he was hospitable, loved beauty, and "his writings often betrayed subtile feeling for artistic form,—a sure mark of intellectual sensuousness." (That this might answer to a portrait of Adams himself speaks, no doubt, to the psychology of the biographer's art.) On the other hand, Jefferson was susceptible to flattery and too devoted to popularity; he was a man "easily elated, unwilling to forebode trouble, devoid of humor, and unable to see himself in any but the heroic light," and a stylist whose innocence occasionally led to comic blunders of expression. Further, he "had the faculty, peculiar to certain temperaments, of seeing what he wished to see, and of believing what he willed to believe." Still, he meant well and, as Louis Marie Turreau observed, "There is something voluptuous in meaning well." The adjective suggested an implication Adams was willing to see: "Jefferson's nature was feminine; he was more refined than many women in the delicacy of his private relations. . . . He was sensitive, affectionate, and, in his own eyes, heroic. He yearned for love and praise as no other great American ever did." Significantly, Adams saw the same quality elsewhere, in Jefferson's Greek chorus: "Randolph was a creature of emotions; with feminine faults he had feminine instincts and insight, which made him often shrink from results of his own acts."[69] As will become evident later, this sense that Virginia and the South were feminine was to grow in Adams's mind, but the theme occurs only sporadically in the *History*.

This was, on balance, a generous portrait. Skeptics of Jefferson pointed to darker qualities. They saw a man vicious in his vendettas, cowardly in his flight from Monticello during the Revolution, hypocritical in preaching virtue but practicing the dark arts of politics, blasphemous in his deism, and debauched in his dalliance with Black Sally. Adams acquitted Jefferson of these charges and, in general, saw Jefferson's vices as but the defects of his virtues. By meaning well Jefferson blundered into doing ill. This generosity was personal, given to the man himself, but influenced by the ideology of democracy. Adams approved of "Jeffersonian ideality" and what it sought to accomplish. This ambition he summarized with sympathy: "Jefferson had hoped to make his country forever pure and free; to abolish war, with its train of debt, extravagance, corruption, and tyranny; to build up a government devoted only to useful and moral objects; to bring upon earth a new era of peace and good-will among men. Throughout the twistings and windings of his course as President he clung to this main idea; or if he seemed for a moment to forget it, he never failed to return and to persist with almost heroic obstinacy in enforcing its lessons."[70]

By comparison, Adams's portrait of Madison is flat, though there is every reason to think that Madison required a fine pencil, too. To be sure, Adams described the "small man, quiet, somewhat precise in manner, pleasant, fond of conversation, with a certain mix of ease and dignity in his address." But he was conscious that Madison was less available as a representative Virginian, because he had wavered so in his ideological loyalties: he "was very far from controlling the voice of Virginia," but appealed to "Northern democrats, semi-Federalists, or 'Yazoo men,' as they were called, who leaned toward him because he, of all the prominent Virginians, was least Virginian." The contrast with Randolph, the touchstone of the Virginia school, needed to be made, therefore:

Madison was cautious, if not timid; Randolph was always in extremes. Madison was apt to be on both sides of the same question, as when he wrote the "Federalist" and the Virginia Resolutions of 1798; Randolph pardoned dalliance with Federalism in no one but himself. Madison was in person small, retiring, modest, with quiet malice in his humor, and with marked taste for closet politics and delicate management; Randolph was tall in stature, abrupt in manner, self-asserting in temper, sarcastic, with a pronounced taste for publicity, and a vehement contempt for those silent influences which more practical politicians called legitimate and necessary, but which Randolph, when he could not control them, called corrupt.[71]

Such qualities led to Madison being underrated, and so he was "a dangerous enemy, gifted with a quality of persistence singularly sure in its results." Adams, too, underrated him, indeed often accused him of banality: "If Madison's fame as a statesman rested on what he wrote as

President, he would be thought not only among the weakest of Executives, but also among the dullest of men, whose liveliest sally of feeling exhausted itself in an epithet, and whose keenest sympathy centred in the tobacco crop." This banality in Madison shaded into quietism, a quality of some use in a time of war: "Nothing . . . was more remarkable than the placidity with which [Madison] commonly met anxieties that would have crushed a sensitive man." But this evenness did not contradict waywardness, though the impetuosity was hard to see because so at odds with the man's manner: "Madison was regarded by his contemporaries as a precise, well-balanced, even a timid man, argumentative to satiety, never carried away by bursts of passion, fretful rather than vehement, pertinacious rather than resolute,—a character that seemed incapable of surprising the world by reckless ambition or lawless acts; yet this circumspect citizen, always treated by his associates with a shade of contempt as a closet politician, paid surprisingly little regard to rules of consistency or caution." Indeed, "he ignored caution in pursuit of an object which seemed to him proper in itself."[72]

It is a curiosity of Adams's view of American history that, though he often talked about the principles of the Constitution, he showed little interest in the history of its creation and so never appraised how important was Madison the political philosopher. This neglect was typical of Adams's day. It was to be the late twentieth century before Madison came to occupy an almost equal space on the pedestal accorded to the Founding Fathers, and then mostly in the minds of modern American conservatives, preoccupied with original intent and so with the most sophisticated and informative of original intenders. Eventually, in 1980, a building came to be named for Madison in Washington, but it was only the newest annex to the Library of Congress, whose main building was then named for Jefferson, while an older annex was given the name of John Adams, by way of bipartisanship.[73] Even now, Madison lacks in the capital a monument comparable to those given to Washington, Jefferson, and Lincoln, and no one thought it necessary to carve the face of "poor Jemmy" (as Washington Irving called him) on the rock face of Mount Rushmore.[74]

True, the Philadelphia Convention of 1787 lay outside of Adams's rubric, though that constriction was a deliberate choice. The chronological emphases of Adams's version of American history were, in fact, odd. Apart from a youthful essay on John Smith and Pocahontas, he was uninterested in colonial history and had little to say about the American Revolution and the making of the Constitution.[75] He ventured some writing on the 1790s, followed by thousands of pages on the period between 1801 and 1817. Thereafter, he had a few dozen pages on the antebellum period. In Adams, then, the meaning of the American experience was compressed within a few scant years, and, given the Southern dominance during those years, the arbitration of that meaning was peculiarly given into the hands of Southerners.

Why his shape for American history was compressed is not easy to understand. He disliked the Puritans and New England, so that put much colonial history out of reach. He was almost pathologically unwilling to talk about his Adams forebears, which made the Revolution, the 1790s, and the 1820s inaccessible. But more important may be that Adams was interested in how political and moral systems worked, but less interested in their invention. So the Revolution and 1787 mattered less to him than the early years of the republic, when the attempt was made to give substance to the principles of the late eighteenth century. One might read this as the instinct of a younger son, someone occupying a junior place in a family run by other people, someone expected to fit in wherever he might, someone who never became a father and so had no experience of being a progenitor.

The narrowing effect, however, was to make the Madison of 1787 unavailable. Still, Adams's tepidness about Madison had other roots, which point to an irony. Madison had, save when most in fealty to Jefferson from the late 1790s to the early 1800s, discerned the movement of his times towards a nationalizing centralization, towards what Adams called semi-Federalism. Being not quite Virginian, but not quite Massachusetts, was what the world came to demand, as Adams was very anxious to demonstrate. One might think this would have made Madison the essential man of the narrative, not Jefferson. But Adams saw the necessity of this movement, more than he approved of its morality, and he reserved his greatest admiration for those who tried to defy the times, however quixotically. Madison was too sensible a man for Adams, the restless sniffer out of lost ideals. More to his taste, unexpectedly, was John Taylor of Caroline, that *"vox clamantis,"* who gets several pages of gently ironic praise for fashioning "his Oceana on the banks of the Rappahannock" as the "reflection of his own virtues."[76]

Adams's other Southerners were more swiftly dispatched. James Monroe was "a very dull man" with "a genius for blunders." In principle, he stood on the conservative wing of the Virginia school, close to Randolph and Taylor, and he entered Madison's cabinet to enforce this standpoint, but in a contest "between Monroe's will and Madison's," it was clear "that Monroe's pliable nature must succumb to Madison's pertinacity, backed as it was by authority." John Marshall was a "great man" (from Adams, this was unusually high praise), "of aristocrats the most democratic in manners and appearance," and possessed an irresistible mind "of no flaw," save in its detestation of Jefferson. This hatred was personal but also ideological, for "the Chief-Justice, a man who in grasp of mind and steadiness of purpose had no superior, perhaps no equal, was bent on enlarging the powers of government in the interests of justice and nationality," scarcely the project of Thomas Jefferson. Nathaniel Macon stood as the representative of North Carolina, a state modest and backward, a modesty justifying its designation as "the healthiest community south of the Potomac," a Southern version of Pennsylvania, a place "neither cultivated nor brilliant in intellect, nor great in thought, industry, energy, or organization," but, for all that, "interesting and respectable," worth a pat on the head. True to this spirit of place, Macon was "a typical, homespun planter, honest and simple, erring more often in his grammar and spelling than in his moral principles, but knowing little of the world beyond the borders of Carolina. No man in America left a better name than Macon; but the name was all he left." Beyond these, many appear in brief cameos: William Lowndes and Littleton Waller Tazewell, Langdon Cheves and William Branch Giles, David R. Williams and Felix Grundy. The idiosyncrasies of these lesser Southerners tend to get lost in generalizations. Williams, for example, "was a typical Carolinian," who had "the overbearing temper which marked his class," but "also the independence and the honesty which went far to redeem their failings."[77]

Hence Adams had some sense of the variety of Southern places, but his imagination was preoccupied with Virginia as the normative

South, a skewing not unusual for his times when the retelling of the Civil War was habitually a narrative of Virginia, but also plausible because of the demographic and political dominance of the state in the early republic.[78] As to the other states in existence by 1817, Adams knew a little of South Carolina, less of North Carolina, and almost nothing of Georgia and Tennessee. He was acquainted with Louisiana almost exclusively for the sake of its purchase, not its character. But he was writing a history of the United States from a national perspective, so his usual question was, what qualities did this senator or representative or president bring from his place to Washington? His preoccupation, thereafter, was how Washington interacted by diplomacy and in war with the outside world, with London, Paris, Madrid, and Saint Petersburg. The *History* gives, indeed, a better history of the British House of Commons than it does of the House of Delegates in Virginia. Of course, Adams noticed when a congressman from Georgia or New Jersey rose to speak on the Louisiana Purchase or the War of 1812, but he was inattentive to the internal history of states and regions, except when they served to explain such interventions on the national scene. And this reflected Adams's view of the meaning of locality. For him, the local did not matter for its own sake, but only as part of the wider texture of nationality.

The final judgment of the *History* is that the Southerners failed. It was usual to attribute this failure to the moral shortcomings of a slave society. This was how John Quincy Adams and Charles Francis Adams had seen the matter. Henry Adams is not innocent of the idea. The Southern propensity for willful individuality, connected by Adams to the experience of slavery, is held responsible for much. Southerners as democrats, because individualists, are deemed inattentive to the premise of democracy, the abridging of individuality in the interests of the whole. Still, it is more striking that Adams cares little about slavery in his narrative. Rather, he plays a deeper game. He gives the Southerners the benefit of the doubt. He makes the Jeffersonians into the quintessential American optimists, the makers of the American Dream.[79] His Jeffersonians repose confidence in the people, attempt a foreign policy that might make war obsolete, promise a government that might be frugal, honest, and scrupulous in the observation of constitutional principles. And what eventuated were national banks, high tariffs, an enlarged military, war, and the betrayal of constitutionality. As Adams had put it in his biography of Gallatin, the Jeffersonians had wished to produce "a fresh race of men" and ventured "a theory of democratic government which he and his associates attempted to reduce to practice." They failed, only incidentally because they were Southerners, primarily because they had overestimated human nature, including their own.[80] The Federalists failed, too, for the opposite reason, because they underestimated human nature. Between this Scylla and Charybdis, America lost its way.

One might say that in the failure of the South lay the failure of America, but this says too much, for Adams thought that anyone would have failed, that circumstances and history would have been too oppressive for anyone, any region, any culture. He famously said to Samuel Tilden that Jefferson and Madison "appear like mere grasshoppers, kicking and gesticulating, on the middle of the Mississippi River. . . . They were carried along on a stream which floated them after a fashion without much regard to themselves." He saw this as a general proposition, not specific to Jefferson and Madison. "This I take to be the result that students of history generally reach in regard to modern times. The element of individuality is the free-will dogma of the science, if it is a science. My own conclusion is that history is simply social development along the lines of weakest resistance, and that in most cases the line of weakest resistance is found as unconsciously by society as by water."[81]

Still, there was a significant residue to Adams's locating of the morality play of American history in the early republic. When he wrote his novel *Democracy*, he was concerned to show how the story of American democracy was a story of decline, not of progress. To show this, he made much of the symbolism of Mount Vernon, and so of the contrast between George Washington's world and the corrupt world of Senator Ratcliffe. He had, in fact, said surprisingly little of critical substance about Washington, either as soldier or statesman, in his historical writings of the 1870s and 1880s. His only estimate was merely conventional, when in *The Life of Albert Gallatin* he observed that "Washington and Jefferson doubtless stand pre-eminent as the representatives of what is best in our national character or its aspirations." And this seems to have been how, from the first, he had thought it useful to see Washington, as a stick to beat modern politicians. So in 1870 he said, "The example of President Washington offered an obvious standard for the ambition of Grant." In 1876 he added, by way of contrast, "In the days of Washington and Jefferson and Madison we should have smiled, not without just pride, and remarked that, republicans though we were, we at least did not make a farce of our government."[82] But the details of this paragon were not explored, save in the fiction of *Democracy*, where to explore the contrast between old virtue and modern vice, Adams used a Virginian character called John Carrington, who serves as a moral arbiter in the novel. In this portrait of Carrington, however, there is a tension. Adams as a participant in the coming and course of the Civil War had been scathing about Southerners. Adams as a historian of the early republic had been, on the whole, generous towards them. So he had to decide which kind of Southerner was Carrington, the early or the late, the Southerner before Randolph and Calhoun's invention of the Slave Power, or the Southerner afterwards. Logically, since Carrington was a Confederate war veteran, it ought to have been the latter, but in fact it was the former. Adams minimized Carrington's identity as a rebel. He is said to have entered the Confederate army reluctantly, to have fought dutifully but unenthusiastically, and nowhere is he connected to slaveholding. Rather, he stands as a type of the lost world of George Washington—simple, plain, rough, honest—a world where men rode well amid a warm landscape of flowers. So Carrington can be available as the critic of 1880, because he stands for the South of 1800, not 1860.

This might seem a strange sleight of hand. Most modern historians would insist that George Washington's world and Jefferson Davis's were, by and large, the same worlds and that Adams's disjunction is implausible. Indeed many of Adams's Northern contemporaries were saying what recent historians are saying. That Adams disagreed needs explanation. One may conjecture that his living in the city of Washington and his fresh intimacy with Southerners led Adams partially to adopt Southern self-explanations. It had become usual for Southerners to claim that secession had little to do with slavery, but was a stand

Marian Adams with group at Mount Vernon. Photograph by Luke C. Dillon, 1887. Courtesy of the Massachusetts Historical Society.

for states rights and self-determination. Richard Taylor's memoirs, for example, dwelled on secession as a response to "the actions and tendencies of the Federal Government," but said nothing about slavery, save to note its unmourned ending.[83] Adams remembered the Slave Power too well to accept such elegant rationalization, but he did argue that there was a declension from the South of George Washington to that of Jefferson Davis, and hence Adams accepted that the cultural moments of 1800 and 1860 were profoundly different. He would not erase slavery from 1860, but he was willing to obscure it in 1800. This interpretation was greatly influential, indeed remained conventional until, at least, the early 1960s.[84]

However, there may have been an influence from old disputes, observed by Adams during his first political education. In the 1850s, there had been several schools about the Slave Power. William Henry Seward had traced its origins to the Constitution itself, especially to the clause that allowed states to count three-fifths of their slaves as part of the population used to calculate political representation, but also to the social psychology of slaveholding. Yet both Seward and Charles Sumner had excused George Washington from membership of the dark conspiracy (as everyone did), but also Thomas Jefferson, which was more contentious. Edmund and Josiah Quincy, from old Massachusetts Federalist stock, saw no reason to exclude Jefferson and saw a continuity from Monticello to the Hermitage. Both of these standpoints made, at least, some effort at respecting chronology, by seeing a starting point for the Slave Power's emergence and a coherent history thereafter. Others were more wayward about timing. The son of Alexander Hamilton, John C. Hamilton, would assert in 1864 that Jefferson had belonged, as had Calhoun—all agreed on Calhoun—but, mysteriously, Andrew Jackson did not. But, then, Hamilton was a Jacksonian democrat.[85] In general, in his *History*, Adams was following Seward's line, but not without the extra frisson of hostility to Andrew Jackson, natural to a grandchild of John Quincy and Louisa Catherine Adams.

In these writings of the 1880s, then, the South mattered deeply to Adams. Later, things changed and the South began to fade into the background. In his middle years, Henry Adams was still committed to an ordinary kind of historical or fictional narrative, in which a writer might feel reasonably confident that certainty and meaning were attainable and could be represented. The South was fitted into these patterns of meaning, sometimes well, sometimes ill. When Adams ceased to believe in such metahistorical patterns, when he came to think that the world made little or no sense, the status of the South in his imagination was to mutate.

CHAPTER FOUR

The South in a Supersensual Multiverse

The life of Henry Adams split in two on the morning of Sunday, December 6, 1885, when he walked out of his home at 1607 H Street to visit a dentist and returned to find his wife dying. She had committed suicide by swallowing photographic chemicals.[1] Her motives for this action do not concern us here, but its profound consequences do. His grief was overwhelming, perhaps also his guilt, but most striking was that he committed himself to one of the more extraordinary acts of repression of which we have record. Once the funeral obsequies were completed, he scarcely spoke of her again in conversation, in correspondence, or in print.[2] Thereafter, anyone who knew him and wished to continue knowing him accepted the bargain of this silence. His friends, relatives, and acquaintances entered the company of Henry Adams on the strict understanding that Clover Adams had never existed, but also with the common knowledge that the clue to the sad, restless, pessimistic, and needy man before them lay in the cataclysmic event of that Sunday morning.

In one sense, he decided to carry on the life they had planned together. He moved into the new Romanesque mansion, designed for them both by H. H. Richardson. Having reached somewhere into the volumes on the first administration of James Madison, he carried on writing his *History*. He sustained the salon they had created with the friends they had made. In another sense, however, he was very much changed, though it took a while for the alteration to register in the physical pattern of his life, because the completion of his history obliged him to live as he had since 1877, by sticking very closely to a life in Washington. (The only major exception was a visit to Japan in 1886.)[3] Indeed it almost seems as though he postponed the psychological change, too, because he tried to write the remainder of his history in the same style, with the same evenness of temper with which he had begun it, despite how little after 1885 he felt even tempered.

When he completed his page proofs in the summer of 1890 and set out for the South Seas, the pattern changed. For the rest of his life, at least until he grew too infirm, he became an inveterate traveler. Later he settled into a rhythm of summers and autumns in Paris, with winters and springs in Washington, and after 1895 reacquired the taste for European travel that had abated after 1880. But in the early 1890s, he sought the distraction of the exotic. He visited Samoa, Tahiti, Australia, Ceylon, Russia, Egypt, Mexico, Cuba, all these places and many more, often for long periods. He bought artifacts, came to like Buddhist art and Ming vases, and developed a knowledge of different histories and cultures, far beyond the transatlantic world that John Adams and John Quincy Adams had inhabited. Henry's engagement with these worlds was complex. Most relevant here is that he greatly extended his appreciation for balmy landscapes, a taste once confined mostly to his engagement with Italy, and he added a stronger attraction for the primitive. He sought healing from trauma and he was helped by many of these places, especially when they seemed unsophisticated and intellectually undemanding. There is no question that he traveled with the intellectual baggage of a cultural imperialist, often with an air of amused condescension towards worlds deemed simpler, more instinctive, somehow marooned in the days of Homer.[4] He tended to see these travels as a revisiting of man's childhood, which was how the new discipline of anthropology and the old discipline of history saw the matter then, though he did not see childhood as innocence and had no patience with Rousseau and noble savages. As importantly, these journeys fed his skittish appreciation of the sensual. The strange foods and tastes, the different seascapes and landscapes, the alien clothing, the noises of startling religions and rituals, the unexpected shapes of bodies, all these changed him. This was the more so as he often traveled, notably in Japan and the South Seas, with the painter John La Farge, who instructed sight and nurtured Adams's modest talent for watercolors.

There was a sexual dimension to all this. Adams spent a lot of time looking at exotic women and thinking about them, though he often claimed that he never did anything with them, and he may not have been lying. In Samoa, in the village of Nua in Tutuila, for example, he and La Farge "passed the day and night in the chief's family, and all the girls of the village—mighty handsome too—kicked about on the mats, sprawling over us to look at our drawings or writings . . . until we seemed all mixed up with naked arms, breasts and legs." In Santiago de Cuba, when with Clarence King, he was very observant in its plaza in the evening of "five hundred exquisite females, lovely as mulatto lilies and graceful as the palm-tree whose height—of a hundred feet—they rival." This was a man who, when he had commissioned his wife's memorial at Rock Creek cemetery, was pleased that the artist had created a "sexless" figure.[5] Later, Adams came to see, more urgently than in his earlier days, that sex was important in history and it is arguable that he had this awakening on these peregrinations.[6] He was to claim that this transformation was obliged to be limited in a Bostonian. When later La Farge thought of publishing something on their Polynesian travels, Adams protested that, apart from letters, "There is no record at all of my part of the journey. In fact, I want none, and should destroy any that I had; for I can imagine few things more incongruous than my poor Bostonian, Harvard College, matter-of-fact Ego, jammed between the South Seas and John La Farge. I felt the absurdity of it then, and I feel it worse now, so that nothing would induce me to touch anything he wrote about it."[7] For all that, the Bostonian ego was changed.

Adams saw the American South as connected to these primitive places, partly via his ideas about race. So, for example, he observed when in Hawaii that he was not attracted by the women, what he called the "old-gold girl," because "long residence in Washington has accustomed us to the color; and, as far as I can see, Maggy would be rather a belle here." So, in Samoa, he wrote, "I can live well enough on native food here, when I famish on native food in Japan and Alabama." So, still in Samoa, he wrote, "I find more to eat in a Samoan hut than in a Carolina town." In Fiji, he observed, "the scenery is very like the Virginian Alleghanies, if you would throw in a few tree-ferns and palms and long, pendent creepers."[8] Likewise, Cuba and Haiti and Mexico seemed to have cultures reminiscent of the South, the more so as he habitually traveled through it to reach them; in his experience, Texas prefaced Mexico and Florida intimated Cuba.

This conjunction was much occasioned by his visiting, for the first time, the South beyond northern Virginia. In the late 1880s, this began with short trips through Virginia and North Carolina to as far south as Savannah, in the company of various male friends. Later, the visits were longer, because his great friend Elizabeth Cameron and her husband, the U.S. senator from Pennsylvania, bought themselves a place at Coffin's Point on Saint Helena Island, South Carolina, and Adams would stay for months. As in the South Seas, he did watercolors.

However, his letters from the South—unlike those from the South Seas—show an indifference to the people around him. For Adams, then, the South seems to have been a landscape and little more, a place of "gnats, mocking-birds, clams and mud-crabs, with occasional couters or terrapin." Just occasionally he would notice the black population, unkindly. So, he reported that his host Don Cameron was "supporting the darkies, who are all washed out of their sand-holes, by paying them fifty cents a day to make a shell road as far as Ward's store;—a mile and a half. Nearly seventy carts have been at work for ten days on this great Roman task, which is now nearly done."[9] In some senses, this was a surprising tendency on Adams's part to see the South as an empty place, save only (and only a little) for its subordinate class. His historical imagination had earlier done the reverse. In his *History*, he had richly peopled the South with whites, but ignored the slaves and little noticed the landscape.

Part of the explanation is cultural. Adams was one of the new Yankee tourists who came South, often to visit run-down Sea Island plantation houses bought by their friends. Tourists usually see more of servants than of the local upper or middle class, and it is possible that the Camerons and Adams never or seldom met the white inhabitants. If Adams did, he never thought it important to mention them, with the significant exception of "old Miss Towne on Saint Helena," that is, the veteran New England schoolteacher who had come in the war as part of the Port Royal Experiment and remained to run the Penn School for ex-slaves.[10]

Coffin's Point, Saint Helena Island, January 1894. Watercolor by Henry Adams. Courtesy of the Massachusetts Historical Society.

From Cottage Window, Coffin's Point, 1894. Watercolor by Henry Adams.
Courtesy of the Massachusetts Historical Society.

Afternoon in January, Coffin's Point, 1894. Watercolor by Henry Adams.
Courtesy of the Massachusetts Historical Society.

But it was more than this. He came seeking what he once described to John Hay as "the warmer natures of the south," because "I . . . like the sun and the tropics, and the world that is not sane and sensible." The South was, to him, counterpoint, something that elicited his gratitude "for the refuge from Washington and the North, where the world seemed . . . more daft than ever before."[11] So the South mattered to him as a cessation, as landscape alone, as an emotion and not a thought.

This impulse meant it was unnecessary for him to seek a knowledge of Southern culture. Selectively, when writing his *History*, he had acquired some command of the South's political literature.[12] This fact can be inferred from the evidence of his extant library.[13] He came to possess a few original and reprinted texts from the colonial period: the writings of Captain John Smith, Hugh Jones, William Stith, and the young George Washington on Virginia; Jerome Hawkey and John Lewger on Maryland; and a collection of South Carolina documents.[14] In addition, he had a modern biography of Smith.[15] He owned most of the modern editions of the writings of the Founding Fathers from Virginia and their immediate Southern successors.[16] He had collected some scarce, original works of political controversy, written by the likes of Robert Goodloe Harper, James Monroe, Robert Smith, and John Taylor.[17] He especially accumulated biographies of the men (and one woman) of this era. Some were pre-1861 publications.[18] Others were postbellum, and, not unexpectedly, among these were several volumes in the American Statesmen series, to which he had himself contributed.[19] Naturally, he acquired works on John Randolph.[20]

For the next generation of Southerners, he had all the writings of John C. Calhoun, the correspondence of Henry Clay, and the memoirs of Thomas Hart Benton.[21] Again, he had political biographies: those of Clay and Benton, plus Andrew Jackson.[22] Of state histories, he had only a smattering. His wife had given him the first two volumes of John Daly Burk's *History of Virginia* in 1874.[23] He also had two standard histories of Louisiana, another of Kentucky, plus a few antiquarian works on Maryland and Virginia.[24] Further, he possessed two of Hugh Blair Grigsby's antebellum studies in Virginian history and biography.[25] There was also David Bailie Warden's 1816 description of the District of Columbia and some early travel accounts reaching into the South.[26]

Absent are works of antebellum Southern belles lettres. There is, to be sure, Augustus Baldwin Longstreet's *Georgia Scenes*, written by the father-in-law of Adams's friend L. Q. C. Lamar. And there is Washington Allston's novel, *Monaldi*. (Later Adams would acquire a biography.)[27] But Allston resided in Massachusetts in later life, and, as noted above, the Sturgis family (the maternal line of Marian Adams) owned several of his paintings, so Allston came to Adams more as a Bostonian than a South Carolinian.[28] Hence Adams knew little or nothing of writers like William Gilmore Simms or George Tucker or Henry Timrod, or even much about proslavery texts. Perhaps his omission of Thomas Dew or George Fitzhugh is unsurprising, for the antislavery mind (like its opponent) tended to quarrel with a rumor, but it is a little more puzzling that Adams owned only two texts that specifically documented the antislavery crusade, in which his father was so engaged, though he did have books by and about New Englanders incidentally opposed to slavery.[29]

Later, even this limited engagement with the literature of the South ebbed. In 1903, he was asked by Edwin Alderman, then president of Tulane University, to recommend the names of those Southerners who had made the greatest contribution to the American character. (Alderman was then planning what was to become the multivolume *The South in the Building of the Nation*.) Adams, in reply, was polite but dismissive: "The southern society has left very little trace in literature of its own. Almost no intimate letters, memoirs, or records of any kind exist to fill a biographical outline. Politically, the southern statesman, like all statesmen, was a self-conscious actor on a stage, and sometimes he acted well, sometimes ill, but his acting, though it became a second nature, was never worth a biography."[30] This was odd coming from a biographer of John Randolph, odder from someone who owned so much Southern political biography.

Likewise, Adams little noticed postbellum Southern writing or even works on the Civil War. On the latter score, indeed, it is hard to show much beyond the biography of Abraham Lincoln coauthored by John Hay, which in 1892 he regarded (whether out of friendship or dispassionate criticism) as "the first work on American history in popular and political importance that has appeared in my time."[31] Adams owned only four works about military campaigns: one about the Mississippi and another on the Shenandoah Valley, both places where Richard Taylor had served; and the memoirs of William T. Sherman (the uncle of Elizabeth Cameron) and Ulysses S. Grant. Otherwise, he had only Horace Greeley's general history, a study of the blockade, and—a personal document—an 1862 pamphlet on the *Trent* affair.[32] As for Southern writing, he knew Owen Wister, though did not like him or his wife ("The Owen Wisters do not amuse me; he has the qualities of his race, and I of mine"), but Adams did read him. He had a copy of Wister's biography of George Washington and liked it.[33] It is possible that Adams read George W. Cable and Joel Chandler Harris, or at least he knew enough about them in 1905 to suggest their names as candidates for election to the National Institute of Arts and Letters. He read some Mark Twain, again without especial attention, though he did admire Twain's 1901 spoof of a diary written by Adam in the Garden of Eden, and in 1917 he acquired an edition of Twain's letters.[34] And he had a copy of Henry Watterson's *Oddities in Southern Life and Character*. Again, personal acquaintance mattered. He had asked Watterson, the somewhat liberal editor of the *Louisville Courier-Journal*, to dinner in 1874 by way of serving the liberal Republican cause, and still knew him in 1901.[35] The rest is silence.

So the South ceased to possess words, but became only a wild landscape in his mind. There was value in such a landscape: it offered a counterpoint to the social damage of pell-mell American industrialization, with which Adams was growing disenchanted. Part of his revulsion was from money grubbing, vulgarity, ugliness, smoke, and grime. Deeper, though, was his reassessment of the role of science in the modern world. In early manhood, he had been a believer in science and seen himself as a historical scientist, though even then he had been uneasy at how science might prove too independent of human will. But such detachment and dispassion had also been science's main attraction. In 1871, he had said of the philosopher: "[He] delights in studying phenomena, whether of his own mind or of matter, with absolute indifference to the results. His business is to reason about life, thought, the soul, and truth, as though he were reasoning about phosphates and square roots; and to a mind fairly weary of self, there is a marvellous relief and positive delight in getting down to the hard pan of science." He abandoned this faith with reluctance. In 1884, when writing to Francis Parkman, he was still of the opinion that "Before long a new school of history will rise which will leave us antiquated. Democracy is the only subject for scientific history. I am satisfied that the purely mechanical development of the human mind in society must appear in a great democracy so clearly, for want of disturbing elements, that in another generation psychology, physiology and history will join in proving man to have as fixed and necessary a development as that of a tree; and almost as unconscious." In 1894, he was more dubious, if holding on. In his presidential remarks to the American Historical Association, he observed that the attempt to create a science of history had made "little progress," though "almost every successful historian has been busy with it, adding, here a new analysis; a new generalization there; a clear and defining connection where before the rupture of idea was absolute; and above all, extending the field of study until it shall include all races, all countries, and all times." The venture might be uncertain, but it was still the only venture worth making. "That the effort to make History a Science may fail, is possible, and perhaps probable; but that it should cease, unless for reasons that would cause all science to cease, is not within the range of experience. Historians will not, and even if they would they cannot, abandon the attempt. Science itself would admit its own failure, if it admitted that man, the most important of all its subjects, could not be brought within its range."[36]

The South was, for Adams, outside the domain of science and industry. This was so, in the minor sense that (as he saw it) the region's intellectuals had not yet assimilated the modern scientific method. As he had told William Henry Trescot of South Carolina in 1876, "We [in the North] are nothing if not scientific. We analyze like chemists; we dissect like surgeons; we construct like architects; we never lose our temper; we are never ornate; we are always practical. . . . The condition of the southern states is a subject on which I have above all things wished to obtain a good article but I have after many efforts abandoned the attempt for the simple reason that all my southern correspondents . . . seemed possessed of the literary theories of fifty years ago, and let their feelings get the better of them."[37] But it was so, in the major sense that Southern society was still before the great divide, still in the preindustrial world, and so still possessed of the social instincts natural to that world.

Before his wife's suicide, Adams had had a low opinion of those who let their feelings get the better of them. He had indicted John Randolph for a want of restraint. In Adams's 1884 novel, *Esther*, where he first interrogated the problem of religion and faith, his heroine refuses to become a believing Christian because she is told that Christianity might comfort her feelings as a woman and offer the prospect of again meeting her family in the afterlife. Of this bribe, Esther asks with indignation, "Why must the church always appeal to my weakness and never to my strength! I ask for spiritual life and you send me back to my flesh and blood as though I were a tigress you were sending back to her cubs. What is the use of appealing to my sex? the atheists at least show me respect enough not to do that!"[38]

In the 1890s, this trust in independence and the capacities of reason began to weaken. By the time Adams came to write *Mont-Saint-Michel and Chartres*, which he finished in 1904, the trust had all but disappeared. In the complex argument of that book lurked this problem of feeling. It was Adams's contention that between the eleventh and thirteenth centuries, "Europe was a unity . . . in thought, will, and object" and that "Christianity was the unit."[39] This unity had been a self-conscious achievement—in philosophy, art, and literature—but had been fiercely contested by the thinkers of the age. At the heart of their debate lay the problem of free will and human capacity, which even for architectural form had implications, discernible for Adams in the transition from the simplicity of the Romanesque to the tense complexity of the Gothic.

Adams set up the Abbey Church of Mont-Saint-Michel in Normandy and the cathedral of Chartres some two hundred kilometers to its southeast as the sites that might best exemplify his thesis. To Adams, that Mont-Saint-Michel was Norman mattered greatly, because to him the Norman represented masculine simplicity and military energy; he embodied a sensibility that was hardheaded, empirical, serious. The "Norman [was] the practical scheme which states the facts, and stops." But Chartres was French; it represented the feminine, not least because it had been dedicated in 1260 as "the Cathedral of the Assumption of Our Lady," the Virgin Mary. Because of her, at Chartres one found grace, gentleness, compassion, pity, all founded on Mary's strength as a queen and a woman. In her cathedral was light, color, sympathy. For Adams, "Chartres expressed . . . an emotion, the deepest man ever felt—the struggle of his own littleness to grasp the infinite." Mary's purpose was to intercede as the representative of mankind between an often pitiless God and his frequently suffering human creation. As Adams put it, "If the Trinity was in its essence Unity, the Mother alone could represent whatever was not Unity: whatever was irregular, exceptional, outlawed; and this was the whole human race." Further, "She knew that the universe was as unintelligible to her, on any theory of morals, as it was to her worshippers, and she felt, like them, no sure conviction that it was any more intelligible to the Creator of it."[40] So her value was this understanding that the world was disorderly, fitted no tidy scheme of morals, and could not be expected to embody justice. Mary held out her hand to mankind, and, touching her, men and women touched pity and warmth.

Adams saw Mont-Saint-Michel and Norman culture as, in part, the analogue of New England. He said so in his letters, written after visiting the abbey in 1895 and going on to the cathedral of Coutances: "I have rarely felt New England at its highest ideal power as it appeared to me, beatified and glorified, in the Cathedral of Coutances," he told his brother Brooks. In the first few pages of *Mont-Saint-Michel and Chartres*, the theme is plainly stated: "From the top of this Abbey Church one looks across the bay to Avranches, and towards Coutances . . . [the] shore, facing us, recalls the coast of New England. The relation between the granite of one coast and that of the other may be fanciful, but the relation between the people who live on each is as hard and practical a fact as the granite itself." What is more elusive is how far Adams saw Chartres as Southern. It seems unlikely that he had the American South specifically in mind, but the imaginative construct of "southern" made by his times in Italy, Spain, Cuba, Fiji, as well as South Carolina, was undeniably present. To move from Normandy to Chartres was, physically, a move southward, from a gloomy, severe, rain-lashed shore to something lighter. But the move was more spiritual than physical. Adams knew that Chartres is not so very far south. Rather, he liked to see Chartres as a Mediterranean outpost. He had a theory that Chartres was deeply influenced by the Languedoc, by its troubadours and cult of courtly love, and (beyond southern France) by the Mediterranean cultures, which the Crusades had brought back to western Europe. So he spoke of "the sunny atmosphere of the Southern poetry" and of "a softer, Southern temper in a happier climate." So he said of the Virgin of Chartres that one might see "a Southern or Eastern type in her face."[41]

Mont-Saint-Michel and Chartres was not a blanket endorsement of the feminine and the Southern. It is, in fact, a book that in its closing pages contends that the achievement of the high Middle Ages was to effect an androgynous synthesis of masculine and feminine, North and South, reason and passion, energy and repose. This was the achievement of Thomas Aquinas, as it was the material accomplishment of the Gothic architects. Pity and compassion alone were not enough. At the last, Saint Thomas was greater than Saint Francis. But Aquinas had to solve the problem posed by Saint Francis and the Virgin, their insight that humanity was fallible and was, by itself, incapable of grasping the unity of the infinite. As Adams saw it, Aquinas had understood that logic and form was needed, not only to embody reason, but also to deal with doubt and suffering. Further, Aquinas had seen, in deference to the Virgin, that logic was inferior to faith and feeling. This was the message that Adams was painfully anxious to communicate in the book's final, extraordinary paragraph, perhaps the most remarkable passage written by an American author, not least for its exquisite but mediated confessional quality. It reads:

> Of all the elaborate symbolism which has been suggested for the Gothic cathedral, the most vital and most perfect may be that the slender nervure, the springing motion of the broken arch, the leap downwards of the flying buttress—the visible effort to throw off a visible strain—never let us forget that Faith alone supports it, and that, if Faith fails, Heaven is lost. The equilibrium is visibly delicate beyond the line of safety; danger lurks in every stone. The peril of the heavy tower, of the restless vault, of the vagrant buttress; the uncertainty of logic, the inequalities of the syllogism, the irregularities of the mental

mirror—all these haunting nightmares of the Church are expressed as strongly by the Gothic cathedral as though it had been the cry of human suffering, and as no emotion had ever been expressed before or is likely to find expression again. The delight of its aspirations is flung up to the sky. The pathos of its self-distrust and anguish of doubt is buried in the earth as its last secret. You can read out of it whatever else pleases your youth and confidence; to me, this is all.[42]

To reiterate, this was not an argument for preferring the feminine to the masculine, the Southern to the Northern, though Adams sometimes came close to saying this. His was a case for androgyny. But, having made the abstract case in *Mont-Saint-Michel and Chartres*, Adams decided to see how the argument might work when applied to the modern American world he had experienced. So he wrote *The Education of Henry Adams*, his memoir-cum-philosophical tract. The two books were self-consciously a pair, and the latter sought to show that, while the Middle Ages had triumphantly but unstably fashioned its vision and embodiment of unity, the modern world under still greater pressures had failed to do so, had gradually lost its grip on the idea of order and surrendered to the confusions of multiplicity. To use the phrase Adams coined, an orderly universe had been succeeded by a disorderly "supersensual multiverse."[43]

One must remember the book's mixed purpose. The *Education* was not just a memoir, though it was that. Adams was old, his friends were dead or dying, and it was natural to remember some, if not all, of what he had seen and known. Many members of his family had plied the trades of memoir and family history. His father had edited the works of John Adams and the diary of John Quincy Adams. His elder brother Charles was to write an autobiography and had once written a biography of their father.[44] His younger brother, Brooks, was to try to write a biography of John Quincy Adams. But memoir was not enough. A second task of the *Education* was to narrate a historical and philosophical stance. As Adams explained to a reader in 1910, "*Mont-Saint-Michel* . . . began the demonstration of the law which . . . the *Education* illustrates." Of these two purposes, memoir and philosophy, the latter was more important. Philosophical conjecture was habitually the preference of his later writings, which desired to set up the abstract over the empirical, which wanted to think facts inferior to imagination. As he put it to Henry Osborn Taylor in 1905, "To me, accuracy is relative. I care very little whether my details are exact, if only my *ensemble* is in scale."[45]

As a young man, Adams had become a historian to gain literary fame, but also because he had thought that studying historical facts would produce historical laws, just as biological facts had produced the laws of Darwinian natural selection.[46] He had presumed that empiricism led to surety. (He had been then much influenced by Auguste Comte, the father of positivism.) In time, Adams claimed that empiricism did no such thing; he alleged that it only produced a mass of indigestible and amoral facts. So he lost interest in historical facts for their own sake and began to work from the other direction. Instead of using history to produce meaning, he used meaning to produce history. As he put it to Henry Morse Stephens in 1916, Adams had started as a teacher at Harvard long ago, with "the usual assumption of unity and continuity as bases" for history, but by 1914 was "driven to doubt," so "I fell back, for my personal needs, on the world of idealism,—on art, poetry, religion, philosophy, &c,—which satisfied my own needs, and which could do without realism or history." But even in 1896, to the historian John Franklin Jameson, he had said: "As History stands, it is a sort of Chinese Play, without end and without lesson."[47]

What you get, if a historian writes a memoir when disbelieving in realism or history, is a book in which facts are used but little respected. Adams thought narrative was about achieving an intellectual and emotional response in a reader. He believed that the only theme worth stating was tragedy. When he demolished his brother's life of John Quincy Adams, it was because he judged Brooks had not understood the tragedy of their grandfather's life. But this was a general principle, much wider than the Adams family. As Henry told Brooks, "I have no scruple, in my own theories, about handling my material in view of a climax, and for artistic purposes, the climax must always tend to tragedy. No one with the intelligence of an average monkey will try to tell a story without leading up to its point." Even in the 1880s, he had thought that narration required the managing of facts and tone. One reason for disliking his own biography of Randolph was that he had allowed Randolph himself too much authority over the book. "If you like 'Randolph,' I am pleased, for you are the only person I was bound to satisfy," he told John T. Morse, the editor of the American Statesmen series, in 1882. "To me it is an unpleasant book, which sins against all my art-canons. The acidity is much too decided. The rule of a writer should be that of a salad-maker; let the vinegar be put in by a miser; the oil by a spendthrift. In this case however the tone was really decided by the subject, and the excess of acid is his." Adams liked more control than this. So, in writing the *Education*, he did not scruple to fix the facts, if thereby the history could be made to work, morally or politically or philosophically. He did this semireluctantly, with a sense of necessity more than virtue, a necessity partly arising from the historian's entrapment in self. As he told George Cabot Lodge in 1903, "The fact, which all the psychologists insist on, that the mind really reflects only itself, is to me the most exasperating thing in the world. Until I read over my own work, I never see the holes and bare spots in my own mind; and only then I feel how hard it is to scratch about, and put on false hair and rouge and a grin. As writers grow old, they all do it, some well, some ill; and call it art."[48]

In the *Education*, Adams had a story to tell. He needed to show how the truths grasped by the twelfth century had ceased to be enactable as truths by the end of the nineteenth century. This meant he needed the same ingredients as he had defined for the Middle Ages, but then he had to demonstrate how the mix of these ingredients had turned out differently by 1900. And he had to use the raw materials of American history, even the raw materials of his own life. This was not easy, though it was possible, at all, because his view of the Middle Ages had been much informed, in the first place, by his American experience. So one decision about narrative was inevitable. Just as once New England had informed his understanding of Normandy while the South had inflected Chartres, so now Normandy would inform New England and Chartres would inflect the South. The difference would be that there could be no modern Aquinas, no one to pull the rabbit of meaning out of the hat.

It turned out to be more complicated than that, on both sides of the equation. He had the problem that his New England contained not one site, but two. Quincy and Boston stood for different things, and strictly speaking, Boston put on a better show as Normandy than did Quincy. Boston was masculinity, power, energy, repressive reason. Quincy was his childhood, so softer. As he put it, "Town was restraint, law, unity. Country, only seven miles away, was liberty, diversity, outlawry, the endless delight of mere sense impressions."[49] As such, Quincy was a sort of quasi-South, but it could not do the work in the narrative that the real South would be asked to do, because Quincy was too minor in the drama of American history. Quincy and Boston would never meet at a Massachusetts version of Gettysburg, but only had an asymmetrical moral rivalry in the mind of the Adamses. So, Quincy could be used only to intimate the great theme to come, could be used only as prelude to Boston, so that Adams could the better convey the wintry sterility of Boston and its mind.

The South enters the narrative in three early places. First, there is the description of his grandmother Louisa Catherine Adams. The second is the tale of visiting Washington when a boy, where he evokes the city's ragged, haphazard, black sensuality, the "May sunshine and shadow," the "thickness of foliage and . . . heavy smells," the "want of barriers, of pavements, of forms; the looseness; the laziness; the indolent Southern drawl; the pigs in the streets; the negro babies and their mothers with bandanas; the freedom, openness, swagger, of nature and man." The third is the characterization of his Harvard classmate William Henry Fitzhugh Lee, commonly known as Rooney, who is shown as tall, handsome, a natural leader, but someone "simple beyond analysis," childlike, with no mind, only temperament.[50] All three of these narrative moments serve the same purpose, to state the theme of the South as the feminine side of American culture, but in its various forms. Louisa Adams is the female in her proper sphere, unintellectual but nurturing. The streets of Washington represent the female in her improper sphere, as an alluring whore who invites from a doorway. Rooney Lee is what happens when the feminine is lodged in a man and female unintellectuality structures male aggression.

Before developing this analysis further, it is worth pausing, as a matter of curiosity, to ask how far one can independently validate Adams's portrait of Rooney Lee. Against the will of Lee's recent biographer, there is little reason to challenge Adams's sense that Lee had intellectual shortcomings, though none as grave as Adams was to charge. At Harvard, certainly, Lee was more interested in rowing than in classes, he piled up debts, and he was much drawn to the fraternity crowd. In his first year, Lee was fifty-sixth in his class, out of ninety-one, and thereafter his standing worsened. (Henry Adams's own standing was not stellar, just forty-fourth at graduation.)[51] But this ill performance was partly because Lee found the recitations to be boring—as did Adams—and, indeed, the two met partly because Lee founded what was called an "eating table," for the purpose of, as his biographer puts it, "learning, discussion, and probing more relevant topics than those in the recitation halls." Still, his father, Robert E. Lee, was realistic about his son's abilities and in a letter of 1856 expressed no loftier ambition than that Rooney might "find it entirely within your power to make a respectable if not a high standing in your class" and observed, with more hope than confidence, "I cannot believe you inferior, I am sure you do not wish to prove yourself so." Hence one might partially agree with Adams's assessment of Rooney's intellect. Unclear, however, is whether Lee was a natural leader, a man who instantly expressed authority. He was, to be sure, a very good cavalry commander in the war, and his men seem to have followed him. And he was very tall—six foot two—and this loftiness, then as now, tended to suggest mastery. (Adams himself was self-consciously short, and the *Education* confesses his difficulty in falling "behind his brothers two or three inches in height, and proportionally in bone and weight.") But there is much evidence that Lee was not masterly, but retiring and modest. John S. Wise of Virginia, who observed Lee during the war, saw a gentleman, to be sure, but one abstemious when it came to drink, someone awkward because of immense hands and feet, and one who was "in company . . . ill at ease." Later, when Lee was in Congress, it was said of him that "he never put himself forward except when duty prompted" and that he was "a simple, kindly, unaffected, modest gentleman" with a "sweet, calm smile." It was his springtime custom, when serving in the House of Representatives, to bring in baskets of roses, which he distributed to his fellow congressmen.[52] This is not the man described by Henry Adams. A photograph of Lee at Harvard shows—at least to my eye—someone uncertain, not someone convinced.

The *Education*'s portrait of Lee as an individual may be true to how Adams had seen Lee in the 1850s, but much had intervened between

William H. F. "Rooney" Lee at Harvard, ca. 1858. Courtesy of the Harvard
University Archives.

1855 and 1907 to make Lee useful as a cultural symbol. If Adams had wanted to say something else about the South, he had other Southern classmates who answered to a different description. There was, for one, Henry Hobson Richardson of New Orleans and Priestley Plantation, who went on to become one of America's leading architects and who remained one of Adams's closest friends, to whom Adams entrusted the design of his Washington home, who instructed Adams in the meaning of Romanesque architecture, a knowledge without which Adams could not have written *Mont-Saint-Michel and Chartres*. But, as a Southerner, Richardson was too complex for Adams's purposes. He could appear in the *Education* as an individual, but not as a type.

So Rooney Lee it was, for making the general point about the South, the point that has for so long depressed Southerners about the world's opinion. It may be worth saying, though—by way of partially lifting the gloom—that, though Adams's judgment of the South and its culture was severe, it was not singular. If one glances over the whole corpus of Adams's writing, there is scarcely a culture he did not find inadequate, especially in its intellectual capacities. He described the English mind as "one-sided, eccentric, systematically unsystematic, and logically illogical." More broadly, he spoke of "the impenetrable stupidity of the British mind." He spoke more fondly of the Germans, but only because they seemed, at least before 1914, unthreatening, and his compliments were ambivalent, at best. In the *Education*, he said: "What he liked was the simple character; the good-natured sentiment; the musical and metaphysical abstraction; the blundering incapacity . . . for practical affairs." Spain was "a hole" with nice weather but occupied by "a good-natured, dirty people who are always apologetic if one does not insult them." Russia was "rotten and decrepit to the core." Australians were a "savage race . . . totally without interest; they have no arts, dances or manners of their own." As for Italy, "If the Italians ever publish anything, I have not found it out. . . . The Italian novel at best is an utterly hopeless and Godforsaken product of intellectual impotence, and I firmly believe that the newspapers now contain all there is of literary life in Italy. The rest is mere imitation so far as I have seen anything."[53] Even the French did not escape, for he was inclined to think that Cartesians were too logical to grasp an illogical world.

This scything extended amply into American culture. New England, of course, he roughly handled. It was, on his account, "narrow, nervous, self-distrustful often, always introspective, uneasy, and till lately, intolerant." Those from the American West were scoundrels: "I never knew more than two or three men born west of the Alleghanies who knew the difference between a gentleman and a swindler." As for "the New York crowd, which seems now to count for society in America," they were "too loathsome for expression."[54] Adams was seldom happy to be around Americans, especially when abroad, and often made Henry James sound starry-eyed about the American mind. Amid this gallery of cultural bunglers, the American South appears as a bungler indeed, but not singularly so.

This does not mean that Adams was somehow anti-American.[55] In fact, he was peculiarly devoted to the project of American nationality. These criticisms showed a duty of care, if also a marked snobbery. Something in the Adams legacy complicated nationality. When criticizing Brooks's manuscript, Henry had observed that their grandfather had been much happier in Saint Petersburg than in Massachusetts, that John Quincy Adams, in fact, "loathed and hated America" and "beyond dispute, he never thought of going home without nausea." And the consequence was that "he, and his son, and his grandchildren had to be trained to profess a passionate patriotism which very strongly resembled cant."[56]

However, there is evidence that the act of remembering, necessary for the writing of the *Education*, revived in Adams the partisan passion of the early 1860s. He was, after all, partly writing a Civil War memoir, a genre that often elicited and strengthened half-forgotten animosities. To be sure, that animosity had never been extinguished, though it had somewhat softened in the late 1870s and 1880s. Still, even then, in his biography of Albert Gallatin, he had written disparagingly (if briefly) of American politics between 1830 and 1849 as offering "as melancholy a spectacle as satirists ever held up to derision." The Whigs he dismissed as, of parties, "the most feeble in ideas and the most blundering in management," whilst "Jacksonian Democracy was corrupt in its methods." American society was then "deeply cankered with two desperate sores: the enormous increase of easily-acquired wealth, and the terribly rapid growth of slavery and the slave power." And, as before discussed, in his biography of John Randolph, he sketched the rise of a proslavery doctrine of states rights, initiated by Randolph and completed by Calhoun. That doctrine, as Adams saw it, was formally in favor of decentralization, but in fact was compelled into using centralized power to protect its interests; he offered a swingeing list of the "triumphs of the slave power": the Louisiana Purchase, the Embargo, the War of 1812, the annexation of Texas, the Mexican War, the Fugitive Slave Law, and the Dred Scott decision.[57]

This condemnation, when applied to the decades before the Civil War, was usually generic rather than ad hominem, but a few individuals were singled out. The genial and charming Henry Clay, though a planter and slaveholder, was often praised by Adams, upon the reasoning that Clay was at least a nationalist and, by dividing the South, "broke, by his immense popularity, the solid ranks of the slaveholding, states rights democracy which Randolph wished to organize." He even wrote of "Clay's nobler genius."[58] Calhoun fared less well. In print, Adams was warily respectful, at least of the War Hawk. In private, however, he had been less impressed. When at Harvard in the academic year of 1876–77, when he had begun to teach American history, he had been compelled to read more widely than before. To that end, he acquired Calhoun's collected works. In May 1877, he sat down to read the *Disquisition on Government* with pen in hand to interject his customary marginalia.[59]

Some of Adams's comments merely characterized. When Calhoun's text observed that "power can only be resisted by power,—and tendency by tendency," Adams wrote in the margin, "Reason has no place in Calhoun's conception of human society." When Calhoun said that, under the influence of the principle of the concurrent majority, "concession would cease to be considered a sacrifice,—would become a free-will offering on the altar of the country, and lose the name of compromise," Adams observed, "This sounds like Sieyes and Robespierre." Some notations, however, challenged Calhoun's command of historical evidence. When the senator observed that government first arose in human society from the necessity to control "a universal state of conflict, between individual and individual," Adams countered by writing, "Pure theory. The Greeks could have taught him better. It was not the conflict of individuals that necessitated government, as Indian society shows, but the military exigencies arising from interests rising from contests between groups." Likewise, when Calhoun suggested that the Norman Conquest "introduced the feudal system, with its necessary appendages, a hereditary monarchy and nobility," the professional reproved the amateur by sniffing, "This is indeed a discovery in history." Adams was wary when Calhoun invoked God. The text observed that, "Constitution is the contrivance of man, while government is of Divine ordination," and the margin protested, "Surely this is wretched stuff."[60]

The philosophical drift of Adams's notations was to criticize Calhoun's cynicism about human reason and the moral underpinnings of nationality. Adams thought there was more to human society than self-interest. For instance, Calhoun had observed that when a political majority exercises its power, "the minority, for the time, will be as much the governed or subject portion, as are the people in an aristocracy, or the subjects in a monarchy." To this, Adams rejoined, "If so, the whole theory and practice of 'His Majesty's Opposition' is false. Calhoun knew better than this. Minorities are an essential part of the government, and affect legislation indefinitely as Calhoun well knew." When Calhoun insisted that the power of a majority tends to create "confusion, corruption, disorder, and anarchy," and so force revolution, Adams was indignant: "This is a mere assertion. No proof is offered. Just the contrary may equally well be asserted. Nations often are purified by the same process; rarely by any other." When Calhoun argued that "in the earliest stages of society, numbers and individual prowess constituted the principal elements of power," Adams demanded, "Prove it! The elements were always complicated. Even numbers and prowess were not simple elements but results of conditions; and intelligence was the most active factor of all." Adams asked, instead, "Is there not a pecuniary and a patriotic interest? a selfish and a common one? Is society so simple a thing that there are no doubts in men's minds as to which of many interests is their true interest?" So, when Calhoun observed that the existence of the concurrent majority would give citizens confidence in being protected and "thereby, not every feeling calculated to weaken the attachment to the whole is suppressed," Adams countered, "This is positively bewildering. To suppress all *action* is to suppress all *feeling*! To link the good and bad, the live and dead together, is to unite both in common devotion to their country."[61]

The political drift of the criticism, however, was Adams's awareness that Calhoun pretended a dispassionate disquisition, while actually devising a political mechanism for the defense of slavery. "What is his 'concurrent majority'?" he asked, by way of summary at the *Disquisition*'s end. "A mere machinery for stereotyping interests and protecting decayed and corrupt ones from the operation of natural laws by giving them political powers. As applied to *the* interest intended to be protected, that of negro slavery, its object and working is obvious. Apply it to any other, and the wretchedly sophistical quality of Calhoun's mind becomes instantly obvious." In 1877, for a liberal Republican, an aspirant historical scientist, and a quasi-Comtean, Calhoun was obliged to be unsatisfactory. For a New Englander, there was a cultural explanation ready to hand. "I am bitterly disappointed. This work reads to me like the crude vagary of a South Carolina planter, half-educated and half-trained. I never in my life was more surprised than with this exhibition of Calhoun's famous intellectual power."[62] Slaveholding kills reason.

Such remarks are not to be found again for several decades, but they resurface and strengthen in the *Education*. The portrait of Rooney Lee is an instance, but most strictures are found in the chapter on the great secession winter, which is unambiguously entitled "Treason." There Adams liberally abused "the cotton-planters," a category he much used, though little explained. It seems to have denoted a distinction between the older slavocracy of Virginian tobacco planters and the parvenus made by the invention of the cotton gin, and so was as much a condemnation of (what in the *Gallatin* he had reprobated as) "the enormous increase of easily-acquired wealth" as it was of slavery's effect. These "cotton-planters" were "stupendously ignorant of the world," and "as a class, [they] were mentally one-sided, ill-balanced, and provincial to a degree rarely known." They formed "a close society on whom the new fountains of power had poured a stream of wealth and slaves that acted like oil on flame."

Significantly, Adams added, such an opinion was a "commonplace of 1900," though a heterodoxy in 1860, because then the reputation of Southerners for statesmanship was so high.[63] After finishing the *Education*, he seldom again lost this passion. In 1909 he went still further in his remembered anger. "I see the age of Andrew Jackson and the cotton-planters much as I see the age of the Valois or Honorius," he wrote to Brooks Adams, "that is, [with] profound horror." The tragedy of John Quincy Adams, indeed, was that he had thrown in his lot with the planters and only understood what he had done, and turned to opposition, when it was too late: "The sum of it, as it affects me, is to prove that he had no business to serve Jefferson or Jackson; that he knew better; that he did it for personal ambition quite as much as for patriotism; and that when he realised what he had done, he—did what he did."[64]

However, in the *Education*, Adams could also find ways to affect a dispassion towards both North and South. On the Northern side of the ledger, he managed even a kindliness towards his grandfather. There he made central a story of refusing to go to school, of his grandfather emerging from the library and taking his hand, of walking the mile to the schoolhouse, and of the absence of reprimand: "During their long walk he had said nothing; he had uttered no syllable of revolting cant about the duty of obedience and the wickedness of resistance to law." The former president is made to seem indulgent, familiar, and patient. The grandson knew better, of course. In his 1869 selection from the papers of his grandmother, the only document from John Quincy Adams he chose to reproduce is a letter that could readily be characterized as embodying "revolting cant about the duty of obedience and the wickedness of resistance to law." His 1909 critique of Brooks Adams's biography is explosive with unforgiving anger towards the old, bald man in the Quincy pew for crimes that were political ("J.Q.A. deliberately acted as tool of the slave oligarchy [especially about Florida], and never rebelled until the slave oligarchy contemptuously cut his throat") and personal (he was "abominably selfish, or absorbed in self, and incapable of feeling his duty to others" and "his dragging his wife to Europe in 1809, and separating her from her children was demonic").[65] But, in the *Education*, John Quincy Adams sat at the center of Quincy and childhood, not at the heart of

American politics, and because Quincy stood for happiness, so must the grandfather. This rhetorical cunning, which could blunder into a generosity of spirit, inflected Adams's scrutiny of American culture. He was anxious to contend that both the antebellum North and the South were anachronistic. In defeat, the South lost, but so in victory did the North. The feminine failed, but so did the masculine. Instinct failed, but so did reason. If the nineteenth century had succeeded as the twelfth century had succeeded, there would have emerged from the struggle of the Civil War a workable synthesis, not just a political Union but a philosophical unity. It did not. Ulysses Grant botched the first part and Adams did not miss using Grant for tragicomic effect, but the whole tendency of the modern world made the second, more important part impossible. The failure was fundamental and vexatious, not least because Adams was an American exceptionalist. He persisted in thinking that the fate of American culture was the fate of the world. If, around him in America, Adams could see no meaning, no sense, he had no hope that any other culture could be modernity's Aquinas.

It was once usual to see Adams as, in effect, writing as a proto-modernist, if by modernism one means the intellectual stance of T. S. Eliot, Virginia Woolf, and the like, those who thought that, though the world might make little sense, at least in art we can fashion meaning.[66] Certainly, the later Adams had marks of the breed: an antidemocratic elitism, a preference for the urban, a mysticism about creativity, a myth of the fall, a fear of the future, an exhilaration about technology, and an unease about the death of God. Recently, however, Adams has been cast as a proto-postmodernist and placed among those who have thought that, not only does the world make little sense, but neither does art.[67] There may be less difference here than some might claim—at best, there may be a difference of emphasis.[68] At varying moments, Adams flirted with both of these paradigms. He was, perhaps, most the postmodernist when he argued in the *Education* that the modern world would require a new way of thinking. As he put it there, "The movement from unity into multiplicity . . . would require a new social mind." This is, after all, what has been said in recent years by critics like Jean-François Lyotard, who thinks that "the Enlightenment narrative, in which the hero of knowledge works towards a good ethico-political end" is dead; that we live in an age marked by "incredulity toward metanarratives"; that "technological transformations . . . have a considerable impact on knowledge"; that "scientific knowledge does not represent the totality of knowledge" and competes only as one narrative among many; that the collapse of paradigms has left us with relationships encoded only in unstable and negotiated "language games" and a self which "exists in a fabric of relations that is now more complex and mobile than ever before"; that hermetically sealed genres have dissolved into fluctuating inter-disciplinarities; and that knowledge is increasingly understood not as truth but something "saleable."[69] These contentions are very close to the argument of *Mont-Saint-Michel and Chartres* and the *Education*.

As he himself tirelessly claimed, Adams came from the old intellectual order. He did not himself have this new social mind, just wit enough to see that what he had been taught about the world was wrong. As he observed after one of the formative moments of his later life, his visit to the Chicago Exposition of 1893, the point of education now was "to learn chaos when one sees it."[70] The old order had seen not chaos, but pattern. It had had the habit of cultural generalization, the notion of social types. As a historian, Adams had been formed by all those writers—Jules Michelet, Alexis de Tocqueville, Hippolyte Taine, Thomas Henry Buckle—who had fashioned generalizations about the French, the English, and the Americans, and so had made it possible to talk about smaller cultural units like New England and the South. A supersensual multiverse would kill all that. Amid this carnage, the death of the South would be certain.

If Adams were a prophet, we would now be living in such a world, in which the idea of the South would be impossible. That I have been writing about the South and you (whoever you are) have been reading, and we may share some understandings, might suggest that Adams was an inadequate prophet. Perhaps so, but the postmodernist insight is more clever than that. There are many literary critics, a few historians, and not a few social critics who think the South as a construct has lost any specificity of meaning, that it has only what individuals make of it at the moment such meaning is asserted, that (to use

Adams's term) the South lives in a supersensual multiverse, like the rest of us.

But there are, at least, two kinds of postmodernists. There are those who come from the Marxist tradition, or any of those social-scientific schools that contend that how we think is grounded in the materiality of how we live. These see postmodernism as a historical situation created by particular social preconditions at a particular moment in time. Among these, most notable are Fredric Jameson and David Harvey. The former explains postmodernism by the emergence of a "late form of capitalism." The latter is so convinced that the sensibility has social and economic groundings that he finds it possible to furnish charts, tables, and graphs that evidence the movements of capital, the acceleration of time, and the compression of space since 1910, even since the Renaissance. These writers are not necessarily sympathetic to the postmodernist habit of mind. Jameson, indeed, is desperate to transcend postmodernism and find "a breakthrough to some as yet unimaginable new mode of representing this last, in which we may again begin to grasp our positioning as individual and collective subjects and regain a capacity to act and struggle which is at present neutralized." Harvey, too, seeks "a meta-theory with which to embrace all these gyrations of postmodern thinking and cultural production."[71] But both accept that this is the way we live now, if not how we ought to live.

The other postmodernists tend to be indifferent to history and materiality because their standpoint has arisen, not from the Marxist tradition, but from poststructuralism and linguistic philosophy; their intellectual genealogy reaches back via Wittgenstein to Nietzsche. For them, postmodernism is a critique of human nature, especially of perception and language. Epistemology, not history, is their queen of disciplines. They look at the fragments discernible in novels or poetry, buildings or actions, and see signs and signifiers of feelings, thoughts, habits, and their kaleidoscopic forms. But they see no internal logic and no external compulsion for these forms. At best, the fragments influence one another, but unstably. Lyotard, though he gestures towards the social influence of technology, is close to this standpoint by his focus upon language games. Whereas the social-scientific postmodernist is gloomy, the philosophical-linguistic post-modernist tends to be optimistic, for in the lessening of external pressure lies the hope of freedom, or at least a chance for playful amusement.

It is unclear which sort of postmodernist was Henry Adams, if indeed he was one, at all. On the one hand, he was trained in social science, committed to history (even if only as a Chinese play), and was deeply unhappy at how the modern world was turning out, indeed could not see how such a new world was sustainable. By his fingernails, he held on to the idea of culture, including that of Southern culture, which he placed in a time anterior to the crisis of order inherent in industrial society. On the other hand, he had worked his way towards a more radical standpoint, for his motives in using history came to be ahistorical. He wanted, above all, to say something about the problem of human perception, about reason and despair, and the South was allocated a role in this passion play. History provided scenes for the play, costumes for the actors, even lines for them to say, but finally the play was not about a place in time, but about the perennial problem of human nature and the universe. In truth, Adams could have distributed the roles differently—for example, given the part of unreason to New England and logic to the South—and his play would have worked as well. But the roles did have to be given to somebody, if the play was to be staged, at all.

It will be clear, by now, why Adams allocated the roles he did. Of some interest, though, is why so many Southerners in the half century after 1918 were willing to accept this assignment. Later Southerners have tended to be impatient, at least with Adams on Rooney Lee. Though he was otherwise sympathetic to Adams, C. Vann Woodward in 1971, when speaking of the notorious passage, was to describe it as a "patronizing quip," and in 1990 Melvin Bradford (at the other end of the ideological spectrum) called the entirety of the *Education* but "supercilious inanities."[72] But earlier was different. In 1948 John Donald Wade could describe Adams, if puckishly, as "Henry the Great." In the 1920s Wilbur Cash, as part of a modernist education that extended to Friedrich Nietzsche and Oswald Spengler, read and admired both the *Education* and *Mont-Saint-Michel and Chartres*. Indeed, when visiting Europe in 1927, the secular Cash went on a pilgrimage to Chartres and was moved to tears by what Adams had instructed him to value. As we have seen, in *The Mind of the South*, Cash used Adams on Rooney Lee as an analytical foundation. After quoting the passage in extenso, Cash wrote, simply, "There it is, then," as though little more need be said.[73]

But even Southern conservatives used Adams. In his essay for *I'll Take My Stand* in 1930, Allen Tate tried to suggest that Adams had tragically sought the qualities that the Old South contained, without knowing it: "He passed his last days in Washington despising the 'ignorant' and 'simple' minds south of the Potomac, . . . never suspecting that his efforts in behalf of defeating this simplicity and ignorance in a recent war did something towards undermining the base of the civilized values he coveted most." But Tate accepted much of what Adams described, though with a twist to transmute shortcoming into virtue. As Tate further explained in 1959, though the Rooney Lee portrait was "unkind," it pointed roughly towards a truth, that the Northern mind was analytical and dialectical, but the Southern was rhetorical; this was easy to misread as conveying "the impression that no Southerner of the past or present was ever given to thought." Rather, "the Southerner always talks to somebody else, and this somebody else, after varying intervals, is given his turn . . . that is to say, the typical Southern conversation is not going anywhere; it is not about anything. *It is about the people who are talking.* . . . This may be the reason why Northerners . . . find the alternating, or contrapuntal, conversation of Southerners fatiguing. Educated Northerners like their conversation to be about ideas."[74]

This theme is to be found in Richard Weaver, too, who in the 1940s inherited the conservatism of the Agrarians, while giving it a richer philosophical complexity. In 1948 he found the Rooney Lee portrait "unflattering," but also "shrewd," because Adams's "prejudices were not of the parochial kind," so Weaver could "give him credit for some true insights in certain parts of this sketch." Like Tate, Weaver had thought that the strength of the Old South resided in an instinctual tenacity, a stress upon living over thinking-about-living, and that this habit found its best expression in "religiousness." Unlike Tate, Weaver came to understand that Adams might have seen more than was self-evident in the *Education*, but clear from *Mont-Saint-Michel and Chartres.*

Indeed in 1958 Weaver suggested that his own conversion from liberalism to conservatism, consummated in 1939 by an epiphany when "driving one afternoon across the monotonous prairies of Texas," was influenced by Adams's version of what John Crowe Ransom had called the "unorthodox defense of orthodoxy." Weaver came to an understanding that "the aim is to strip aside the clichés of generalization, the slogans which are preserved only because they render service to contemporary institutions, and of course to avoid the drug of economic interpretation. Henry Adams felt an impulse to do something like this amid the hullaballoo of his America, and his enquiry led him—this bloodless, self-questioning descendant of New England Puritans—to ponder the mystery of the Virgin."[75]

Both Tate and Weaver were deeply troubled by the direction of industrial modernity. It was logical to turn to Adams, who had fashioned the most compelling image in American prose of modernity's disorder. This helped them over his being a New Englander, even one capable of what Donald Davidson (when criticizing Cash in 1941) called "puling bits of malice." But Davidson saw the main point in 1957, if not without an adjustment of chronology. Ours, he wrote, "is a culture from which the idea of divinity has more or less evaporated and in which, therefore, religion is no longer the arbiter of knowledge. This is what our society has been in the process of becoming ever since the sixteenth century—slowly at first, but, since the beginning of the industrial revolution, with accelerated speed observed and predicted by Henry Adams."[76]

The richness, not to say contradictions, in Adams's oeuvres allowed Southerners the freedom to move between Rooney Lee, the Virgin, and the Dynamo, and so create an Adams to serve their purposes.[77] (Though they seldom ventured earlier than the late works.)[78] As Robert Penn Warren was to observe in 1970, "[Adams] is interesting and has the secondary value of a kind of cultural hero who enacted an important role, perhaps more important than his actual writing."[79] Not least, Adams was available as a model for the elegiac patrician, a type with which the postbellum South was much endowed, in a Southern world where the sense of living after "the War" lingered even to 1941, if not longer. William Alexander Percy of Mississippi best exemplified this type, and he performed the role in admiring knowledge of how Adams had done it.[80] In Percy's case, there was the bonus of a familial connection to 1603 H Street. In 1918, Percy had returned from his service on the Western Front and landed in New York, to be greeted by his cousin Janet Longcope. He was depressed, she was sympathetic, and she thought he might be helped by reading *Mont-Saint-Michel and Chartres*, a copy of which she later sent to him. As it happened, she had known Adams, for she had lived near Lafayette Square during the war while her husband (a professor of medicine at Columbia University) had advised the government. She had visited during Adams's last winter and so found "an old, old man," one "who could have written Ecclesiastes there was such a taste of ashes in his philosophy." But, knowing her cousin, she discerned "that you would have been interested by him."[81] So it proved, for Percy liked the book, paid his ritual respects by visiting Chartres, and moved on to a reading of Adams's philosophical memoir. Indeed, he would be deeply influenced by the *Education* in writing its Southern analogue, published by Alfred Knopf in 1941 as a companion piece to Cash's *Mind of the South*.

The Adams touches in *Lanterns on the Levee: Recollections of a Planter's Son* are abundant. There is an opening evocation of the birthplace, rich in flora: "the water-oak, the pecan, the cypress, and the sweet-gum." There is an old woman, who connects to a vanishing past: "exquisite slender white hands, usually folded in idleness on her lap . . . she smelled faintly of orris-root." There is a claim that the older world was stuck in antiquated tastes: "a library . . . [with] leather-bound sets of the *Spectator*, the *Edinburgh Review*, the works of Mr. Goldsmith and Mr. Pope, *Tom Jones* and *A Sentimental Journey*." There is an awareness that the modern world has bred a vulgar and incompetent politics, which shuts out the patrician: "Anybody who was anybody must feel *noblesse oblige*" and "I have witnessed a disintegration of that moral cohesion of the South which had given it its strength and its sons their singleness of purpose and simplicity." There is even attendance at Harvard, where not all in education was good: "Whatever I learned in class was absorbed and left no conscious memories." There is the southern European experience: "the hill-towns of Italy, particularly Perugia; my first nightingale at Nîmes; my first Greek temple at Paestum; the brumal gold interior of St. Mark's before it was cleaned." There is the call from the alma mater to instruct what was unknown: "my ignorance of English literature was a real handicap, because, after all, that was what I was supposed to be teaching." There is the effect of war: "The North destroyed my South; Germany destroyed my world." There is a melancholy landing in New York, after the war is over: "I have never before or since felt so incapable of emotion, so dead inside." There is an acquisition of, if not nieces, then nephews: "I found myself, unprepared, with the responsibility of directing young lives in a world that was changing and that seemed to me on the threshold of chaos." There is a grave, guarded by a statue, to be visited: "[a] bronze figure of a brooding knight, sunshine flowing from his body as indicated in low relief on the stone stele behind." Above all, there is a haunting by ancestors.[82]

To be sure, much was unlike Adams. The narrative is first person; Percy is aware of the individuality of servants and neighbors, ignored in the *Education*; the prose is more lush; the uncertainty is more palpable; there is a greater acknowledgment of pleasure and happiness; the figure of the father is less abstract; combat in war is experienced, not missed; the problem of race is more pressing and debated; there are few philosophical disquisitions. The *Education* was an influence upon, not a template for Percy.

This Southern *nachleben* for Henry Adams was, in one sense, unexpected. Southern culture in 1850 gave little hint that later Southerners would acquiesce in Adams's diagnosis of the Southern question. In the antebellum years, there were very few Southern writers interested in being considered peculiarly gifted in the heart, if this meant a lesser quotient of intellectuality, and these tended to be influenced by a simplified Romanticism. Charleston's Ada McElhenney, for example, drafted a passionate review of Tennyson in 1854, but was conscious that such warmth opposed her culture's preferences. "[It is] no profound or analytical review, of that most exquisite poem 'The Princess,'" she told her editor, "all that I write must come from the heart, not from the head. And so I implore you not to exclude any article from the Magazine, in order to publish mine, for in all probability it will be laughed at." But, some years earlier, Thomas Dew of Virginia had thought that even women, notoriously thought to be emotional, preferred a world of reason: "There is no recommendation so great in a woman's eyes as a well cultivated understanding. Perhaps the most royal road to woman's heart is through the region of the intellect." A premise of balance was customary: heart and head should be coequal. An address by the Presbyterian divine Benjamin Morgan Palmer was praised in 1852 because it did "credit to his head & heart," just as Ann Hardeman, the Mississippi spinster, remembered and valued her sister Mary for having "many virtues & noble qualities of heart & head." Similarly, Alfred Huger of Charleston admired Cleland Kinloch because "his Intellect commanded my confidence & reverence: and his kindness filled my heart!"[83]

It was common, of course, to see the North as unreasoning and unbalanced, because of its religious zeal and abolitionism. Nothing was more habitual than to speak of "the mad fanaticism of the North" and to suggest, as Mitchell King did, that Northerners were uninterested in logic: "The fanaticism of abolitionism is as much offended by a correction of mistakes and misstatements, and by a refutation of erroneous arguments—as by any mere rudeness—and is very apt to consider a strong difference of opinion however politely expressed, as a personal insult." Hence it was common for Southerners to contend that their cultural role was to offer reason. Stay cool, was the advice that Francis Hawks, a Southern expatriate in New York, offered to the president of the University of North Carolina in 1860: "Use no violence against 'incendiaries & abolition emissaries' but scrupulously follow the law, abjure passion."[84] So antebellum Southerners found the contemporary Northerners who spoke of the South as irrational, as Adams himself spoke in 1860, to be themselves irrational. None of this is surprising: to be adversary often requires doubt about an opponent's lucidity.

Military victory was to give Northern judgments a cultural authority over Southerners, who had lost an old role but not yet found a new one. Recovery required a reassessment, both emotional and intellectual; of the two, the emotional was more pressing. The language of war and defeat spoke of honor, loyalty, courage, bitterness, regret, and grief. Henry Grady, that impresario of the sentimental, evoked the "footsore Confederate soldier . . . ragged, half-starved, heavy-hearted, enfeebled by want and wounds, having fought to exhaustion, [who] surrenders his gun, wrings the hands of his comrades in silence, and lifting his tear-stained and pallid face for the last time to the graves that dot, old Virginia hills, pulls his gray cap over his brow and begins the slow and painful journey." In this passage, eight adjectives denoted a state of feeling, but none a state of mind. Even the less sentimental, like Grace King of New Orleans, presumed that a postbellum life meant dealing with trauma, which must be cured more in the heart than the head. In her diary, she wrote of how "the great events of our lives roll over us and pass away—They do not roll and pass ineffectually—they wash over us & so alter the whole of us. . . . Heart-breaking & heart-making episodes have an intrinsic value—our vigilant, business-like brain cannot afford to let them pass."[85]

So New Southerners came to concede that New Englanders had possessed the better minds. In 1902 Edwin Mims, then of North Carolina, argued that Massachusetts between 1830 and 1875 had achieved a "pre-eminent position" in American culture and deserved imitation: "If we adopt the results of New England's experience in the manufacture of cotton goods, why should we be provincial enough to exclude its ideas?" he asked. To soften this admission, it became common to suggest that Southerners had had the better hearts, with the qualities of "courage, fidelity, purity, hospitality, magnanimity, honesty, and truth." Reformers customarily conjectured that, to train intellects equal to the modern world and to Boston, Southerners needed a new texture of emotions on which to found their minds. As William Preston Few, the president of Duke University, said, Southerners should be strong, free, steady, wholehearted, intrepid, and no longer "temporizing, truckling, or compounding with fears."[86] And, naturally, to learn such lessons, they had to read the New Englanders, with a marked preference for sympathetic postbellum writers, over the hostile likes of Wendell Phillips and William Lloyd Garrison. In their essays, Mims and Few showed themselves much read in the likes of Oliver Wendell Holmes, Charles W. Eliot, Charles Eliot Norton, Barrett Wendell, and Charles Francis Adams Jr., though also some of the older canonical New England authors such as Emerson, Longfellow, and Lowell.

Hence *The Education of Henry Adams* did not enter into a Southern discourse innocent of the context that had made Adams, or unprepared for what he might say. Adams's cultural power came to reside in his offering the South a role in intellectual modernism, which valued the heart, but cared less for the head. As Robert Penn Warren put it in 1973, doubtless of his own younger self, the *Education* "found its fame . . . after the First World War when knowledge of the fragmentation and inner paradoxes of the modern world was no longer the privilege of the learned, subtle, and disenchanted mind of the aged Adams, but was appropriated by the romantic melancholy of a generation of college sophomores as well as by that of their elders." Modernists saw this value in instinct, if only by default, because they saw little evidence of rationality in the wasteland of Passchendaele and could see a kind of sense in the shell-shocked veteran who (as in *Mrs. Dalloway*) impaled himself upon iron railings. As Erich Auerbach was to observe of Virginia Woolf's *To the Lighthouse*: "[Her] speakers no longer seem to be human beings at all but spirits between heaven and earth, nameless spirits capable of penetrating the depths of the human soul, capable too of knowing something about it, but not of attaining clarity as to what is in process there," because "exterior events have actually lost their hegemony, they serve to release and interpret inner events, whereas before [Woolf's] time . . . inner movements preponderantly function to prepare and motivate significant exterior happenings."[87]

Many modernist Southerners accepted this mission of expressing inclarity, this task of speaking from within, the more so as Shiloh had anticipated Passchendaele in slaughter. Allen Tate's great ode to the Confederate dead asked, "What shall we say who have knowledge / Carried to the heart?" William Faulkner's Nobel Prize acceptance speech in 1950 pointed to "the problems of the human heart in conflict with itself which alone can make good writing because only that is worth writing about, worth the agony and the sweat."[88]

Hence Southerners took Adams's slur and made it a cultural asset, though few noticed that he always meant more than a slur. For, when Adams said of Rooney Lee that the latter had temperament but could not analyze an idea, this was not only a criticism. There was a wistfulness in the characterization, almost an envy, for a man who in 1898 had written, "My wildest ambition is no longer to have ideas, far less to carry them out," and a man who once composed "A Prayer to the Virgin of Chartres" and asked her to "help me to feel!"[89] But

Adams knew, too, that feeling was not enough. Mind mattered, too. A great issue of Southern culture since Adams—since Wilbur Cash, Allen Tate, and William Faulkner, and since the ebbing of the ideological legacy of the Civil War—has been whether, in consenting to represent the heart in American culture, Southerners did not overly slight the value of the head.

Notes

ABBREVIATIONS

CFA2   Charles Francis Adams Jr.
CMG   Charles Milnes Gaskell
EC   Elizabeth Cameron
EHA   *The Education of Henry Adams: An Autobiography* (Boston and New York: Houghton Mifflin, 1918)
HA   Henry Adams
HU   Houghton Library, Harvard University, Cambridge, Massachusetts
JH   John Hay
JQA   John Quincy Adams
JM1   Henry Adams, *History of the United States of America during the First Administration of James Madison*, 2 vols. (New York: Charles Scribner's Sons, 1890)
JM2   Henry Adams, *History of the United States of America during the Second Administration of James Madison*, 3 vols. (New York: Charles Scribner's Sons, 1891)
JR   Henry Adams, *John Randolph* (Boston, Mass.: Houghton Mifflin, 1882)
LCA   Louisa Catherine Adams
LHA   J. C. Levenson, Ernest Samuels, Charles Vandersee, Viola Hopkins Winner, eds., *The Letters of Henry Adams*, 6 vols. (Cambridge, Mass.: Harvard University Press, Belknap, 1982–88)
LMHA   Ward Thoron, ed., *The Letters of Mrs. Henry Adams, 1865–1883* (Boston, Mass.: Little, Brown, 1936)
MHA   Marian Hooper Adams
MHS   Massachusetts Historical Society, Boston, Massachusetts

MSMC Henry Adams, *Mont-Saint-Michel and Chartres*, introduction by Ralph Adams Cram (1913; repr., Boston, Mass.: Houghton Mifflin, 1933)

RWH Robert W. Hooper

TJ1 Henry Adams, *History of the United States of America during the First Administration of Thomas Jefferson*, 2 vols. (New York: Charles Scribner's Sons, 1889)

TJ2 Henry Adams, *History of the United States of America during the Second Administration of Thomas Jefferson*, 2 vols. (New York: Charles Scribner's Sons, 1890)

Preface

1. *EHA*, 57–58.

2. W. J. Cash, *The Mind of the South* (1941; repr., New York: Alfred A. Knopf, 1969), 102; on Cash's postwar influence, see especially Jack Temple Kirby, "Passion and Discontinuities: A Semicycle of *Mind*, 1941–1991," in *W. J. Cash and the Minds of the South*, ed. Paul D. Escott (Baton Rouge: Louisiana State University Press, 1992), 207–25.

3. This is the title of an essay, commissioned by Adams for the *North American Review*; see William Henry Trescot, "The Southern Question," *North American Review* 123 (October 1876): 249–80.

4. "Some Aspects of the Southern Question" (1926), in David Forgacs, ed., *An Antonio Gramsci Reader: Selected Writings, 1916–1935* (New York: Schocken Books, 1988), 171–85.

5. As is customary for the Lamar Lectures, I gave three lectures in Macon. But, for reasons of length and focus, it has seemed sensible to subdivide the second lecture into what now forms chapters 2 and 3.

6. I would single out, especially, the suggestive remarks in John J. Conder, *A Formula of His Own: Henry Adams's Literary Experiment* (Chicago, Ill.: University of Chicago Press, 1970), 98–112, and Christopher E. G. Benfey, *The Great Wave: Gilded Age Misfits, Japanese Eccentrics, and the Opening of Old Japan* (New York: Random House, 2003), 112–17, of which I became aware when finishing the manuscript of these lectures.

CHAPTER ONE
The Sable Genius of the South

1. Paul C. Nagel, *Descent from Glory: Four Generations of the John Adams Family* (New York: Oxford University Press, 1983), 10–11.

2. On the Brooks family, as well as the courtship of Charles Francis Adams

and Abigail Brown Brooks, see Paul C. Nagel, *The Adams Women: Abigail and Louisa Adams, Their Sisters and Daughters* (New York: Oxford University Press, 1987), 244–60.

3. Robert J. Brugger, *Maryland: A Middle Temperament, 1634–1980* (Baltimore, Md.: Johns Hopkins University Press, 1988), 113–14, 140, 162.

4. According to the Web site for his Maryland plantation, Rose Hill; see http://www.co.frederick.md.us/parks/RoseHill%20History.htm.

5. See the Web site of the "John Pope Villa" at http://www.popevilla.org.

6. Nagel, *Adams Women*, 186, 198–243; HA to CMG, 5 November 1868, *LHA*, 2:5–6. Curiously, the *Education* mistakenly dates John Quincy Adams's congressional career from 1833: see *EHA*, 18.

7. Louisa Adams, for example, observed to Abigail Brooks Adams in the early 1840s that women should "preach the equality which God originally assigned to the Sexes as it regards intellectual capacity": quoted, without annotation, in Nagel, *Adams Women*, 262.

8. John Quincy Adams also purchased a flour mill from Louisa's cousin George, though against her advice. See Nagel, *Adams Women*, 237, and Pernilla Holmes and Sabina Wiedenhoeft, "The History of the Columbia Mills," a description written for the Office of Architectural History and Historic Preservation of the Smithsonian Institution, online at http://www.si.edu /oahp/holthous/mills.htm. George Johnson managed the mill after the purchase in 1823 until John Adams (JQA's son) took over in about 1828. When John died in 1834, it was nominally delegated to Charles Francis Adams, who in turn delegated the management to Nathaniel Frye, Louisa's brother-in-law.

9. HA to CFA2, 3 November 1858, HA to Abigail Brooks Adams, 1 July 1860, *LHA*, 1:4–5, 180; Nagel, *Adams Women*, 166.

10. The editors of the Adams letters do cite a reference before 1869, but (unusually for them) in error. In a letter of 1863, Adams suggests that his sister Mary shows signs of "the old Johnson blood cropping out, and faint traces of Mrs John reappearing here and there," and a note seems to indicate that this means Louisa Catherine Adams. In fact, "Mrs John" habitually meant his aunt Mary Hellen Adams, as Chalfant and another letter make clear. For the misattribution, see HA to CFA2, 17 July 1863, *LHA*, 1:373; for the correct attribution, HA to Charles Francis Adams, 30 June 1869, *LHA*, 2:39–40; and, for confirmation, Edward Chalfant, *Better in Darkness: A Biography of Henry Adams, His Second Life, 1862–1891* (Hamden, Conn.: Archon Books, 1994), 141–42.

11. David McCullough, *John Adams* (New York: Simon & Schuster, 2001), 103–4, 134; Martin B. Duberman, *Charles Francis Adams, 1807–1886* (Stanford, Calif.: Stanford University Press, 1960), 56–79, 100.

12. The moment of absorption is unclear. When, in late 1856, he reviewed William Phillips's *The Conquest of Kansas, by Missouri and Her Allies* for the *Harvard Magazine*, his tone was neutral: "It is valuable as a documentary history; and as giving the Free State version of the unhappy difficulties in Kansas, it also has its value. In these exciting times we cannot read such accounts with that impartiality with which we read Tacitus and Livy, and therefore are apt to throw them aside as falsehoods, or let our passions run to the other extreme and take them as perfect both in truth and style. But we can say at least that to those who wish to read an interesting history; to those who have any desire to shudder with horror or be touched by tales of mournful suffering; to those who wish to learn what the Free State settlers have to say in their own defence; and to those who wish to plunge at once headlong into the midst of the political questions that are swaying the country so violently from side to side, this book will give complete satisfaction." See bound volume, marked "Articles &c from the Harvard Magazine. 1855–6–7–8. By Henry Brooks Adams of the Class of 1858," HA Library, MHS.

13. Leonard L. Richards, *The Slave Power: The Free North and Southern Domination, 1780–1860* (Baton Rouge: Louisiana State University Press, 2000), 5; HA to CFA2, 23 November 1859, *LHA*, 1:67.

14. HA to CFA2, 18 December 1860, 8 January 1861, 26 March 1860, *LHA*, 1:208, 219, 105.

15. JQA to the Rev. Charles W. Upham, 2 February 1837, in Adrienne Koch and William Peden, eds., *The Selected Writings of John and John Quincy Adams* (New York: Alfred A. Knopf, 1946), 389. The passage is ambiguous about its referent. "The Sable Genius of the South" may mean John C. Calhoun alone or, more likely, the South and Calhoun confounded.

16. HA to Brooks Adams, 13 March 1909, *LHA*, 6:240.

17. HA to CFA2, 22 December 1860, 13 February 1861, *LHA*, 1:211, 231.

18. It did not see publication until 1909–10, when Charles Francis Adams Jr. put it into the *Proceedings of the Massachusetts Historical Society*.

19. There is a good exposition of Seward on the Slave Power in Richards, *Slave Power*, 4–8.

20. HA, "The Great Secession Winter of 1860–61," in *The Great Secession Winter of 1860–61 and Other Essays by Henry Adams*, ed. George Hochfield (New York: Sagamore Press, 1958), 3–4, 13, 15, 20.

21. Ibid., 29–30.

22. HA to Abigail Brooks Adams, 4 March 1860, *LHA*, 1:98.

23. Friedrich von Geroldt to Alexander von Humboldt, 25 August 1856, Alexander von Humboldt to Varnhagen von Ense, 31 July 1854, 21 November 1856, in *Letters of Alexander von Humboldt, Written between the Years 1827 and*

1858, to Varnhagen von Ense, trans. Ludmilla Assing (London: Trübner, 1860), 251–53, 234–35, 263–64; Alexander von Humboldt, *Cosmos: A Sketch of a Physical Description of the Universe*, trans. E. C. Otté, 4 vols. (London: Henry G. Bohn, 1849), 1:368. On the Assings and Varnhagen, see Maria Diedrich, *Love across Color Lines: Ottilie Assing and Frederick Douglass* (New York: Hill and Wang, 1999).

24. HA, "Secession Winter," 30.

25. On Holmes and the "Soldier's Faith," see David W. Blight, *Race and Reunion: The Civil War in American Memory* (Cambridge, Mass.: Harvard University Press, Belknap Press, 2001), 95–96.

26. *Charles Francis Adams, 1835–1915: An Autobiography* (Boston and New York: Houghton Mifflin, 1916), 114–67; HA to Frederick William Seward, 14 February 1862, HA to CFA2, 23 January 1863, *LHA*, 1:283, 327.

27. David Donald, *Charles Sumner and the Coming of the Civil War* (New York: Alfred A. Knopf, 1961), 51. Adams was later tartly to observe: "Mr. Sumner, both by interest and instinct, felt the value of his English connection, and cultivated it the more as he became socially an outcast from Boston society by the passions of politics. He was rarely without a pocket-full of letters from duchesses and noblemen in England": *EHA*, 30. The definitive text of New England Anglophilia is Ralph Waldo Emerson, *English Traits* (Boston, Mass.: Phillips, Sampson, 1856).

28. HA to CFA2, 15 March 1862, *LHA*, 1:285; *TJ1*, 1:146.

29. HA to CFA2, 11 April 1862, *LHA*, 1:290.

30. HA to CFA2, 25 November 1864, *LHA*, 1:458.

31. The scholars who have emphasized this influence include Robert Dawidoff, *The Genteel Tradition and the Sacred Rage: High Culture versus Democracy in Adams, James, and Santayana* (Chapel Hill: University of North Carolina Press, 1992); J. C. Levenson, *The Mind and Art of Henry Adams* (Boston, Mass.: Houghton Mifflin, 1957); Brooks D. Simpson, *The Political Education of Henry Adams* (Columbia: University of South Carolina Press, 1996).

32. HA to CFA2, 22 October 1867, 8 May, 16 May 1862, *LHA*, 1:555, 295, 299.

33. HA to CFA2, 16 May 1862, *LHA*, 1:299.

34. HA to CFA2, 20 November 1863, HA to John Gorham Palfrey, 23 August 1866, HA to CFA2, 1 March 1867, 8 May 1867, 22 June 1869, *LHA*, 1:408, 509, 524, 533, 2:39.

35. HA, "The Session," in *Great Secession Winter*, 66.

36. HA to Thomas Baring, 2 February 1869, *LHA*, 2:16.

37. HA, "The Session, 1869–1870," in *Historical Essays* (New York: Charles Scribner's Sons, 1891), 384–85.

38. HA to CFA2, 14 July 1865, 10 October 1862, *LHA*, 1:498, 312.

39. Edward Chalfant, *Both Sides of the Ocean: A Biography of Henry Adams, His First Life, 1838–1862* (Hamden, Conn.: Archon Books, 1982), 63.

40. There is an account of the dinner in *CFA2: Autobiography*, 90–91.

41. HA to CMG, 5 October 1869, *LHA*, 2:46; Max I. Baym, *The French Education of Henry Adams* (New York: Columbia University Press, 1951), 20; catalog of the HA Library, August 1858, HA Papers, MHS.

42. HA to Edward Atkinson, 1 February 1869, *LHA*, 2:15.

43. HA, "Civil Service Reform," in *Great Secession Winter*, 101–5 (quotations on 101–2).

44. HA, "Session, 1869–70," 367–70.

45. James P. Young, *Henry Adams: The Historian as Political Theorist* (Lawrence: University Press of Kansas, 2001), 2, citing Russell L. Hanson and W. Richard Merriman, "Henry Adams and the Decline of the Republican Tradition," *American Transcendental Quarterly* 4 (September 1990): 161–83.

46. He is mentioned in HA to CFA2, 23 November 1859, and his book in HA to CFA2, Rome, 17 May 1860, *LHA*, 1:67, 143.

47. George Stillman Hillard, *Six Months in Italy*, 2 vols. (Boston, Mass.: Ticknor, Reed, and Fields, 1853), 1:unpaginated preface, 12.

48. HA to CFA2, 23 April 1860, *LHA*, 1:133.

49. HA to CFA2, 17–18 December 1858, 9 February, 13 March 1859, *LHA*, 1:8, 21, 28.

50. HA to Abigail Brooks Adams, 8 April, 6 May 1860, HA to CFA2, 11 April, 16 April, 23 April 1860, *LHA*, 1:116, 121–22, 124–25, 129, 137.

51. HA to Abigail Brooks Adams, 6 May 1860, HA to CMG, 3 March 1865, *LHA*, 1:137, 480.

52. See, for example, *TJ1*, 1:130; *EHA*, 355, 414. In each of these passages, the word "wander" is associated with "south," so the sense is palpable that a Southern place conferred freedom.

53. Charles Eliot Norton to Francis Child [1855], quoted in Kermit Vanderbilt, *Charles Eliot Norton: Apostle of Culture in a Democracy* (Cambridge, Mass.: Harvard University Press, Belknap, 1959), 76; Norton to Arthur Hugh Clough, 5 April 1855, and Norton to James Russell Lowell, 6 April 1855, in Sara Norton and M. A. DeWolfe Howe, eds., *Letters of Charles Eliot Norton: With Biographical Comment*, 2 vols. (Boston, Mass.: Houghton Mifflin, 1913), 1:123, 125. For a discussion of this issue, see Michael O'Brien, "Italy and the Southern Romantics," in *Rethinking the South: Essays in Intellectual History* (Baltimore, Md.: Johns Hopkins University Press, 1988), 84–111.

54. *EHA*, 16–19.

55. HA to CMG, 19 April 1869, *LHA*, 2:25. On the location of his re-

searches, see Chalfant, *Better in Darkness*, 147, 181–82, 696 n. 2. Chalfant, however, has (what I believe to be) an overly dramatic view of Adams's relationship to his grandmother, since he argues that "her death brought on an extreme response: he felt that she and he were a single being. One can say that Henry *lived* this idea. He saw to it that her life would find its continuation and male variant in his life": see Chalfant, *Better in Darkness*, 5.

56. "Notes towards a Memoir of His Grandmother Louisa Catherine Johnson Adams," HA Miscellaneous Papers (MS Am 1217), HU.

57. The manuscripts of Louisa Adams are now in the Adams Family Papers, MHS, though I consulted them in the microfilm edition, a copy of which is owned by the Cambridge University Library. Her papers occupy reels 264–80.

58. HA to Brooks Adams, 18 February 1909, Brooks Adams Letters to HA (MS Am 1751), HU.

59. See especially the "List of Books read this Winter 1812–13," at the end of her "Diary, 22 October 1812–15 February 1814 (Saint Petersburg)" (reel 264).

60. Entries for 10 March 1819, 4 March, 25 April 1820, LCA Diary (reel 265) (hereinafter LCA Diary [265]).

61. On Byron, see the entries for 1 August 1821 and 27 December 1822, LCA Diary (266 and 265); on Moore and an incident on 26 July 1806 when Moore was in Washington, see LCA, "The Adventures of a Nobody," 193 (reel 269), (hereinafter LCA, "Adventures").

62. Entry for 15 March 1821, LCA Diary (265).

63. Entries for 1 August, 29 January, 11 February 1821, 16 December 1822, LCA Diary (265, 266).

64. The remark is to be found in the midst of a long, undated essay on the New Testament in LCA Diary (268), begun circa November 6, 1835; this essay seems to have been written in 1838 or 1839, so she probably was referring to Emerson's Harvard Divinity School address of July 24, 1838.

65. LCA, "Adventures," 159.

66. *EHA*, 19.

67. Entry for 17 June 1839, LCA Diary [268].

68. "Record of a Life or My Story, July 23rd 1825," 31–32 (reel 265) (hereinafter LCA, "Record of a Life").

69. See "Louisa Catherine Adams Campaigns for the Presidency," in Catherine Allgor, *Parlor Politics: In Which the Ladies of Washington Help to Build a City and a Government* (Charlottesville: University Press of Virginia, 2000), 147–89.

70. On this, see Joan Ridder Challinor, "Louisa Catherine Johnson Adams: The Price of Ambition" (Ph.D. diss., American University, 1982), 333–44.

71. LCA, "Adventures," 125.

72. LCA, "Record of a Life," 24; Nagel, *Adams Women*, 161.

73. LCA, "Adventures," 113, 117; *EHA*, 18.

74. She is mentioned only as a fact, not a character with a history in *CFA2: Autobiography*, 9. Lodge went on to explain, "The Mendelian law of the dominant and recessive qualities would appear to apply"; Henry Cabot Lodge, "Memorial Address," in *CFA2: Autobiography*, xvi.

75. MHA to RWH, 14 May 1882, *LMHA*, 384.

76. Nagel, *Adams Women*, 178–81.

77. LCA, "Record of a Life," 40–41; "Adventures," 123.

78. The following is based on Challinor, "Price of Ambition," esp. 27–38.

79. LCA, "Adventures," 38; Abigail Adams to JQA, 20 May 1796, and to LCA, 14 April 1815, quoted in Challinor, "Price of Ambition," 188, 547.

80. *Population Schedules of the Fourth Census of the United States, 1820* (Washington, D.C.: National Archives, 1959), reel 5, page 97.

81. JQA to Abigail Adams, 16 August 1796, quoted in Challinor, "Price of Ambition," 146. Challinor observes of Louisa's mother, Catherine: "It was . . . an English, not an American household, she managed: a house with well-trained servants, their roles carefully designated in a strict hierarchical order" ("Price of Ambition," 65).

82. LCA, "Record of a Life," 75; "Adventures," 160, 170–71; *TJ1*, 2:227; entry for 5 March 1821, LCA Diary (265).

83. LCA, "Record of a Life," 40, 60; entries for 11 December 1822, 28 December 1819, and 19 February 1823, LCA Diary (265); LCA, "Adventures," 137.

84. Entry for 1 March 1836, LCA Diary (268); entries for 9 and 11 December 1819, 20 January 1821, LCA Diary (265).

85. Entries for 20 December 1822, 30 January 1821, LCA Diary (265); LCA, "Record of a Life," 26; "Adventures," 162.

86. Entries for 1 March 1819, 3 April 1820, LCA Diary (265).

87. Entry for 24 December 1835, LCA Diary (268); entries for 11 February, 3 January, 15 February 1820, LCA Diary (265).

88. LCA, "Stray Thoughts" (reel 268).

89. LCA, "Record of a Life," 40; entry for 24 July 1821, LCA Diary (266).

90. "Adventures," 229. His name is given in the entry for 5 August 1809, in Charles Francis Adams, ed., *Memoirs of John Quincy Adams, Comprising Portions of His Diary from 1795 to 1848*, 12 vols. (Philadelphia, Pa.: J. B. Lippincott, 1874–77), 2:3.

91. Entry for 21 December 1819, LCA Diary (266); *1820 U.S. Census*, reel 5, page 97. The schedules make no mention of a young, free black woman,

though Constance Green says that an Arbella Jones, who went on to be educated at St. Agnes's in Baltimore and to run one of the best "colored schools" in Washington in the 1850s, had been "a free servant in John Quincy Adams' household when he was Secretary of State": see Constance McLaughlin Green, *Washington, Village and Capital, 1800–1878* (Princeton, N.J.: Princeton University Press, 1962), 184. Unfortunately, there is no annotation that verifies the claim.

92. In 1820, the household of William Steuben Smith had one female slave under fourteen and another between the ages of fifteen and twenty-five; since, otherwise, the household contained only Smith and his wife, Catherine Johnson Smith, it is very likely that these were Smith's property. In 1820, likewise, the household of Nathaniel Frye and Carolina Johnson Frye contained a male slave aged between fourteen and twenty-five, as well as a free colored female over forty-five. Later, the 1850 census shows Johnson Hellen, Louisa's nephew, in possession of a thirteen-year-old black female slave. See *1820 U.S. Census*, reel 5, pages 10 and 88; *Population Schedules of the Seventh Census of the United States, 1850* (Washington, D.C.: National Archives and Records Service, 1964), reel 57, schedule 2, 4th Ward. On Hellen, see Nagel, *Adams Women*, 235.

93. *U.S. Census*, reel 57, page 84; undated document about servants, which follows LCA, "Adventures"; entry for 21 December 1821, LCA Diary (265).

94. Entry for 16 February 1820, LCA Diary (266). She says "D. S. Cook," but "Daniel Pope Cook" is correct.

95. Entry for 29 January 1821, LCA Diary (266); LCA, "Adventures," 173.

96. Entries for 13 March 1820, 8 and 28 February 1821, 19 December 1823, 4 June 1836, LCA Diary (265, 268).

97. Nagel, *Adams Women*, 173; LCA, "Adventures," 176, 159; entry for 28 August 1836, LCA Diary (268).

98. She did this often. Other diaries seem to be addressed to her brother and husband, though how this worked is something of a mystery, unless she periodically showed the diary to the designated person, or transcribed passages into letters.

99. Entries for 6 December 1819, 5 March 1821, 1 September 1836, LCA Diary (265, 268).

CHAPTER TWO
The Little Society of Washington

1. HA to CMG, 14 June 1876, 25 October 1870, 22 May 1871, *LHA*, 2:275, 84, 110.

2. HA to JH, 9 January 1892, *LHA*, 3:599.

3. HA to Charles Eliot Norton, 13 January 1871, HA to Sir Robert Cunliffe, 31 August 1875, *LHA*, 2:97, 235.

4. HA to Hugh Blair Grigsby, 9 October 1877, *LHA*, 2:323; HA to Mabel Hooper La Farge, 22 February 1906, J. C. Levenson, et al., *Supplement to the Letters of Henry Adams*, 2 vols. (Boston, Mass.: Massachusetts Historical Society, 1989), 2:1906-2; HA to Harriet Taylor Upton, 16 February 1887, HA to JH, 16 November 1890, HA to Henry Cabot Lodge, 31 July 1876, *LHA*, 3:54, 346, 2:284.

5. HA to CMG, 14 June 1876, *LHA*, 2:275.

6. Kaledin wisely observes, "The historical rumors about his [HA's] impotence must, of course, remain just that" (Eugenia Kaledin, *The Education of Mrs. Henry Adams*, 2d ed. [Amherst: University of Massachusetts Press, 1994], 146); on Sumner, see David Donald, *Charles Sumner and the Rights of Man* (New York: Alfred A. Knopf, 1970), 314–16.

7. On this, see Joseph F. Byrnes, *The Virgin of Chartres: An Intellectual and Psychological History of the Work of Henry Adams* (Rutherford, N.J.: Fairleigh Dickinson University Press, 1981), 25.

8. Edward Chalfant, *Better in Darkness: A Biography of Henry Adams, His Second Life, 1862–1891* (Hamden, Conn.: Archon Books, 1994), 764–65 n. 21; HA to CMG, 22 August 1877, *LHA*, 2:316.

9. Henry James, "Pandora," in *Henry James: Complete Stories, 1874–1884*, ed. William L. Vance (New York: Library of America, 1999), 838; *EHA*, 317.

10. Quoted in James H. Whyte, *The Uncivil War: Washington during the Reconstruction, 1865–1878* (New York: Twayne, 1958), 16.

11. HA to CMG, 13 February 1874, *LHA*, 2:188; Chalfant, *Better in Darkness*, 129, 149–50; Paul C. Nagel, *The Adams Women: Abigail and Louisa Adams, Their Sisters and Daughters* (New York: Oxford University Press, 1987), 238.

12. Hans Trefousse, *Andrew Johnson: A Biography* (New York: W. W. Norton, 1989), 208; Chalfant, *Better in Darkness*, 128; Donald, *Sumner and the Rights of Man*, 268–77, 289–95, 312–20; Glyndon G. Van Deusen, *William Henry Seward* (New York: Oxford University Press, 1967), 269; Russel B. Nye, *George Bancroft: Brahmin Rebel* (New York: Alfred A. Knopf, 1944), 280.

13. MHA to RWH, 31 January 1882, *LMHA*, 338.

14. *TJ1*, 1:187. On this see, especially, James Sterling Young, *The Washington Community, 1800–1828* (New York: Harcourt, Brace & World, 1966), 65–83 (quotation on 75).

15. Henry James was in Washington too briefly to be a reliable judge, but he did observe that in the Bonnycastle/Adams salon there was "an occasional senator, whose movements and utterances often appeared to be re-

garded with a mixture of alarm and indulgence," but "members of the House were very rare": James, "Pandora," 839.

16. HA to Sir John Clark, 6 March 1881, *LHA*, 2:420–21; *EHA*, 261.

17. *EHA*, 101.

18. James, "Pandora," 837.

19. Kathryn Allamong Jacob, *Capital Elites: High Society in Washington, D.C., after the Civil War* (Washington, D.C.: Smithsonian Institution Press, 1995), 9.

20. Not unimportant was the fact that Southern families tended more often to bring their families to live with them: on this, see Jacob, *Capital Elites*, 38.

21. He was referring to his sojourn in 1860–61: see *Charles Francis Adams, 1835–1915: An Autobiography* (Boston and New York: Houghton Mifflin, 1916), 48, 49.

22. Jacob, *Capital Elites*, 29–30.

23. "Series A 195–209: Population of States by Sex, Race, Urban-Rural Residence, and Age: 1790 to 1970," in U.S. Bureau of the Census, *Historical Statistics of the United States on CD-Rom: Colonial Times to 1970—Bicentennial Edition* (Cambridge: Cambridge University Press, 1997), 1:24–37.

24. Constance McLaughlin Green, *Washington, Capital City, 1879–1950* (Princeton, N.J.: Princeton University Press, 1963), 89.

25. Ibid.

26. MHA to RWH, 5 December 1880, *LMHA*, 240. The claim about trying white servants comes from Chalfant, *Better in Darkness*, 819 n. 23, though his evidence is unclear.

27. Henry James to E. L. Godkin, 22 January 1882, Edwin Lawrence Godkin Papers, HU, quoted in Chalfant, *Better in Darkness*, 434, 819 n. 21; James, "Pandora," 839.

28. HA to Theodore F. Dwight, 2 October 1885, *LHA*, 2:631; on the separate building, see Chalfant, *Better in Darkness*, 414.

29. HA to CMG, 26 February 1892, *LHA*, 4:3.

30. It is possible she was first employed in 1884. At least, in commenting upon her death in 1909, the editors of the Adams letters remark that she had been HA's housekeeper "for twenty five years": see *LHA*, 6:248 n. 1.

31. Chalfant, *Better in Darkness*, 498; Edward Chalfant, *Improvement of the World: A Biography of Henry Adams, His Last Life, 1891–1918* (Hamden, Conn.: Archon Books, 2001), 18. In 1890, Gray was being paid $50 a month and Wade $33; in each case, part of their salary was $15 for board; see HA to Theodore F. Dwight, late June 1890, *LHA*, 3:244.

32. MHA to RWH, 30 October 1881, *LMHA*, 294; Maggie Wade to Louisa

Hooper, 24 December 1900–3 January 1901, HA Family Papers (accession # 93M-35 [b]), HU.

33. For example, HA to Mabel Hooper, 22 August 1890: "If you want your Easter visit to Washington, you need only go there. Maggy and William will take care of you, but you will have to order in a cook and keep house." See Levenson, et al., *Adams Letters Supplement*, 1:1890-11.

34. HA to Sir John Clark, 29 May 1892, *LHA*, 4:13. In addition, Wade accompanied Adams to the Columbian Exposition in Chicago in 1893: see HA to EC, 8 October 1893, *LHA*, 4:132.

35. HA to Rebecca Dodge Rae, 23 August 1898, HA to Louisa Hooper, 7 January 1907, HA to Anna Cabot Mills Lodge, 12 May 1909, in Levenson, et al., *Adams Letters Supplement*, 1:1898-31, 2:1907-1, 1909-18; HA to EC, 5 June 1892, *LHA*, 4:16.

36. Chalfant, *Better in Darkness*, 504; Chalfant, *Improvement of the World*, 420–21, 476; Alfred Worcester to Louisa Hooper Thoron, 20 September 1930, R. P. Blackmur Correspondence Concerning Henry Adams (MS Am 1750–1750.2), HU; HA to EC, 10 November 1914, *LHA*, 6:665.

37. Maggie Wade to Louisa Hooper, 6 September (on which Louis Hooper Thoron, presumably, has conjectured "[1898]"), HA Family Papers (accession # 93M-35 [b]), HU; all subsequent Wade letters can be assumed to be in this collection.

38. Wade to Hooper, "Wed. Dec 30th" [1905?]; however, in the years covered by the Wade correspondence, 30 December fell on a Wednesday only in 1903 and 1908, and the former date seems more likely for this letter.

39. Wade to Hooper, 4 November [1901?].

40. Wade to Hooper, 24 December 1900–3 January 1901, 29 November [1907? 1908?], 20 December 1903, 11 July [no year suggested].

41. See, especially, her consolatory letter on the death of Edward Hooper: Wade to Hooper, "Friday July 5th" [1901].

42. HA to Ward Thoron, 15 May 1909, *LHA*, 6:248.

43. HA to Brooks Adams, 2 April 1898, *LHA*, 4:556; Wade to Hooper, 29 November [1907 or 1908?], 24 December 1900–3 January 1901, 8 April [1898], 22 January [no year suggested].

44. Wade to Hooper, 6 September 1898. On the marriage, see HA to Mabel Hooper, 2 September 1898, *LHA*, 4:611–12.

45. Maggie Wade to "My Dear Young Ladies," 4 May 1904.

46. Wade to Hooper, 8 April [1898], 29 November [1907? 1908?], Wade to "My Dear Young Ladies," 4 May 1904; Wade to Hooper, "Saturday 13th" [no year suggested].

47. Mary Clemmer Ames of the New York *Independent*, as quoted in Jacob, *Capital Elites*, 57.

48. Jacob, *Capital Elites*, 202–3. Constance Green, however, observes that the association "wielded little influence": Constance McLaughlin Green, *Washington, Village and Capital, 1800–1878* (Princeton, N.J.: Princeton University Press, 1962), 333.

49. Entry for 10 January 1883, Violet Blair Janin Diary, Albert and Violet (Blair) Janin Collection, Huntington Library, San Marino, California, quoted in Jacob, *Capital Elites*, 207.

50. So Adams described Lincoln: see *EHA*, 107.

51. Adams appears in several of Vidal's novels, though most fully in Gore Vidal, *Empire: A Novel* (New York: Random House, 1987), which contains a good portrait of the Adams-Hay circle in the 1890s. See also "The Four Generations of the Adams Family" (1976) in Gore Vidal, *United States: Essays, 1952–1992* (1993; repr., London: Abacus, 1994), 644–63.

52. Taylor was born in 1812, Lamar in 1825, Lowndes in 1834, and Randolph in 1839.

53. The evidence for this is HA's visiting list, which reads, less than clearly: "Taylor, Mrs. / Gen. & Mrs. 10 Nov"; Chalfant, *Better in Darkness*, 690 n. 74. There seems to be no clear evidence for the claim, advanced by Parrish, that Adams met Taylor at the White House in 1850: see T. Michael Parrish, *Richard Taylor, Soldier Prince of Dixie* (Chapel Hill: University of North Carolina Press, 1992), 489.

54. HA to CMG, 28 November 1878, *LHA*, 2:349.

55. For the following account, I draw upon Parrish, *Richard Taylor*.

56. For Olmsted's account of the Taylor plantation, see Charles E. Beveridge and Charles Capen McLaughlin, eds., David Schuyler, asst. ed., *Slavery and the South, 1852–1857*, vol. 2 of *The Papers of Frederick Law Olmsted*, gen. ed. Charles Capen McLaughlin (Baltimore, Md.: Johns Hopkins University Press, 1981), 210–14, 464–65, 470.

57. Adams was usually severe on those who broke promises, but he excused Taylor for it: see HA to Henry Cabot Lodge, 29 January 1879, *LHA*, 2:351.

58. HA to Samuel L. M. Barlow, 20 March 1879, *LHA*, 2:354; MHA to RWH, 23 January 1881, *LMHA*, 259.

59. Richard Taylor to MHA, "Tuesday" [January 1879], and L. Q. C. Lamar to MHA, 25 December 1880, HA Papers, MHS; *EHA*, 322, 185.

60. For the following, I rely on James B. Murphy, *L. Q. C. Lamar: Pragmatic Patriot* (Baton Rouge: Louisiana State University Press, 1973).

61. HA to CMG, 28 November 1878, *LHA*, 2:349; on the absenteeism, see Murphy, *L. Q. C. Lamar*, 217, 221–22, 231–32; Lucius Quintus Cincinnatus Lamar, "The Eulogy of Sumner," in *Southern Prose and Poetry for Schools*, ed. Edwin Mims and Bruce R. Payne (New York: Charles Scribner's Sons, 1910), 363, 371 n. 1.

62. Neil R. McMillen, *Dark Journey: Black Mississippians in the Age of Jim Crow* (Urbana: University of Illinois Press, 1989), 38; MHA to RWH, 13 February 1881, *LMHA*, 264; Henry James, quoted in Leon Edel, *Henry James: The Middle Years, 1882–1895* (1962; New York: Avon Books, 1978), 30.

63. On Lowndes, see Carl J. Vipperman, *William Lowndes and the Transition of Southern Politics, 1782–1822* (Chapel Hill: University of North Carolina Press, 1989).

64. *TJ1*, 1:151; entry for 19 January 1823, LCA Diary, Adams Family Papers, MHS (reel 265).

65. This is pieced together from the editorial note in *LHA*, 2:437; HA to EC, 18 January 1910, *LHA*, 6:299; HA to Louisa Hooper, Thursday, 20 January 1910, Levenson, et al., *Adams Letters Supplement*, 2:1910-3; and MHA to RWH, 22 January 1882, *LMHA*, 333.

66. HA to Mary Leiter Curzon, 30 December 1895, *LHA*, 4:353. The genealogical Web sites are: http://www.hillmanc.fsnet.co.uk/lowndes.htm (which gives circa 1870) and http://www.usgennet.org/usa/topic/historical /southernnewyork/s_ny_4.htm (which also claims that Lucius Tuckerman "built a large house on the corner of Sixteenth and I Streets, Washington, in what was then the Corcoran Gardens, where he had a fine collection of paintings, and with his wife and daughters, Mrs James Lowndes and Miss Emily Tuckerman, exercised a notable hospitality"). The view that his marriage was after 1880 is expressed in *LMHA*, 240 n. 2.

67. HA to James Lowndes, 26 September 1888, Levenson, et al., *Adams Letters Supplement*, 1:1888-9; MHA to RWH, 16 January, 9 January 1881, 12 February 1882, 30 October 1881, 4 June 1882, *LMHA*, 257, 254, 347, 294, 390; HA to JH, 29 August 1883, *LHA*, 2:509–10.

68. MHA to RWH, 15 April 1883, *LMHA*, 440.

69. *LMHA*, 440 n. 2. The Boston Atheneum in 1827 did an exhibition of Allston's paintings, among them *Katherine, Petruchio, Grumio and the Tailor*, owned by Mrs. George W. Sturgis; see Nathalia Wright, ed., *The Correspondence of Washington Allston* (Lexington: University Press of Kentucky, 1993), 238.

70. Kaledin, *Mrs. Henry Adams*, 16–18; Willie Lee Rose, *Rehearsal for Reconstruction: The Port Royal Experiment* (1964; repr., New York: Vintage Books, 1967), 21–36, 50–51, 59, 80, 90, 206–7, 221–22, 388; Otto Friedrich, *Clover*

(New York: Simon and Schuster, 1979), 59–60; Marian Hooper to Annie, 8 May 1861, Adams-Thoron Papers, MHS.

71. MHA to RWH, 1 January, 12 March 1882, *LMHA*, 316, 363.

72. MHA to RWH, 30 January 1881, *LMHA*, 261, for the pleasantness; MHA to RWH, 23 January 1881, HA Papers, MHS, for the dying: "Mr Tucker gave a most interesting account of an interview with Calhoun on his deathbed in which he vehemently deprecated being a disunionist—but his life outweighed that dying statement." On Randolph, see W. Hamilton Bryson, *Legal Education in Virginia, 1779–1979: A Biographical Approach* (Charlottesville: University Press of Virginia, 1982), 624–38.

73. MHA to RWH, 19 February, 5 November 1882, 4 February 1883, 17 April 1881, *LMHA*, 350, 395, 420, 283–84; MHA to Anne Palmer, Monday 24th, n.d. [circa spring 1884], letter beginning "Many, many thanks," Hooper-Adams Papers, MHS.

74. M. R. B. McA——, "Addendum from the Third Edition 1947: Edgehill," in Sarah N. Randolph, *The Domestic Life of Thomas Jefferson: Compiled from Family Letters and Reminiscences* (1871; repr., Charlottesville: University Press of Virginia, 1978), 435–36; HA to Hugh Blair Grigsby, 30 August, 7 September 1877, *LHA*, 2:317–19; Merrill D. Peterson, *The Jefferson Image in the American Mind* (New York: Oxford University Press, 1960), 232, 291–92.

75. Chalfant, *Better in Darkness*, 365–66. There is no letter describing the Monticello visit, only one that indicates its imminence: see MHA to RWH, 4 May 1878, HA Papers, MHS: "On Thursday morning our three women go back to Boston & we by 8.30 train to Edgehill Va. near Charlottesville to pass two days with Miss Randolph—she is to show H. Monticello—her grandfather [*sic*] Jefferson's home."

76. Peterson, *Jefferson Image*, 231–38 (quotation on 237). For evidence of her burial, see "Persons Buried at the Monticello Graveyard, 1773–1997," at http://www.monticello.org/reports/people/burials.html. On the general context of Monticello in the late nineteenth century, see Melvin I. Urofsky, *The Levy Family and Monticello, 1834–1923: Saving Thomas Jefferson's House* (Monticello: Thomas Jefferson Foundation, 2001).

77. HA to George Bancroft, 9 March 1885, asks Bancroft to propose Lamar as a member of the Metropolitan Club in Washington: *LHA*, 2:578. See also HA to Francis Parkman, 4 October 1881, *LHA*, 2:440–41, and MHA to RWH, 1 January 1882, *LMHA*, 316.

78. HA to EC, 18 January 1910, *LHA*, 6:299.

79. The letters with Grigsby begin in August 1877 and continue for about two years: *LHA*, 2:314–15, 317–23, 329, 337, 339, 370–71. He also corre-

sponded at Grigsby's suggestion with William Wirt Henry, the grandson and biographer of Patrick Henry: *LHA*, 2:317–18, 320–21. On Grigsby's standing as a historian of Virginia, pertinent is Michael O'Brien, *Conjectures of Order: Intellectual Life and the American South, 1810–1860*, 2 vols. (Chapel Hill: University of North Carolina Press, 2004), 2:636–53.

CHAPTER THREE
American Types

1. I here briefly summarize an argument developed in several places: see Michael O'Brien, "On Observing the Quicksand," *American Historical Review* 104 (October 1999): 1202–7; Michael O'Brien, "William Gilmore Simms," *Southern Cultures* 5 (summer 1999): 107–12; and a revised piece on "Regionalism," forthcoming in a new edition of the *Encyclopedia of Southern Culture*.

2. Adams himself was troubled by the linguistic difficulties occasioned by this hierarchy. As he observed in 1909, when Brooks Adams used the phrase "the United States has": "'The United States has' or have. I always used the singular, and now think I was wrong. I ought always to have said 'The Union.'" See comment on 69, line 24, of the manuscript biography of JQA, in HA to Brooks Adams, 18 February 1909, Brooks Adams Letters to HA (MS Am 1751), HU.

3. On the Midwest, see Andrew R. L. Cayton and Peter S. Onuf, *The Midwest and the Nation: Rethinking the History of an American Region* (Bloomington: Indiana University Press, 1990), and Andrew R. L. Cayton and Susan E. Gray, eds., *The American Midwest: Essays on Regional History* (Bloomington: Indiana University Press, 2001).

4. Stephen Nissenbaum, "New England as Region and Nation," in *All Over the Map: Rethinking American Regions*, Edward L. Ayers, et al. (Baltimore, Md.: Johns Hopkins University Press, 1996), 40–41.

5. In 1890, Charles's annual income was $167,000, though it halved during the depression of the 1890s before recovering. In 1947, Harold Dean Cater estimated Henry's annual income at $25,000. There are surviving accounts for the years 1913–14 and 1916–18. The first year, 1913, is fairly typical in showing an income of $14,933.73 and an expenditure of $7212.61. But these accounts do not seem to be comprehensive. They document his trust income and investments, but seem to focus on his New England expenses, with no mention of disbursements in Washington. See Edward Chase Kirkland, *Charles Francis Adams, Jr., 1835–1915: The Patrician at Bay* (Cambridge, Mass.: Harvard University Press, 1965), 173–74; Harold Dean Cater, ed., *Henry Adams and His Friends: A Collection of His Unpublished Letters* (Boston, Mass.:

Houghton Mifflin, 1947), xcii; "Current Account of Henry Adams, Esq., for the year ending December 31, 1913," Adams-Thoron Papers, MHS.

6. CFA2 Diary, 31 December 1912, quoted in Kirkland, *Patrician at Bay*, 209.

7. That the historian should enter the political arena is the burden of his presidential address to the American Historical Association in 1901: see CFA2, "An Undeveloped Function," in *Lee at Appomattox and Other Papers* (Boston, Mass.: Houghton Mifflin, 1902), 274–338.

8. CFA2, Memorabilia, 1888–1893, 3 May 1891, 283, and CFA2 Diary, 25 March 1890, quoted in Kirkland, *Patrician at Bay*, 4, 210; Edward Chalfant, *Better in Darkness: A Biography of Henry Adams, His Second Life, 1862–1891* (Hamden, Conn.: Archon Books, 1994), 628, 619, 530.

9. Henry Cabot Lodge, "Memorial Address," in *Charles Francis Adams, 1835–1915: An Autobiography* (Boston and New York: Houghton Mifflin, 1916), lv, lvii; HA to Brooks Adams, 18 February 1909, Brooks Adams Letters to HA (MS Am 1751), HU.

10. I say "few" because, inexplicably, Gore Vidal has written, "Henry was a writer of genius even though his brother Charles wrote rather better prose": see Gore Vidal, *United States: Essays, 1952–1992* (1993; London: Abacus, 1994), 659.

11. CFA2, *Massachusetts, Its Historians and History* (Boston and New York: Houghton Mifflin, 1894), 94, 67–68, 84, 98–99, 103. On CFA2 reading Comte in 1865, see *CFA2: Autobiography*, 179.

12. CFA2, "The Ethics of Secession," in *Studies Military and Diplomatic, 1775–1865* (New York: Macmillan, 1911), 203–31; CFA2, "Lee's Centennial," in *Studies Military and Diplomatic, 1775–1865* (New York: Macmillan, 1911), 291–343. Useful on this is David W. Blight, *Race and Reunion: The Civil War in American Memory* (Cambridge, Mass.: Harvard University Press, Belknap Press, 2001), 359–60.

13. CFA2, "Lee at Appomattox," in *Lee at Appomattox and Other Papers* (Boston, Mass.: Houghton Mifflin, 1902), 1–19; CFA2, *Trans-Atlantic Historical Solidarity* (Oxford: Clarendon Press, 1913).

14. CFA2, *Massachusetts*, 9–10. As most readers will know, the case for the significance of New England religion for even American secular ideology was later to be made by Perry Miller and, in partial imitation, by Sacvan Bercovitch: see Perry Miller, *The New England Mind: The Seventeenth Century* (New York: Macmillan, 1939); Perry Miller, *The New England Mind: From Colony to Province* (Cambridge, Mass.: Harvard University Press, 1953); Sacvan Bercovitch, *The Puritan Origins of the American Self* (New Haven, Conn.: Yale University Press, 1975).

15. This was a family belief, even though the Adams brothers disagreed on most things. Compare Brooks Adams, *The Emancipation of Massachusetts: The Dream and the Reality* (1887; repr., Cambridge, Mass.: Houghton Mifflin, 1962), 213: "The clergy . . . trod their appointed path with the precision of machines, and, constrained by an inexorable destiny, they took that position of antagonism to liberal thought which has become typical of their order. And the struggles and the agony by which this poor and isolated community freed itself from its gloomy bondage, the means by which it secularized its education and its government, won for itself the blessing of free thought and speech, and matured a system of constitutional liberty which has been the foundation of the American Union, rise in dignity to one of the supreme efforts of mankind." On the sibling discord, mostly taking the form of the disparagement of Brooks, see Perry Miller, "Introduction," in Brooks Adams, *Emancipation of Massachusetts*, v–xl.

16. CFA2, *Massachusetts*, 2, 107, 97, 105; CFA2, *Historical Solidarity*, 36; CFA2, "A National Change of Heart," in *Lee at Appomattox*, 271.

17. CFA2, *Historical Solidarity*, 178, 66, 49, 137–38; CFA2, "Secession," 221, 230; CFA2, "Lee's Centennial," 303–5.

18. JQA Address, 4 July 1821, Adams Family Papers, quoted in William Earl Weeks, *John Quincy Adams and American Global Empire* (Lexington: University Press of Kentucky, 1992), 21. The next few sentences are based on Weeks, but see also James E. Lewis Jr., *The American Union and the Problem of Neighborhood: The United States and the Collapse of the Spanish Empire, 1783–1829* (Chapel Hill: University of North Carolina Press, 1998), 96–220.

19. Quoted in Ernest N. Paolino, *The Foundations of the American Empire: William Henry Seward and U.S. Foreign Policy* (Ithaca, N.Y.: Cornell University Press, 1973), 7. Paolino argues, however, that Seward was uninterested in significant American acquisitions beyond North America but did contemplate an American commercial hegemony in world affairs, which would require coaling stations that might control the sea lanes, necessary for American shipping, naval and mercantile.

20. CFA2, "Undeveloped Function," 326; Kirkland, *Patrician at Bay*, 137.

21. See, especially, CFA2, *"Imperialism" and "The Tracks of Our Forefathers"* (Boston, Mass.: Dana Estes, 1899).

22. In his business days, he had defended the "survival of the fittest" in railroad policy, too: on this, see Robert C. Bannister, *Social Darwinism: Science and Myth in Anglo-American Social Thought* (Philadelphia, Pa.: Temple University Press, 1979), 87, quoting CFA2, *The Federation of the Railroad System* (Boston, Mass.: Estes and Lauriat, 1880), 10.

23. CFA2, *Imperialism*, 10–11, 16.

24. Ibid., 18; CFA2, *Massachusetts*, 9, 107.

25. Barrett Wendell, "American Literature," in *Stelligeri and Other Essays Concerning America* (New York: Charles Scribner's Sons, 1893), 143–44. HA owned a copy of Barrett Wendell, *The Mystery of Education, and Other Academic Performances* (New York: Charles Scribner's Sons, 1909).

26. On Tyler, see Kermit Vanderbilt, "Moses Coit Tyler and the Rise of American Literary History," in *American Literature and the Academy: The Roots, Growth, and Maturity of a Profession* (Philadelphia: University of Pennsylvania Press, 1986), 81–104.

27. Moses Coit Tyler, *A History of American Literature, 1607–1676* (1878; repr., London: Sampson Low Martson, Searle, & Rivington, 1879), 80, 84–86, 90.

28. Tyler, *American Literature, 1607–1676*, 92, 98, 112, 100, 170, 192; Moses Coit Tyler, *A History of American Literature, 1676–1765* (1878; repr., London: Sampson Low Martson, Searle, & Rivington, 1879), 204–97.

29. Tyler, *American Literature, 1607–1676*, 192.

30. I adapt a quotation attributed by Adams to Edward Gibbon. "Adams never tired of quoting the supreme phrase of his idol Gibbon, before the Gothic cathedrals: 'I darted a contemptuous look on the stately monuments of superstition' ": *EHA*, 386. This quotation has much vexed scholars. In 1945 R. P. Blackmur was fruitlessly hunting through Gibbon's writings to find it; see R. P. Blackmur to Louisa Hooper Thoron, 15 October 1945, R. P. Blackmur Correspondence Concerning Henry Adams (MS Am 1750–1750.2), HU. Ernest Samuels has surmised, however, that this was never said by Gibbon, but seems to have been cobbled together by Adams from sentences in Gibbon's French Journal of 1763 and the *Memoirs*; on this, see *The Education of Henry Adams*, ed. Ernest Samuels (1918; repr., Boston, Mass.: Houghton Mifflin, 1974), 653 n. 34.

31. Carl L. Becker, *Cornell University: Founders and the Founding* (Ithaca, N.Y.: Cornell University Press, 1944), 43–65; Howard Henry Peckham, *The Making of the University of Michigan, 1817–1967* (Ann Arbor: University of Michigan Press, 1967), 47, 55, 57, 82, 85; C. Vann Woodward, *Origins of the New South, 1877–1913* (1951; repr., Baton Rouge: Louisiana State University Press, 1971), 437; William P. Trent, "Introduction," in John Bell Henneman, ed., *History of the Literary and Intellectual Life of the South*, vol. 7 of *The South in the Building of the Nation*, ed. Julian A. C. Chandler, 12 vols. (Richmond, Va.: The Southern Historical Society, 1909), xviii.

32. Joseph A. Conforti, *Imagining New England: Explorations of Regional Identity from the Pilgrims to the Mid-Twentieth Century* (Chapel Hill: University of North Carolina Press, 2001), 79–262 (quotations on 185).

33. Earl N. Harbert, *The Force So Much Closer Home: Henry Adams and the Adams Family* (New York: New York University Press, 1977), 157.

34. Henry Adams, *Novels, Mont Saint Michel, The Education*, ed. Ernest Samuels and Jayne N. Samuels (New York: Library of America, 1983), 99.

35. Useful on this topic is Robert L. Dorman, *Revolt of the Provinces: The Regionalist Movement in America, 1920–1945* (Chapel Hill: University of North Carolina Press, 1993). On Mumford, see especially Casey Nelson Blake, *Beloved Community: The Cultural Criticism of Randolph Bourne, Van Wyck Brooks, Waldo Frank, and Lewis Mumford* (Chapel Hill: University of North Carolina Press, 1990).

36. Though Dawidoff's claim that Adams's works "remain heartless and merciless in their refusal of community" seems too strong: see Robert Dawidoff, *The Genteel Tradition and the Sacred Rage: High Culture versus Democracy in Adams, James, and Santayana* (Chapel Hill: University of North Carolina Press, 1992), 73.

37. Advocates of the importance of Western history understandably resent this indifference; see Noble E. Cunningham Jr., *The United States in 1800: Henry Adams Revisited* (Charlottesville: University Press of Virginia, 1988) for such a complaint. However, the frequency of Adams's later visits to the Far West, usually in the company of Clarence King, has meant that Adams sometimes appears in cultural histories of the West, but also in fiction; for an instance of the latter see, especially, Wallace Stegner, *Angle of Repose* (Garden City, N.Y.: Doubleday, 1971).

38. On this, see Fulmer Mood, "The Origin, Evolution, and Application of the Sectional Concept, 1750–1900," in *Regionalism in America*, ed. Merrill Jensen (Madison and Milwaukee: University of Wisconsin Press, 1951), 38–47. Adams owned a copy of Jedidiah Morse, *The American Gazetteer: Exhibiting, in Alphabetical Order, a Much More Full and Accurate Account, Than Has Been Given, of the States, Provinces, Counties, Cities, Towns, Villages, Rivers, Bays, Harbours, Gulfs, Sounds, Capes, Mountains, Forts, Indian Tribes, and New Discoveries, on the American Continent, Also of the West-India Islands* (Boston, Mass.: S. Hall et al., 1797).

39. William Lee Miller, *Arguing about Slavery: John Quincy Adams and the Great Battle in the United States Congress* (1996; repr., New York: Vintage Books, 1998), 28.

40. *TJ1*, 1:75–107 (quotation on 87).

41. *TJ1*, 1:310, 105, 211; *TJ2*, 1:6.

42. *TJ1*, 2:188; *JM2*, 2:1, 229.

43. William Dusinberre, *Henry Adams: the Myth of Failure* (Charlottesville: University Press of Virginia, 1980), 113.

44. The story is told in Cater, *Adams and His Friends*, cv–cvi, but Edward Chalfant, *Improvement of the World: A Biography of Henry Adams, His Last Life, 1891–1918* (Hamden, Conn.: Archon Books, 2001), 686 n. 67, makes a good case that Cater misdated the incident to April 1917 and that November of that year is more probable.

45. *TJ1*, 1:108–30 (quotations on 116, 117, 114–15), 264–65; *TJ2*, 1:367.

46. *TJ1*, 1:131–55 (quotations on 137–38), 37, 59.

47. To this, one might add his successors. Especially indignant about Adams's medieval theme is Cunningham, *United States in 1800*.

48. *TJ1*, 1:17.

49. Oscar Cargill, "The Mediaevalism of Henry Adams," in *Essays and Studies in Honor of Carleton Brown*, ed. Percy Waldron Long (New York: New York University Press, 1940), 318, 320. Norman Cantor is still more dismissive, even of *Mont-Saint-Michel and Chartres*; see Norman F. Cantor, *Inventing the Middle Ages: The Lives, Works, and Ideas of the Great Medievalists of the Twentieth Century* (New York: William Morrow, 1991), 44.

50. HA, "The Primitive Rights of Women," in *Historical Essays* (New York: Charles Scribner's Sons, 1891), 1–41; HA, "The Anglo-Saxon Courts of Law," in *Essays in Anglo-Saxon Law* (Boston, Mass.: Little, Brown, 1876), 1–54; *EHA*, 293.

51. "As Regius Professor at Oxford, [Stubbs] gives dignity to the study of history. Even yet this study stands at that University in comparatively slight esteem, overshadowed as it still is by the prescriptive authority of the classics; and the present work is doubly valuable if it is an evidence that Oxford intends at last to interest herself seriously in the history of England, and to tolerate no longer that indifference which has thus far left the national annals in the hands of Scotchmen or amateurs" (HA, "Stubbs's 'Constitutional History of England,'" in *Sketches for the North American Review by Henry Adams*, ed. Edward Chalfant [Hamden, Conn.: Archon Books, 1986], 114). This was, presumably, a rebuke to David Hume, whose historical work was conspicuously absent from Adams's pantheon of great historians, but not only his historical work. It is, in fact, striking that there is not a single reference to Hume in the *Education* or in the six volumes of the Adams letters.

52. HA, "Anglo-Saxon Courts," 1–2.

53. HA, "Primitive Rights," 7, 5, 38.

54. Ibid., 15–16; HA, "Stubbs," 114.

55. HA, "Anglo-Saxon Courts," 3, 21.

56. HA, "Von Holst's History of the United States," in *The Great Secession Winter of 1860–61 and Other Essays by Henry Adams*, ed. George Hochfield (New York: Sagamore Press, 1958), 287.

57. *JM2*, 3:220–24.

58. Ibid., 3:223–26.

59. HA to JH, 3 September 1882, 8 October 1882, HA to John T. Morse Jr., 9 April 1881, *LHA*, 2:468, 475, 424. For examples of critics who derogate the Randolph biography, see R. P. Blackmur, *Henry Adams*, ed. Veronica A. Makowsky (New York: Harcourt Brace Jovanovich, 1980), 10, and John J. Conder, *A Formula of His Own: Henry Adams's Literary Experiment* (Chicago, Ill.: University of Chicago Press, 1970), 8. More appreciative are George Hochfield, *Henry Adams: An Introduction and Interpretation* (New York: Barnes & Noble, 1962), 34–43, and Robert A. Hume, *Runaway Star: An Appreciation of Henry Adams* (Ithaca, N.Y.: Cornell University Press, 1951), 79–83.

60. *EHA*, 181; *TJ1*, 1:268.

61. *JR*, 6, 11–12.

62. Ibid., 278–80, 306, 261.

63. Ibid., 272.

64. HA, *The Life of Albert Gallatin* (Philadelphia, Pa.: J. B. Lippincott, 1879), 154, 267; *JR*, 250, 252, 249.

65. *TJ1*, 1:268, 2:151–52; *TJ2*, 2:379.

66. *TJ2*, 1:22; *TJ1*, 1:148, 154, 143–44.

67. *TJ1*, 1:187, 277.

68. To this, he added: "Jefferson's really creditable philosophy broke down, but I don't blame him for anything more than being a sentimentalist, while I blame his people for being neither sentimental nor practical nor anything but venal." See HA to Brooks Adams, 18 February 1909, Brooks Adams Letters to HA (MS Am 1751), HU.

69. *TJ1*, 1:238, 323–24, 144, 2:202; *TJ2*, 1:159, 164, 205, 58; *JM1*, 1:362.

70. *TJ1*, 1:199; *TJ2*, 2:464.

71. *TJ1*, 1:188; *TJ2*, 1:120–21.

72. *JM1*, 1:11, 176, 310; *JM2*, 2:230.

73. On this, see http://www.loc.gov/loc/walls/adams.html.

74. "As to Jemmy Madison,—oh, poor Jemmy!—he is but a withered little apple-john," quoted in *TJ1*, 1:189.

75. He owned many works on the subject, however, though they were somewhat slanted towards New England's revolutionary history. See HA, "Captaine John Smith: Sometime Governour in Virginia, and Admirall of New England," (1867) in *Historical Essays*, 42–79.

76. *JM2*, 3:195, 197.

77. *TJ2*, 1:413, 2:435; *JM1*, 2:59; *TJ1*, 1:192–94, 148–49, 267.

78. On Virginia and the writing of Civil War history, see Thomas L. Connelly, *The Marble Man: Robert E. Lee and His Image in American Society* (Baton

Rouge: Louisiana State University Press, 1977), and Thomas L. Connelly and Barbara Bellows, *God and General Longstreet: The Lost Cause and the Southern Mind* (Baton Rouge: Louisiana State University Press, 1982).

79. One should note that Adams conflated Southerners and Jeffersonians, and was fairly oblivious of the existence of Southern Federalists, apart from John Marshall.

80. HA, *Albert Gallatin*, 491–92.

81. HA to Samuel J. Tilden, 24 January 1883, *LHA*, 2:491.

82. HA, *Albert Gallatin*, 267; HA, "The Session, 1869–1870," in *Historical Essays*, 370; HA, "The Independents in the Canvass," in *Great Secession Winter*, 306.

83. Richard Taylor, *Destruction and Reconstruction: Personal Experiences of the Late War*, ed. Charles P. Roland (1879; repr., Waltham, Mass.: Blaisdell Publishing, 1968), 234, 236.

84. Perhaps most notably in the various works of Clement Eaton: see Clement Eaton, *Freedom of Thought in the Old South* (Durham, N.C.: Duke University Press, 1940); Eaton, *The Growth of Southern Civilization, 1790–1860* (New York: Harper & Row, 1961); and Eaton, *The Mind of the Old South* (Baton Rouge: Louisiana State University Press, 1964).

85. I draw here upon Leonard L. Richards, *The Slave Power: The Free North and Southern Domination, 1780–1860* (Baton Rouge: Louisiana State University Press, 2000), 21–27.

CHAPTER FOUR

The South in a Supersensual Multiverse

1. Edward Chalfant, *Improvement of the World: A Biography of Henry Adams, His Last Life, 1891–1918* (Hamden, Conn.: Archon Books, 2001), 501–4, best scrutinizes fact and fiction in accounts of the death.

2. Or, at least, he was silent until about February 1917. According to Chalfant, then Aileen Tone broke the rule of never asking about Marian Adams: "During a drive, she told him she wished their silence about his wife were broken. He replied that he would like nothing better! Soon he slipped into a habit of talking to her almost volubly about a woman she had never known: 'your aunt Clover.'" Chalfant, *Improvement of the World*, 507.

3. On this, see Christopher E. G. Benfey, *The Great Wave: Gilded Age Misfits, Japanese Eccentrics, and the Opening of Old Japan* (New York: Random House, 2003), 109–75.

4. However, Adams was not unaware of the effect of Western power on non-Western cultures, and his book on Tahiti has fierce passages on this subject: see HA, *Memoirs of Arii Taimai e Marama of Eimeo, Teriirere of Tooarai,*

Terrinui of Tahiti, Tauraatua i Amo (1901; repr., New York: Scholars' Facsimiles and Reprints, 1947), 136–39.

5. HA to JH, 16 October 1890, 27 February 1894, HA to Theodore Roosevelt, 16 December 1908, *LHA*, 3:301, 4:167–68, 6:198.

6. The theme can be found earlier, in a different form, in HA, "The Primitive Rights of Women," in *Historical Essays* (New York: Charles Scribner's Sons, 1891), 1–41, first written in 1876.

7. HA to EC, 31 December 1897, *LHA*, 4:511.

8. HA to EC, 8 September 1890, 2 July 1891, HA to JH, 16 October 1890, HA to William Hallett Phillips, 13 December 1890, *LHA*, 3:272, 499, 302, 370.

9. HA to Mabel Hooper, 21 February 1892, HA to JH, 16 January 1894, *LHA*, 4:2, 155–56.

10. HA to EC, 4 February 1893, *LHA*, 4:87; even this reference was made not in South Carolina but in conversation with Boston relatives in Washington. On Towne, see Willie Lee Rose, *Rehearsal for Reconstruction: The Port Royal Experiment*, introd. by C. Vann Woodward (1964; repr., New York: Vintage Books, 1967).

11. HA to JH, 7 September 1895, 3 February 1894, HA to EC, 3 February 1894, *LHA*, 4:319, 160, 159.

12. It should be remembered that the following discussion is of books published before the publication of Adams's *History*, though it is possible (if mostly unlikely) that he purchased some of them after 1890.

13. The evidence from his library takes two forms. Firstly, there are books now in the possession of Case Western Reserve University that were given by Adams at various times in the 1890s to a university with a close connection to John and Helen Hay; a typescript list, compiled by Mary Eleanor Streeter in 1946, is in the HA Papers, MHS. Secondly, there are the books owned by the Massachusetts Historical Society, which are most of the volumes on Adams's shelves in Lafayette Square when he died. The Boston collection used to be housed in a room at the Society, but is now stored off-site. Its old card catalog is no longer accessible to researchers, who are now asked to use the "Abigail" electronic catalog, which allows one separately to browse items from the "Henry Adams Library." However, only about 80 percent of the old catalog has been transferred to the new, so conclusions are obliged to be tentative.

14. John Smith, *The Generall Historie of Virginia, New-England, and the Summer Isles* (London: Printed by I. D[awson] and I. [Haviland] for Michael Sparkes, 1624); John Smith, *The Last Will and Testament of Captain John Smith with Some Additional Memoranda Relating to Him* (Cambridge, Mass.: J. Wilson and Son,

1867); John Smith, *A True Relation of Virginia*, ed. Charles Deane (1608; repr., Boston, Mass.: Wiggin and Lunt, 1866); Hugh Jones, *The Present State of Virginia* (1724; repr., New York: Joseph Sabin, 1865); William Stith, *The History of the First Discovery and Settlement of Virginia* (1747; repr., New York: Joseph Sabin, 1865); George Washington, *The Journal of Major George Washington Sent by the Hon. Robert Dinwiddie to the Commandant of the French Forces in Ohio* (New York: Joseph Sabin, 1865); Francis L. Hawks, ed., *A Relation of Maryland Reprinted from the London Edition of 1635* (New York: Joseph Sabin, 1865); B. R. Carroll, ed., *Historical Collections of South Carolina*, 2 vols. (New York: Harper & Brothers, 1836).

15. Charles Dudley Warner, *Captain John Smith (1579–1631) Sometime Governor of Virginia, and Admiral of New England. A Study of His Life and Writings* (New York: Henry Holt, 1881).

16. Jared Sparks, ed., *The Writings of George Washington Being His Correspondence, Addresses, Messages, and Other Papers, Official and Private*, 12 vols. (New York: Harper & Brothers, 1847); Consul Willshire Butterfield, ed., *The Washington-Crawford Letters. Being the Correspondence Between George Washington and William Crawford, from 1767 to 1781, Concerning Western Lands* (Cincinnati, Ohio: R. Clarke, 1877); Henry Augustine Washington, ed., *The Writings of Thomas Jefferson: Being His Autobiography, Correspondence, Reports, Messages, Addresses, and Other Writings, Official and Private*, 9 vols. (Philadelphia, Pa.: J. B. Lippincott, 1869–71); James Madison, *Letters and Other Writings of James Madison*, 4 vols. (Philadelphia, Pa.: J. B. Lippincott, 1865); John Marshall, *The Writings of John Marshall, Late Chief Justice of the United States, upon the Federal Constitution* (Boston, Mass.: James Munroe, 1839); Alexander Hamilton, James Madison, and John Jay, *The Federalist, on the New Constitution* (Washington, D.C.: Thompson & Homans, 1831).

17. James Monroe, *A View of the Conduct of the Executive in the Foreign Affairs of the United States, Connected with the Mission to the French Republic, During the Years 1794, 5, and 6* (Philadelphia, Pa.: Benjamin Franklin Bache, 1797); Robert Goodloe Harper, *Observations on the Dispute between the United States and France* (Boston, Mass.: Printed for the subscribers, 1798); *The Address of the Minority in the Virginia Legislature to the People of That State Containing a Vindication of the Constitutionality of the Alien and Sedition Laws* (Richmond, Va.: A. Davis, 1799); Stephen Cullen Carpenter, *Memoirs of the Hon. Thomas Jefferson, Secretary of State, Vice-President, and President of the United States of America Containing a Concise History of Those States, from the Acknowledgment of Their Independence : With a View of the Rise and Progress of French Influence and French Principles in That Country*, 2 vols. (New York: Printed for the Purchasers, 1809); *Important State Papers: Documents Accompanying the President's Message to Congress, November 29, 1809* (Boston,

Mass.: Boston Gazette Office, 1809); Robert Smith, *Robert Smith's Address to the People of the United States* (n.p., 1811); *Message from the President of the United States, Communicating Further Information Relative to the Pacific Advances Made on the Part of This Government to That of Great Britain* (Washington City: Roger C. Weightman, 1812); James Monroe, *Mr. Monroe's Letter on the Rejected Treaty, between the United States and Great Britain, Concluded by Messrs. Monroe and Pinkney: Also, the Treaty Itself, and Documents Connected with It* (Portland, Maine: Gazette Press, 1813); John Taylor, *An Inquiry into the Principles and Policy of the Government of the United States* (Fredericksburg, Va.: Green and Cady, 1814); John Taylor, *Construction Construed, and Constitutions Vindicated* (Richmond, Va.: Shepherd & Pollard, 1820); George M. Bibb, *An Exposition of the Meaning of the Clause in the Constitution of the United States: That "No State Shall Pass any Ex Post Facto Law, or Law Impairing the Obligation of Contracts": And an Examination of the Opinions of the Court of Appeals of Kentucky, in the Cases of Blair vs. Williams and Lapsley vs. Brashear, in Petition for Re-Hearing* (Frankfort, Ky.: Amos Kendall, 1824); Robert Goodloe Harper, *Plain Reasons of a Plain Man: For Preferring Gen. Jackson to Mr. Adams, as President of the United States* (Baltimore, Md.: Benjamin Edes, 1825).

18. John Marshall, *The Life of George Washington, Commander in Chief of the American Forces*, 5 vols. (Philadelphia, Pa.: C. P. Wayne, 1804–7); William Wirt, *Sketches of the Life and Character of Patrick Henry*, 3d ed. (Philadelphia, Pa.: James Webster, 1818); Henry Wheaton, *Some Account of the Life, Writings, and Speeches of William Pinkney* (New York: J. W. Palmer, 1826); Theodore Dwight, *The Character of Thomas Jefferson as Exhibited in His Own Writings* (Boston, Mass.: Weeks, Jordan, 1839); Henry Lee, *Observations on the Writings of Thomas Jefferson with Particular Reference to the Attack They Contain on the Memory of the Late Gen. Henry Lee*, 2d ed. (Philadelphia, Pa.: J. Dobson, 1839); Henry Stephens Randall, *The Life of Thomas Jefferson*, 3 vols. (New York: Derby & Jackson, 1858). In addition, he had William H. Safford, ed., *The Blennerhassett Papers: Embodying the Private Journal of Harmon Blennerhassett, and the Hitherto Unpublished Correspondence of Burr, Alston, Comfort Tyler, Deveraux, Dayton, Adair, Miro, Emmett, Theodosia Burr Alston, Mrs. Blennerhassett, and Others, Their Contemporaries* (Cincinnati, Ohio: Moore, Wilstach, Keys, 1861).

19. Cornélis Henri de Witt, *Thomas Jefferson; étude historique sur la démocratie Américaine* (Paris: Didier et ce, 1871); Robert C. Winthrop, *Washington, Bowdoin, and Franklin as Portrayed in Occasional Addresses* (Boston, Mass.: Little, Brown, 1876); Daniel Coit Gilman, *James Monroe in His Relations to the Public Service during Half a Century, 1776–1826* (Boston and New York: Houghton Mifflin, 1883); Allan B. Magruder, *John Marshall* (Boston and New York: Houghton Mifflin, 1885); Lucia Beverly Cutts, ed., *Memoirs and Letters of Dolly Madison*

(Boston, Mass.: Houghton Mifflin, 1886); Moses Coit Tyler, *Patrick Henry* (Boston and New York: Houghton Mifflin, 1887); Moncure Daniel Conway, *Omitted Chapters of History Disclosed in the Life and Papers of Edmund Randolph, Governor of Virginia: First Attorney-General United States, Secretary of State* (New York and London: G. P. Putnam's Sons, 1888).

20. Lemuel Sawyer, *A Biography of John Randolph, of Roanoke with a Selection from His Speeches* (New York: W. Robinson, 1844); Hugh A. Garland, *The Life of John Randolph of Roanoke*, 13th ed., 2 vols. in 1 (New York: D. Appleton, 1860); Powhatan Bouldin, *Home Reminiscences of John Randolph of Roanoke* (Danville, Va.; Richmond, Va.: The author; Clemmitt & Jones, 1878); Daniel Bedinger Lucas, *John Randolph of Roanoke: His Convictions, and Their Influence upon His Public Career. An Address Delivered before the Literary Societies of Hampden-Sidney College, June 13, 1883* (New York: Economical Print, 1884).

21. Richard K. Crallé, ed., *The Works of John C. Calhoun*, 6 vols. (New York: D. Appleton, 1854–57); Calvin Colton, ed., *The Private Correspondence of Henry Clay* (New York: A. S. Barnes, 1856); Thomas Hart Benton, *Thirty Years' View; or, a History of the Working of the American Government for Thirty Years from 1820 to 1850: Chiefly Taken from the Congress Debates*, 2 vols. (New York: D. Appleton, 1875).

22. Carl Schurz, *Life of Henry Clay* (Boston and New York: Houghton Mifflin, 1887); Theodore Roosevelt, *Life of Thomas Hart Benton* (Boston and New York: Houghton Mifflin, 1887); John Henry Eaton, *The Life of Andrew Jackson Major-General in the Service of the United States: Comprising a History of the War in the South, from the Commencement of the Creek Campaign, to the Termination of the Hostilities before New Orleans* (Philadelphia, Pa.: S. F. Bradford, 1824).

23. John Daly Burk, *The History of Virginia from Its First Settlement to the Present Day*, 2 vols. (Petersburg, Va.: Dickson & Pescud, 1804–5); the Streeter listing of the Western Reserve gift notes, in volume 1, the inscription, "Henry Adams from his wife. July 11, 1874."

24. François Barbé-Marbois, *The History of Louisiana, Particularly of the Cession of the Colony to the United States of America with an Introductory Essay on the Constitution and Government of the United States* (Philadelphia, Pa.: Carey & Lea, 1830); Charles Etienne Artur Gayarré, *History of Louisiana*, 4 vols. in 3 (New York: William J. Widdleton, 1866–67); Humphrey Marshall, *The History of Kentucky. Exhibiting an Account of the Modern Discovery; Settlement; Progressive Improvement; Civil and Military Transactions; and the Present State of the Country*, 2 vols. (Frankfort, Ky.: G. S. Robinson, 1824); George Adolphus Hanson, *Old Kent: The Eastern Shore of Maryland; Notes Illustrative of the Most Ancient Records of Kent County, Maryland, and of the Parishes of St. Paul's, Shrewsbury and I. U. and Genealogical Histories of Old and Distinguished Families of Maryland* (Baltimore, Md.:

J. P. Des Forges, 1876); Esmeralda Boyle, *Biographical Sketches of Distinguished Marylanders* (Baltimore, Md.: Kelly, Piet, 1877); William Meade, *Old Churches, Ministers and Families of Virginia*, 2 vols. (Philadelphia, Pa.: J. B. Lippincott, 1857); Samuel Mordecai, *Virginia, Especially Richmond, in by-Gone Days; with a Glance at the Present: Being Reminiscences and Last Words of an Old Citizen*, 2d ed. (Richmond, Va.: West and Johnston, 1860).

25. Hugh Blair Grigsby, *The Virginia Convention of 1776* (Richmond, Va.: J. W. Randolph, 1855); Hugh Blair Grigsby, *Discourse on the Life and Character of the Hon. Littleton Waller Tazewell* (Norfolk, Va.: J. D. Ghiselin, Jun., 1860).

26. David Bailie Warden, *A Chorographical and Statistical Description of the District of Columbia the Seat of the General Government of the United States* (Paris: Smith, 1816); Christian Schultz, *Travels on an Inland Voyage through the States of New York, Pennsylvania, Virginia, Ohio, Kentucky and Tennessee, and through the Territories of Indiana, Louisiana, Mississippi, and New-Orleans Performed in the Years 1807 and 1808; Including a Tour of Nearly Six Thousand Miles*, 2 vols. (New York: Isaac Riley, 1810); John Melish, *Travels in the United States of America, in the Years 1806 and 1807, and 1809, 1810, and 1811 Including an Account of Passages betwixt America and Britain, and Travels through Various Parts of Britain, Ireland, and Canada: With Corrections, and Improvements, to 1815*, 2 vols. (Philadelphia, Pa.: John Melish, 1815); Morris Birkbeck, *Notes on a Journey in America, from the Coast of Virginia to the Territory of Illinois* (London: J. Ridgway, 1818); *Ohio Valley Historical Series: Miscellanies: 1, a Tour in Ohio, Kentucky and Indiana Territory, in 1805 by Joseph Espy; 2, Two Western Campaigns in the War of 1812 by Samuel Williams; 3, the Leatherwood God by R. H. Taneyhill*, Ohio Valley Historical Series, no. 7 (Cincinnati, Ohio: R. Clarke, 1871). Later he acquired Benjamin Henry Latrobe, *The Journal of Latrobe. Being the Notes and Sketches of an Architect, Naturalist and Traveler in the United States from 1796 to 1820* (New York: D. Appleton, 1905).

27. Augustus Baldwin Longstreet, *Georgia Scenes: Characters, Incidents, &c., in the First Half Century of the Republic / by a Native Georgian*, 2d ed. (1835; repr., New York: Harper & Brothers, 1874); Washington Allston, *Monaldi: A Tale* (Boston, Mass.: Charles C. Little and James Brown, 1841); Jared Bradley Flagg, *The Life and Letters of Washington Allston* (New York: Charles Scribner's Sons, 1892).

28. Something similar could be said of a postbellum text by George Henry Calvert, who resided after 1840 not in his native Maryland but in Newport, Rhode Island; George Henry Calvert, *Brief Essays and Brevities* (Boston, Mass.: Lee and Shepard, 1874).

29. *A Memorial to the Congress of the United States on the Subject of Restraining the Increase of Slavery in New States to be Admitted into the Union* (Boston, Mass.: Sewell Phelps, 1819); Richard Hildreth, *Despotism in America or, An Inquiry*

into the Nature and Results of the Slave-Holding System in the United States (Boston, Mass.: Whipple and Damrell, 1840).

30. HA to Edwin A. Alderman, 10 February 1903, *LHA*, 5:455.

31. HA to Charles W. Eliot, 12 June 1892, *LHA*, 4:21; John G. Nicolay and John Hay, *Abraham Lincoln: A History*, 10 vols. (New York: Century, 1890).

32. Francis Vinton Greene, *The Mississippi* (New York: Charles Scribner's Sons, 1882); George E[dward] Pond, *The Shenandoah Valley in 1864* (New York: Charles Scribner's Sons, 1883); William Tecumseh Sherman, *Memoirs of Gen. William T. Sherman*, 2 vols. (New York: D. Appleton, 1875); Ulysses S. Grant, *Personal Memoirs of U. S. Grant*, 2 vols. (New York: C. L. Webster, 1885–86); Horace Greeley, *The American Conflict: A History of the Great Rebellion in the United States of America, 1860–64*, 2 vols. (Hartford, Conn.: O. D. Case, 1865); James Russell Soley, *The Blockade and the Cruisers* (New York: Charles Scribner's Sons, 1883); *Correspondence Relative to the Case of Messrs. Mason and Slidell* (Washington, D.C.: n.p., 1862).

33. Owen Wister, *The Seven Ages of Washington: A Biography* (New York: Macmillan, 1907); HA to EC, 11 January 1903, HA to Owen Wister, 20 March 1908, *LHA*, 5:438, 6:128.

34. HA to JH, 9 May 1905, HA to EC, 8 April 1901, *LHA*, 5:657–58, 233; Albert Bigelow Paine, ed., *Mark Twain's Letters*, 2 vols. (New York: Harper & Brothers, 1917).

35. Henry Watterson, *Oddities in Southern Life and Character* (Boston, Mass.: Houghton Mifflin, 1883); HA to Samuel Bowles, 23 April 1874, and HA to EC, 18 February 1901, *LHA*, 2:191–92, 5:200.

36. HA to CMG, 18 April 1871, HA to Francis Parkman, 21 December 1884, HA to Herbert Baxter Adams, 12 December 1894, *LHA*, 2:106, 563, 4:228–29.

37. HA to William Henry Trescot, 9 August 1876, *LHA*, 2:286.

38. HA, *Novels, Mont Saint Michel, The Education*, ed. Ernest Samuels and Jayne N. Samuels (New York: Library of America, 1983), 333.

39. *MSMC*, 32.

40. Ibid., 55, 104, 261, 274.

41. HA to Brooks Adams, 8 September 1895, *LHA*, 4:321; *MSMC*, 2, 230, 237, 146.

42. *MSMC*, 377.

43. *EHA*, 461. On Adams and gender, see Duco van Oostrum, *Male Authors, Female Subjects: The Woman Within/Beyond the Borders of Henry Adams, Henry James, and Others*, Postmodern Studies 14 (Amsterdam: Rodopi, 1995).

44. Charles Francis Adams, ed., *The Works of John Adams, Second President of the United States*, 10 vols. (Boston, Mass.: Little, Brown, 1856); Charles Francis

Adams, ed., *Memoirs of John Quincy Adams, Comprising Portions of His Diary from 1795 to 1848*, 12 vols. (Philadelphia, Pa.: J. B. Lippincott, 1874–77); *Charles Francis Adams, 1835–1915: An Autobiography* (Boston and New York: Houghton Mifflin, 1916); CFA2, *Charles Francis Adams* (Boston and New York: Houghton Mifflin, 1900).

45. HA to Raphael Pumpelly, 19 May 1910, HA to Henry Osborn Taylor, 17 January 1905, *LHA*, 6:341, 5:628.

46. William Dusinberre, *Henry Adams: The Myth of Failure* (Charlottesville: University Press of Virginia, 1980) persuasively argues that the later Adams suppressed the evidence for his earlier impulse towards fame, thereby leaving the impression that his early career had only been dedicated to scientific investigation.

47. HA to Henry Morse Stephens, 15 January 1916, HA to John Franklin Jameson, 17 November 1896, *LHA*, 6:716, 4:440.

48. HA to Brooks Adams, 18 February 1909, HA to John T. Morse Jr., 19 November 1882, HA to George Cabot Lodge, 22 April 1903, *LHA*, 6:229, 2:479, 5:490.

49. *EHA*, 8.

50. *EHA*, 44–45, 57–59 (quotation about Lee on 57).

51. Edward Chalfant, *Both Sides of the Ocean: A Biography of Henry Adams, His First Life, 1838–1862* (Hamden, Conn.: Archon Books, 1982), 89.

52. Mary Bandry Daughtry, *Gray Cavalier: The Life and Wars of General W. H. F. "Rooney" Lee* (Cambridge, Mass.: Da Capo Press, 2002), 24, 197, 311, 299; Robert E. Lee to W. H. F. Lee, 1 November 1856, Lee Family Papers, Library of Congress, quoted in Daughtry, *Gray Cavalier*, 28–29; *EHA*, 6.

53. *EHA*, 180, 122, 83; HA to CMG, 24 October 1879, 25 July 1870, HA to Henry Cabot Lodge, 4 August 1891, HA to William Hallett Phillips, 8 October 1891, *LHA*, 2:379, 76, 3:519, 553.

54. HA to Hugh Blair Grigsby, 9 October 1877, HA to Sir Robert Cunliffe, 12 November 1882, HA to CMG, 15 June 1894, *LHA*, 2:323, 477, 4:194.

55. This is, in effect, the contention of Robert Dawidoff, *The Genteel Tradition and the Sacred Rage: High Culture versus Democracy in Adams, James, and Santayana* (Chapel Hill: University of North Carolina Press, 1992).

56. HA to Brooks Adams, 18 February 1909, *LHA*, 6:228.

57. HA, *The Life of Albert Gallatin* (Philadelphia, Pa.: J. B. Lippincott, 1879), 635–36; *JR*, 272–73.

58. *TJ1*, 1:134; *JR*, 285, 274.

59. Nothing else in the six volumes received the same attention.

60. John C. Calhoun, *A Disquisition on Government and a Discourse on the Con-*

stitution and Government of the United States, ed. Richard K. Crallé (Columbia, S.C.: A. S. Johnston, 1851), 12, 69, 4, 99, 8, in HA Library, MHS.

61. Ibid., 23, 42, 61–62, 27–28, 48.

62. Ibid., 107.

63. *EHA*, 100.

64. HA to Brooks Adams, 18 February, 13 March 1909, *LHA*, 6:229, 240.

65. *EHA*, 13; HA to Brooks Adams, 18 February 1909, Brooks Adams Letters to HA (MS Am 1751), HU: these sentiments are keyed to 429 of Brooks Adams's manuscript.

66. For this argument, see especially John Carlos Rowe, *Henry Adams and Henry James: The Emergence of a Modern Consciousness* (Ithaca, N.Y.: Cornell University Press, 1976).

67. John Carlos Rowe, "Introduction," in *New Essays on The Education of Henry Adams*, ed. John Carlos Rowe (Cambridge: Cambridge University Press, 1996), 19–20.

68. To put the matter formally, I am doubtful of Fredric Jameson's claim that postmodernism is not "little more than one more stage of modernism (if not, indeed, of the even older romanticism)," because "a mutation in the sphere of culture has rendered such attitudes archaic" (Fredric Jameson, *Postmodernism, or, the Cultural Logic of Late Capitalism* [London: Verso, 1991], 4). Instead, I incline to David Harvey's view that "there is much more continuity than difference between the broad history of modernism and the movement called postmodernism . . . the latter [being] a particular kind of crisis within the former" (David Harvey, *The Condition of Postmodernity: An Enquiry into the Origins of Cultural Change* [Cambridge, Mass.: Blackwell, 1990], 116).

69. *EHA*, 498; Jean-François Lyotard, *The Postmodern Condition: A Report on Knowledge*, trans. Geoff Bennington and Brian Massumi (1984; repr., Manchester: Manchester University Press, 1986), xxiii–xxiv, 4, 7, 10, 15, 24–26, 39, 51. On the saleable, compare Adams's anecdote about his Harvard students in the 1870s: "Their faith in education was so full of pathos that one dared not ask them what they thought they could do with education when they got it. Adams did put the question to one of them, and was surprised at the answer: 'The degree of Harvard College is worth money to me in Chicago' " (*EHA*, 305–6).

70. HA to Lucy Baxter, 18 October 1893, *LHA*, 4:133.

71. Jameson, *Postmodernism*, 54; Harvey, *Postmodernity*, 337.

72. C. Vann Woodward, "The Elusive Mind of the South," in *American Counterpoint: Slavery and Racism in the North-South Dialogue* (Boston, Mass.: Little, Brown, 1971), 264; M. E. Bradford, "The Vocation of Norman Pod-

horetz," in *The Reactionary Imperative: Essays Literary and Political* (Peru, Ill.: Sherwood Sugden, 1990), 32. For Woodward's other usages of Adams, see C. Vann Woodward, *Origins of the New South, 1877–1913* (1951; repr., Baton Rouge: Louisiana State University Press, 1971), 290; Woodward, "A Southern Critique for the Gilded Age: Melville, Adams, and James," in *The Burden of Southern History*, rev. ed. (1960; repr., Baton Rouge: Louisiana State University Press, 1968), 109–40; Woodward, *Thinking Back: The Perils of Writing History* (Baton Rouge: Louisiana State University Press, 1986), 111; Woodward, "Henry Adams (1838–1918)," in *The Future of the Past* (New York: Oxford University Press, 1989), 342–48.

73. John Donald Wade, "A Bet on the Bottom Man," in *Selected Essays and Other Writings of John Donald Wade*, ed. Donald Davidson (Athens: University of Georgia Press, 1966), 80; Bruce Clayton, *W. J. Cash: A Life* (Baton Rouge: Louisiana State University Press, 1991), 48, 57; W. J. Cash, *The Mind of the South* (1941; repr., New York: Alfred A. Knopf, 1969), 101–2 (quotation on 102).

74. Allen Tate, "Remarks on the Southern Religion," in Twelve Southerners, *I'll Take My Stand: The South and the Agrarian Tradition* (1930; repr., Baton Rouge: Louisiana State University Press, 1980), 171; Tate, "A Southern Mode of the Imagination," in *Essays of Four Decades* (1959; repr., New York: William Morrow, 1970), 584–85.

75. Richard M. Weaver, "Lee the Philosopher," and "The Older Religiousness in the South," in *The Southern Essays of Richard M. Weaver*, ed. George M. Curtis III and James J. Thompson Jr. (Indianapolis, Ind.: Liberty Press, 1987), 172, 134–46; John Crowe Ransom, *God without Thunder: An Unorthodox Defense of Orthodoxy* (New York: Harcourt, Brace, 1930); Richard M. Weaver, "Up from Liberalism," in *In Defense of Tradition: Collected Shorter Writings of Richard M. Weaver, 1929–1963*, ed. Ted J. Smith III (Indianapolis, Ind.: Liberty Fund, 2000), 37, 39–40.

76. Donald Davidson, *Still Rebels, Still Yankees and Other Essays* (1957; repr., Baton Rouge: Louisiana State University Press, 1972), 203, 124–25.

77. See, among literary critics, Lewis P. Simpson, *The Dispossessed Garden: Pastoral and History in Southern Literature* (Athens: University of Georgia Press, 1975), 11; Marion Montgomery, *Possum: And Other Receits for the Recovery of "Southern" Being* (Athens: University of Georgia Press, 1987), 80–81. Among historians, in 1961 Clement Eaton was using the Rooney Lee passage to frame a chapter on "The Southern Mind in 1860," with only an implied demurral: Clement Eaton, *The Growth of Southern Civilization, 1790–1860* (1961; repr., New York: Harper & Row, 1963), 295–96.

78. A belated exception was the critic C. Hugh Holman, who refers to the *History*: see C. Hugh Holman, *The Roots of Southern Writing: Essays on the*

Literature of the American South (Athens: University of Georgia Press, 1972), 108. An earlier instance is Allen Tate's poem, "Fragment of a Meditation," begun in 1928 and completed in 1935. It seems to speak of the *History*: "I'll go back seventy years / And more to the great Administrations : / Yet six had gone and all the public men / Whom doctrine and an evil nature made / Were only errand boys beaten by the sun / While Henry Adams fuddled in the shade" (Allen Tate, *Poems* [Chicago, Ill.: Swallow Press, 1961], 84). On the dating of the poem, see Allen Tate to Andrew Lytle, 21 December 1928, in Thomas Daniel Young and Elizabeth Sarcone, eds., *The Lytle-Tate Letters: The Correspondence of Andrew Lytle and Allen Tate* (Jackson: University Press of Mississippi, 1987), 15.

79. Robert Penn Warren to R. W. B. Lewis and Cleanth Brooks, 16 July 1970, in James A. Grimshaw, ed., *Cleanth Brooks and Robert Penn Warren: A Literary Correspondence* (Columbia: University of Missouri Press, 1998), 311. Warren was to write the entry on Adams in Cleanth Brooks, R. W. B. Lewis, and Robert Penn Warren, *American Literature: The Makers and the Making* (New York: St. Martin's Press, 1973), 2:1475–87. It is, on the whole, an appreciative piece, which mentions Rooney Lee without interest and mainly sees Adams as a modernist. Warren's critical judgment was that Adams had been a failure as a novelist ("Adams had no shred of novelistic instinct, no capacity for letting character or feeling burst into light by a word or gesture, and no ear whatsoever for dialogue"), a success as a historian (though Warren does not dwell on the *History*), but most triumphant in *Mont-Saint-Michel and Chartres* ("a symbolist poem . . . . [that] stood in much the same relation to its time as did Matthew Arnold's poem 'The Scholar Gypsy,' which bewails the 'divided aims' of the modern world, or Melville's *Clarel*, or Eliot's *The Waste Land*, or Faulkner's *The Sound and the Fury*"). Warren was less effusive about the *Education*, but still thought it "a work of art . . . [with] the urgency of personal experience and the commanding force of a dramatic structure."

80. The Percy/Adams link has been often observed: see Richard H. King, *A Southern Renaissance: The Cultural Awakening of the American South, 1930–1955* (New York: Oxford University Press, 1980), 90; Fred Hobson, *Tell about the South: The Southern Rage to Explain* (Baton Rouge: Louisiana State University Press, 1983), 280–86; Bertram Wyatt-Brown, *The House of Percy: Honor, Melancholy, and Imagination in a Southern Family* (New York: Oxford University Press, 1994), 4, 157, 217, 283; Lewis Baker, *The Percys of Mississippi: Politics and Literature in the New South* (Baton Rouge: Louisiana State University Press, 1983), 126.

81. Wyatt-Brown, *House of Percy*, 217; Baker, *Percys of Mississippi*, 76, 126.

82. William Alexander Percy, *Lanterns on the Levee: Recollections of a Planter's*

Son (New York: Alfred A. Knopf, 1941), 4, 8, 7, 74, 122, 111, 140, 156, 223, 310, 345. The sculptor of the memorial to LeRoy Percy was influenced by Saint-Gaudens's Adams memorial: on this, see Wyatt-Brown, *House of Percy,* 3–4.

83. Ada A. McElhenney to Julian Mitchell, 3 April 1854, Julian Mitchell Papers, South Carolina Historical Society, Charleston, S.C.; Thomas R. Dew to B. Franklin Dew, 10 May 1841, Dew Family Manuscripts, Special Collections Department, Early Gregg Swem Library, College of William and Mary, Williamsburg, Va.; G. T. Snowden to James Henley Thornwell, 25 August 1845, James Henley Thornwell Papers, Presbyterian Historical Society, Montreat, N.C.; entry for 9 February 1858, Ann Hardeman Diary, Mississippi Department of Archives and History, Jackson, reprinted in Michael O'Brien, ed., *An Evening When Alone: Four Journals of Single Women in the South, 1827–67,* Publications of the Southern Texts Society (Charlottesville: University Press of Virginia, 1993), 282; Alfred Huger, fragment of letter, circa May 1854, Letterpress Book, Alfred Huger Papers, Manuscripts and Special Collections Department, William R. Perkins Library, Duke University, Durham, N.C.

84. Iveson L. Brookes to Rev. Welham Heath, 20 March 1849, Iveson L. Brookes Papers; Mitchell King to James J. McCarter, 22 September 1856, draft letter in looseleaf letterbook, Mitchell King Papers; Francis L. Hawks to David L. Swain, 3 January 1860, David L. Swain Papers, all in Southern Historical Collection, Wilson Library, University of North Carolina, Chapel Hill, N.C.

85. "The New South" (1886), in Joel Chandler Harris, ed., *Life of Henry W. Grady, Including His Writings and Speeches* (New York: Cassell, 1890), 86; Melissa Walker Heidari, ed., *To Find Her Own Peace: Grace King in Her Journals, 1886–1910,* Publications of the Southern Texts Society (Athens: University of Georgia Press, 2004), 55.

86. Edwin Mims, "The Renaissance in New England," *South Atlantic Quarterly* 1 (July 1902): 224; Thomas Nelson Page, *The Old South: Essays Social and Political* (1892; repr., New York: Charles Scribner's Sons, 1906), 51; "President Eliot and the South" (1909), in Robert H. Woody, ed., *The Papers and Addresses of William Preston Few, Late President of Duke University* (Durham, N.C.: Duke University Press, 1915), 259.

87. Brooks, Lewis, and Warren, *American Literature,* 2:1482–83; Erich Auerbach, *Mimesis: The Representation of Reality in Western Literature,* trans. Willard Trask (Princeton, N.J.: Princeton University Press, 1953), 532, 538.

88. "Ode to the Confederate Dead" (1928, revised in 1937), in Tate, *Poems,* 23; William Faulkner, "Address upon Receiving the Nobel Prize for Literature: Stockholm, December 10, 1950," in *Essays, Speeches and Public Letters of*

William Faulkner, ed. James B. Meriwether (London: Chatto & Windus, 1967), 119.

89. HA to Anna Cabot Mills Lodge, 24 August 1898, *LHA*, 4:609; HA, *Letters to a Niece and Prayer to the Virgin of Chartres* (Boston and New York: Houghton Mifflin, 1920), 133.

Index

Adams, Henry (*continued*)
Washington society, place in, 46,
47–49, 58–59, 72
—Works: *Democracy,* 46, 59, 68,
85–86, 109–10; "Great Secession
Winter," 6, 9; *John Randolph,*
97–101, 130–31, 137; *Life of Albert
Gallatin,* 71, 97, 100–101, 109–10,
136, 139; *Mont-Saint-Michel and
Chartres,* 126–29, 135, 142, 144,
145, 147, 185 (n. 79). See also
Education of Henry Adams, The
(HA); *History of the United States*
(HA)
Adams, John (1735–1826), 4, 34,
41–42, 105, 129; political career
of, xii, 1, 2, 28, 78
Adams, John (1803–34), 155 (n. 8)
Adams, John Quincy, 2, 4, 23, 79,
89, 129, 136, 155 (n. 8); in District
of Columbia, 3, 47–48, 49, 50;
HA on, 4, 23–24, 140–41; and
LCA, 2, 27, 32, 33; political career
of, xii, 1, 6, 30, 47–48, 50; and
slavery, 4–5, 35–36, 37, 108,
160–61 (n. 91)
Adams, Louisa Catherine. *See*
Johnson, Louisa Catherine (later
Adams)
Adams, Mary Hellen, 155 (n. 10)
African Americans. *See* blacks;
servants; slaves and slavery
Agrarians, Southern, 145
Alabama, 61
Alaska, 80
Alderman, Edwin, 123
Alleghanies, 117
Allston, Washington, 68, 123, 166
(n. 69)

American Historical Association,
75, 125
American Indians, 88, 94
American Party, 8, 61
American Revolution, 31, 103, 106,
174 (n. 75)
American Statesmen series, 98, 122,
131
American Universal Geography, The
(Jedidiah Morse), 87
androgyny, 128, 129
Anglo-Saxons, 78, 79, 80–81, 92, 94,
95–96
Antiques, 58, 59
Aquinas, Thomas, 128, 131, 141
Arnold, Matthew, 185 (n. 79)
Arthur, Chester, 67
Aryan race, 94–95
Asia, 97. *See also entries for specific
countries*
Assing, Ludmilla, 8
Assing, Ottilie, 8
Association of the Oldest
Inhabitants of the District of
Columbia, 58, 165 (n. 48)
Auerbach, Erich, 151
Australia, 135

Bancroft, George, 48, 167
(n. 77)
Barbour, James, 35
Barlow, Samuel Latham Mitchell,
62
Barnes, Overton, 38
Benton, Thomas Hart, 122
Bercovitch, Sacvan, 169 (n. 14)
Beverly Farms, 67
Bey, Aristarchi, 59
Bible, 37, 81

blacks, 37–38, 52, 63, 68, 80, 160–61
(n. 91); HA on, 10, 13, 14–15,
118, 132
Black Sally, 103
Blackwood's, 24–25
Blaine, James G., 48–49, 65
Bonnycastle, Alfred, 47, 162–63
(n. 15)
Boston, Mass., 3, 35, 78; HA and, xii,
3, 4, 43–44, 45–46, 117, 131–32
Botkin, B. A., 86
Breckinridge, John C., 61
Brent (groom), 52, 55
Britain and the British, 10–11,
32–33, 63, 80, 86. *See also* England
and the English
British Turf Club, 62
Brooke, Catherine, 86
Brooks, Peter Chardon, 1
Brown, Ann Hart, 35
Bruce, Blanche K., 63
Buchanan, Andrew, 34
Buchanan, James, 61
Buckle, Thomas Henry, 142
Burk, John Daly, 122
Burke, Edmund, 80
Byron, George Gordon Lord, 25

Cable, George Washington, 74, 124
Calhoun, John C., 40, 67, 69, 102,
122, 137–39, 156 (n. 15), 167
(n. 72); and slavery, 100, 110, 112,
137, 139
Calvert, George Henry, 180 (n. 28)
Calvinism, 40, 76, 83, 102
Cambridge, Mass., 43–44
Cameron, Donald, 48, 118
Cameron, Elizabeth, 48, 118, 124
capitalism, 74, 92, 143

Cargill, Oscar, 92
Carlisle, John Griffin, 69
Carlyle, Thomas, 25
Carrington, John, 59, 67, 85–86, 110
Carroll, Charles, 37
Cartesians, 135
Cash, Wilbur, xi, xiii, 144–45, 146,
152
Cater, Harold Dean, 168 (n. 5), 173
(n. 44)
Chalfant, Edward, 159 (n. 55)
Charleston, S.C., 91
Chartres, 126–28, 131, 144–45, 147,
151
Chicago Exposition of 1893, 142,
164 (n. 34)
China, 98
Christianity, 44, 71, 94, 126; Louisa
Adams and, 25, 37; and slavery,
37, 68; Unitarianism, 68, 76. *See
also* Calvinism; religion
Clay, Henry, 25, 40, 67, 122, 137
Cleveland, Grover, 63
climate, 18–20, 44–45, 50–51, 116,
128
Comte, Auguste, 130
Conforti, Joseph, 85
Connecticut, 88, 102
*Conquest of Kansas by Missouri and Her
Allies, The* (William Phillips), 156
(n. 12)
conservatism, 79, 86, 87, 88–89, 96,
105, 107, 145–46; HA and, 13–14,
17
Constitution, U.S., 13, 14, 78, 105,
106, 112
Constitution of Massachusetts
(1780), 78
Cook, Daniel Pope, 39

May, James, 15

Mayflower Compact, 84

McElhenney, Ada, 148

McKinley, William, 11, 79

medievalism, 91–92, 94–96. *See also*
Middle Ages

Melville, Herman, 185 (n. 79)

Mexican War, 5, 80, 137

Mexico and Mexicans, 61, 80, 81,
117–18

Michelet, Jules, 142

Middle Ages, 128, 129, 131, 141. *See
also* medievalism

Middle States, 85–86, 87, 88, 89–90,
91. *See also entries for specific states*

Midwest, 74, 83

Miller, Perry, 169 (n. 14)

Mims, Edwin, 150

Mind of the South, The (Cash), xi, 145,
147

Mississippi, 59, 65, 124, 146

Mississippi State University, 63

Missouri, 35

modernism, 141, 144, 151, 183
(n. 68), 185 (n. 79)

modernity, 11, 100, 109, 124–25,
144, 146, 147; construction of
meaning and, 131, 141–42, 151;
in contrast to medieval, 12, 82,
91–92, 94, 95–96, 125

Monroe, James, 107

Monticello, 71, 103

Mont-Saint-Michel, 126, 127

Mont-Saint-Michel and Chartres (HA),
126–29, 135, 142, 144, 145, 147,
185 (n. 79)

Moore, Thomas, 25

Morrill Act, 84

Morse, Jedidiah, 84, 87

Morse, John T., 131

Mount Vernon, 109

Mumford, Lewis, 86

Murfree, Mary, 74

nationalism, 71, 79, 90, 96–97, 137,
138; HA and, 9–12, 17, 96, 136,
141; and regionalism, 73–74, 85,
86, 87, 108

New Basin Canal, 61

New England, 1, 7, 15, 63, 65, 157
(n. 27), 169 (n. 14); as analogue
of Mont-Saint-Michel and
Normandy, 127–28, 131; cultural
hegemony of, 6, 13, 74, 76, 78–79,
81–85, 149–50; HA on, 13, 44–46,
85, 87–89, 90, 91, 99, 100, 106,
136; HA's identification with, xii,
17, 21, 29, 43, 146; LCA and, 20,
34, 36–37; and rationality, 12, 125,
148, 149–50

New Orleans, La., 61

New South, 59, 63, 150

New York, 46–47, 89–90, 136, 148

Nicholas, Wilson Cary, 71

Nietzsche, Friedrich, 143, 144

Nissenbaum, Stephen, 74

Normandy and Norman, 126–27,
137

North. *See* New England

North American Review, 24, 43, 92

North Carolina, 107, 108

North/South dialectic, 19–20, 84,
94, 122, 127–28, 129, 158 (n. 52)

Norton, Charles Eliot, 19–20, 150

Nuth, Mr., 31

"Ode to the Confederate Dead"
(Tate), 151

Odum, Howard, 86
Oedipus, 103
Olmsted, Frederick Law, 61
Oregon, 80
Oxford University, 173 (n. 51)

Palmer, Benjamin Morgan, 149
Passchendaele, 151
Patapsco Female Institute, 71
Pennsylvania, 47, 86, 88, 89, 90, 100
Percy, William Alexander, 146–48
Philadelphia, Pa., 47, 89, 90
Philadelphia Convention, 105
Phillips, Wendell, 150
Phillips, William, 156 (n. 12)
Pocahontas, 106
Polk, James K., 80
Polynesia, 117, 175 (n. 4)
Pontchartrain, Lake, 61
Port Royal experiment, 13, 68, 118
positivism, 130
postmodernism, 141–44, 183 (n. 68)
Powhatan, 55
primitive, 116–18
psychology, 131
Puritans, 76, 78, 84, 106

Quincy, Edmund, 112
Quincy, Josiah, 112
Quincy, Mass., xii, 3; HA on, 4, 24,
  44, 131–32, 140–41; LCA and, 20,
  25, 28–29, 30, 35

race and racism, 9, 148; CFA2 on,
  78, 79, 80–81; HA on, 14–15, 54,
  94–95, 117. See also Anglo-Saxons;
  blacks; Indians, American
Randolph, John, 38–40, 62, 69, 90,
  102, 103, 107; HA on, 72, 97–101,

104, 126, 130–31; and the Slave
  Power, 110, 137
Randolph, Sarah Nicholas, 59,
  71–72
Randolph, Thomas Jefferson, 71
Randolph, Thomas Mann, 71
Ransom, John Crowe, 146
Ratcliffe, Silas, 59, 85, 109
Reconstruction, 13–14, 16, 78
regionalism, 73–74, 85–91, 108;
  CFA2 and, 76, 78–79
religion, 57, 81, 89, 90, 95, 116,
  138, 145; and HA's later works,
  126–29, 130, 141, 146, 151; in
  New England, 7, 36, 76, 78,
  83, 84–85, 87–88, 149, 169; and
  slavery, 37, 68. See also Calvinism;
  Christianity
republic and republicanism, 5, 10,
  32–33, 73, 88; HA on, 7–8, 9,
  16–17, 105, 110; in New England,
  78, 84
Republican Party, 4, 5, 8, 13, 69, 89,
  124, 139
Rhode Island, 38
Richardson, Henry Hobson, 68, 69,
  115, 135
Rock Creek, 3, 117
Romanesque, 126, 135
Romanticism, 17, 25–26, 148, 183
  (n. 68)
Roosevelt, Theodore, 79
Russia, 24, 80, 135

Saint Helena Island, S.C., 118, 119,
  120, 121
Saint Petersburg, 63, 136
Samoa, 45, 117
Santiago de Cuba, 117

Schneidekoupon, Hartbeest, 85

science, 11, 87, 94, 97, 124–26, 182 (n. 4)

Scott, Dred, 137

Scott, Thomas A., 62

Scott, Walter, 25

secession, of Southern states, xii, 5, 61, 76, 89, 139; states' rights and, 100, 110, 112

sensuality, 117, 132

sentimentality, 148–50, 174 (n. 68)

servants, 52, 54, 56–58, 118, 148, 160–61 (n. 91), 163 (n. 26); Louisa Adams and, 28, 32, 37–38, 160 (n. 81). *See also* slaves and slavery; *and entries for specific servants*

Seward, Frederick William, 10

Seward, William Henry, 5, 7, 48, 49, 80, 112, 170 (n. 19)

Shaw, Robert Gould, 68

Sherman, William T., 124

Shiloh, battle of, 151

Simms, William Gilmore, 123

Slave Power, 6, 110; HA on, 7–8, 16, 20, 72, 112, 136–37

slaves and slavery, 4–5, 7, 51, 68, 78–79, 80; Calhoun and, 139; HA on, 4–9, 10, 12–15, 91, 108, 112, 118, 123, 139; Lamar and, 63; Louisa Adams on, 4, 35–38; R. Taylor and, 61; states' rights and, 100, 110, 112, 136–37

Smith, John, 82, 106

Smith, William Steuben, 3, 34, 161 (n. 92)

Sohm, Rudolph, 92

South, dialectic of, with North. *See* North/South dialectic

South, New, 59, 63, 150

South Carolina, 20, 67, 69, 90, 91, 108, 127

South Seas, 116, 117, 118

Spain, 80, 135

Spengler, Oswald, 144

Staël, Madame de, 25

states' rights, 79, 96, 100, 110, 112, 137

Stevens, Thaddeus, 61

Stubbs, William, 92, 95, 173 (n. 51)

Sturgis family, 69, 123

Sumner, Charles, 5, 9, 14, 61, 112; and Alice Hooper, 46, 48; and England, 11, 157 (n. 27); Lamar's eulogy for, 63, 65

Supreme Court, U.S., 63, 95

Tahiti, 175 (n. 4)

Taine, Hippolyte, 142

Talbot, Margery, 52

Tate, Allen, 145, 146, 151, 152, 185 (n. 78)

Taylor, John, 106–7

Taylor, Richard, 59, 60, 61–62, 63, 65, 69, 72, 112, 124

Taylor, Zachary, 59

Tennessee, 108

Tennyson, Alfred Lord, 148

Texas, 80, 118, 137

Texas and Pacific Railroad, 62, 65

Thirteenth Amendment, 13

Thrasher, J. S., 8

Timrod, Henry, 123

Tocqueville, Alexis de, 12, 142

Tone, Aileen, 89, 175 (n. 2)

Towne, Miss, 118

treason, 88–89, 139

Trent, William P., 84

Trent affair, 124